Working with Children
and Their Families

Also available from Lyceum Books, Inc.

Working with Children and Their Families

Karen V. Harper-Dorton
West Virginia University

Martin Herbert
Emeritus Professor at the University of Exeter

LYCEUM
BOOKS, INC.

Chicago, Illinois

Acknowledgments

We are indebted to all the families in our lives—our families, families we have worked with, and families we encounter—who have taught us so much about those things they celebrate and those things about which they grieve.

First published in 1988 by the British Psychological Society, St. Andrews House, 48 Princess Road East, Leicester, LE1 7DR, in association with Routledge Ltd, 11 New Fetter Lane, London, EC4P 4EE.

Published by

LYCEUM BOOKS, INC.
5758 S. Blackstone Ave.
Chicago, Illinois 60637
773/643-1903 (Fax)
773/643-1902 (Phone)
lyceum3@ibm.net
http://www.lyceumbooks.com

ISBN 0-925065-28-5

Library of Congress Cataloging-in-Publication Data

Harper-Dorton, Karen V., 1942–
    Working with children and their families / Karen V. Harper-
    Dorton,
Martin Herbert.
        p.   cm.
    Includes bibliographical references.
    ISBN 0-925065-28-5 (alk. paper)
    1. Social work with children   2. Family social work.
I. Herbert, Martin.   II. Title.
HV713.H17   1997
362.7—dc21   99-24858
                                                         CIP

Contents

v

Contents

Contents

14. EVALUATION: AN INTEGRAL COMPONENT OF
PRACTICE PROCESSES AND OUTCOMES 250
Why Evaluate?
  Constraints in Evaluating Programs and Practices
Program and Practice Evaluation
  Program Evaluation
  Practice Evaluation
Professional Responsibility for the Practice of Evaluation
  Ethical Practice
Summary and Comment

Epilogue 263

APPENDICES

FIGURES AND TABLES

Contents

Preface

We all know that each child and each family is different, yet society and indeed our world depends on our children and families to populate, nurture, and manage the world for all of us. Children and families are at the very base of our existence and are intrinsic to the social construction of our civilization. We all know about children and families from our experiences of growing up and perhaps parenting. It is likely that many of you reading this book will bring your experiences of working with children and families to each chapter. Intended for students and practitioners in the broad field of human services, particularly social workers, this book informs its readers about intervention, empowerment of those we serve, and evaluation of our work as practitioners.

The range of interventions made in the lives of children and families is as broad as the collection of professionals and paraprofessionals who provide services. Social workers, counselors, medical professionals, psychologists, and others engage children and families in treatment intended to reduce or alleviate suffering and problems. Regardless of the intervention, helping has the potential to build upon the strengths of children and families in their processes of becoming empowered, both as individuals and as family systems. As intervention ends and children and families live their lives, it is hoped that their encounters with professionals and with intervention will contribute to greater self-direction, self-sufficiency, quality of life, and positive images of self and others. This book conveys improved quality of living as the outcome most desired by ourselves as helpers and for clients as consumers of our services. As clients take charge of their lives and happiness, they experience a new sense of self and ability to be assertive and powerful enough to take at least some control over their lives.

It is this sense of empowerment that has the potential to nurture individuals' coping, confidence, success, and growth in personal, economic, social, and political realms.

Locke, Garrison, and Winship (1998) caution that the term "empowerment" is overused to the extent that it is at risk of losing its meaning for most purposes. Nevertheless, "empowerment" as found in social work literature conveys images of increased personal strength, growth in self-esteem, health, self-confidence in the pursuit of personal happiness, and potentials for greater assertiveness, leadership, and participation at all levels of our social environment (Hodges, Burwell, and Ortega, 1998; Kopp, 1989; Parsons, Gutierrez, and Cox, 1998; Saleeby, 1997; and Simon, 1998). Becoming empowered is a process of development and change that occurs sometimes through treatment and often in response to life experiences of success or positive reinforcement. Regardless of the modality of intervention that may be offered along the range of human and social systems, that is, the individual, family, group, community, organization, or society, accentuating autonomy, self-direction, success, and competence are empowering, particularly for the client units of children and families who live in communities and social networks.

It is this process of assessment, intervention, change, development, and individual and family empowerment that is at the center of our work with children and families that we write about. Building upon the strengths of children and families, we begin with assessment, give examples of intervention, and bring attention to underlying theories and assumptions. We complete the journey at the point of community and social networks, the natural and common environment where people live and nurture others.

Leo Tolstoy observed that "all happy families resemble each other, every unhappy family is unhappy in its own way." The first part of this quotation may not be altogether true, but the second half certainly is. This means that as the reader you cannot expect simple answers to questions. Every child, every parent, and all families are unique; so no generalized advice can meet all cases, every circumstance, or a particular individual's special difficulty.

Written for those who work with parents, adolescents, and children in various family contexts, this expanded edition strengthens the emphases of the earlier edition. Theoretical approaches to understanding behavior are expanded and aspects of helping that are psychological and social in what they have to offer are brought into focus. Attention is given to assessing and intervening in personal relationships and interactions that take place within families and the problems to which they commonly give rise—not only for their members, but also for the community in which they reside. New chapters address empowering children and families to go beyond their immediate problem solution and find renewed involvement in social and community networks. The final chapter discusses the importance of evaluating both our practices and programs as we answer demands for accountability and enter new and changing service environments which now include managed care and requirements for briefer treatment and cost containment.

This book is not prescriptive as there are no shortcuts to understanding families or to engaging them in problem resolution. But, we hope that ways of assessing and thinking about family problems and intervening in problem situations are communicated. Further, the scope of family troubles and various psychological and social assessments and approaches for intervention is extensive, and a comprehensive review would be well beyond the scope of this book. However, readers are encouraged to explore the literature cited throughout the volume for those theories, techniques, and practice and research methodologies of particular interest to them.

Part 1, "Taking Account of Children and Their Families," introduces you to the multiplicity of family problems and approaches for assessment. A variety of theoretical models presented for understanding and assessing human behavior include social learning, medical, psychometric, personal construct, psychodynamic, family process, empirical research, and ecological systems. The case of the Hayes family is introduced and continues throughout the book. This case demonstrates assessment and intervention from a social learning perspective.

Part 2, "Understanding Development and Change of Families and Children," presents stages of normal growth and development and provides comparisons of problem behaviors both in the family and in the social environment. Child and parenting behaviors and responsiveness are discussed and include problems such as emotional and physical abuse and neglect, family breakup, loss and change, patterns of parenting, and issues in single-parent and reconstituted families.

Part 3, "You as Helper," addresses the process of intervention, from initial assessment through goal setting, intervention, and termination. Methods and techniques for contracting and working with children and families are discussed. Professional concerns for competent practice are raised in this part.

Part 4, "Empowerment of Families and Evaluation of Practice," highlights the importance of carrying growth and new skills for self-sufficiency beyond the agency and into daily living in homes and communities. The merit of extending client empowerment into social and community networks is presented. Mentoring is presented as an important extension of agency-based intervention and can link family and social networks. The common concern of evaluating effectiveness and efficiency of practice and programs is explored in this section, relating both to professional accountability and the changing human service arena of managed care and cost containment. Considerations for ethical practice of evaluation and service delivery are presented.

Illustrative case material throughout the book highlights linking theory and practice with evaluation. Flow charts and checklists are included to assist you in assessing client situations and monitoring your interventions and outcomes. The appendices include examples of actual work with parent groups and a vignette of a child abuse case.

Recognizing that no single theory is adequate for application to all problems in the practice of working with families and children, we hope that the variety and scope of theories and techniques presented will serve in our quest to strengthen and empower families in their daily lives. Based on the premise that children and families have capacities for growth and change, building on their strengths is central to this book. Finally, professional accountability and assessment of our work bring us to our own potential for extending and building personal and professional competence.

PART I
Taking Account of Children and Their Families

Let us imagine for the moment, and for many it will be close to actual experience, that you are faced with several clients—a family—clamouring for help, with what seems like a very large and very daunting number of what to them seem insoluble problems. Everyone is thoroughly miserable, except the teenager who claims to be "above it all." The mother feels hemmed in between the demands of Grandmother, who lives with them, and the commands of a fretful, strong-willed toddler. Father is feeling truly middle-aged and rather anxious. He faces the possibility of being laid off, and he feels he gets little sympathy, or for that matter, attention from his wife who seems wrapped up in the children. Grandmother is worried about her health and finds the children noisy and impolite, although she does enjoy making a fuss of the youngest. The middle child, aged ten, feels rejected and is having trouble at school; she is beginning to refuse to go—to the concern of her parents. The house is tense; and the atmosphere, particularly in the mornings, fraught with bickering and tears.

Given this sort of situation, where on earth do you start? It must be said that this is but one of an immense variety of scenarios which might unfold before the social worker or some other professional who works with parents and children. The problem, indeed, may be a lot worse and more menacing.

Families are all different and come with a variety of problems. Some are stressed and define their lives as problematic for them. Others are multiproblem with serious issues such as deep resentment, violence, abuse, impoverishment, mental illness, terminal health problems, children in custody of others, children for whom they seek custody, and many other crises.

1

It is misleading to think that troubled families will be troubled in the same ways just as it is misleading to assume that all children live in two-parent families. Families have many forms including biological families, stepfamilies, families with only one parent, adoptive families, gay or lesbian families, biracial families, and reconstituted families. Families and children are our most valuable social unit and must be treated with dignity and respect for the importance they bear in our world.

Of course, the threshold of vulnerability or annoyance varies from person to person; one individual's "devastating" life-event has "nuisance value" only for another hardy being. But everyone deserves at least the dignity of being heard, and attended to with due concern, while the magnitude of their problems and the possible need for intervention are assessed. And therein lies a difficulty: what *is* a problem, and when can a problem be considered to be serious, especially in the realm of psychosocial events involving human relationships and interactions, or with which this book is mainly concerned?

There has been a move away from putting children with problems into categories with names such as physically handicapped, mentally subnormal, delicate, maladjusted, subject to specific learning disability, and so on. Current practice is to access the needs of individual children relative to their circumstances. *Special needs* are specified in terms of what the child requires above and beyond those requirements normally supplied for all children. Thus they might include psychological or speech therapy, special diets, medication, aids to mobility, physiotherapy, and special educational provision or accommodation for learning disabilities. Along with the moves goes a trend toward wider integration of children into the community. This concept of community care requires a close alliance between professionals and parents.

This is not a book about intervention into details of different disabilities and special needs in their accommodation. Instead, it is about problem solving and helping strategies which can be applied to a variety of situations and problems that might involve children and their families. Basic knowledge and skills are presented for use with families in search of solutions to problems. Assessment and short-term intervention are presented to empower and support permanency of families in their community context. In the process of learning to work with families, many fine resources are available to deepen information. For example, resources include: major theoretical approaches to family therapy (Becvar and Becvar, 1996), clinical interviewing with children (Greenspan and Greenspan, 1991), strengths and problems in contemporary families (Mason, Skolnick, and Sugarman, 1998), and children with disabilities (Seligman and Darling, 1997). Troubled families often experience and sometimes seek help with problems such as:

Children
- Children with behavioral (management) problems
- Children with emotional problems (for example, fears, phobias)
- Children with special needs (disabilities)
- Children who have been fostered or adopted
- Children who have been abused

Adults
- Parents who cannot cope (for example, who are unskilled or simply demoralized)
- Parents who are unresponsive, unattached to their children
- Parents who are abusive, who lack self-control
- Parents who argue and don't communicate (for example, marital problems)
- Parents in reconstituted, divorced, and stepfamilies

In the chapters that follow we shall be considering the following questions:

Question 1. **What**, precisely, is the nature of the problem(s) the client(s) want help with?

Question 2. **Why** have these problems arisen, and why (with time) have they not gone away?

Question 3. **How** can I help my clients, or better still, help them to help themselves?

All members of the helping professions are faced constantly with *choices* for themselves and their clients. In this, their role

3

is similar to that of parents and their children. The choices parents make, and the decisions they take, have a potent influence not only on the way their offspring will "turn out," but also how enjoyable and *relatively* problem-free their journey from childhood, through adolescence, and on to adulthood proves to be.

This book is intended to help you to assess problems and to initiate actions that stimulate change in families who are "stuck" in self-defeating, unproductive, and growth-inhibiting patterns of living. Information about child development, child-rearing, and family relationships will be provided. Information provided is intended to help the reader gain basic knowledge and understanding that lead to *practical strategies* for helping parents, and helping children learn to help themselves.

CHAPTER 1

Assessing Children and Their Families: Where to Begin

One of your earliest choices is where to concentrate your attention in what may present itself as a welter of conflicting claims, complaints, and accusations. Some of the problems will reside mainly within an individual, such as fear, but even then they will have repercussions. The individual's parents (or partner) worry about his or her suffering. Or the problems put constraints on the activities of the family, such as when vacations are not possible because a mother is agoraphobic, feeling anxious about leaving the house, and panicky in a crowded shopping center.

Other problems arise from the relationships and interaction such as the give-and-take transactions between people. For example:

- Mother–Father   Disagreements about the children, quarrels over decisions, other marital difficulties.
- Parent(s)–Child   Management difficulties, disappointments over the child's achievement or lack of them.
- Child–Parent(s)   Resentments about being "babied," complaints about unfairness, favoritism.
- Child–Child   Sibling rivalry, jealousy.

Your client(s) may be one of these persons—a child refusing to go to school, one or both parents angry or disengaged, or all of the family members feeling unhappy. You might even have to work more widely in the neighborhood, at the school, or with other agencies in the community. Who the client is, is in fact an unclear question, and one to which we shall have to return.

5

Some workers like to have all the family members at their interviews, some prefer to see the parent(s) first of all, with or without the children present, and then gradually work their way around to talking to other key members of the household. Whichever way you tackle the initial interviews, you are trying to assess *what* is going on, what the problems are, under what circumstances they occur, and what changes (i.e., outcomes) would be desirable for a viable and happier situation to be created or restored for the family.

Exploration: Observing, Asking, Listening

To explore the "what" question, you will bring your observation, questioning, and listening skills when you meet with the family. This meeting, an interaction, is the process of the family seeking intervention or asking for help and the professional assessing and exploring in order to at least clarify the problem as presented. This coming together to gather information is the interview. It is the process of defining the problem, offering help, and agreeing to work together toward an initial plan for finding a solution to the problem, that begins the intervention process. Asking a series of questions, engaging in exploration for facts, and practicing open and careful listening occur during an interview. Insoo Kim Berg (1994) offers a careful description of interviewing processes and techniques from the initial stage of intervention through defining the problem, setting goals, contracting for intervention, conducting a session, and terminating the intervention. Interviewing is a skill, shaped by the methodology or theoretical approach that most informs the professional. The interview is the starting place, the springboard to intervening in problem configurations in the lives of families and children. It is the medium for initial assessment and for intervention and determination of outcomes of the intervention. Interviewing is not an end in itself but a tool to assessment and treatment and is explored later in Part I.

Before we look at particular approaches to assessment from which the professional can choose in his or her endeavor to help a family, there is an important general consideration: the perspective or model to help to be adopted. Cliff Cunningham and Hilton Davis (1985), authors of a book on children with special needs, have a useful device for working out where you stand with regard to your role vis-à-vis your client: on the one hand, the *expert model* and on the other, the *consumer model*. The *transplant model* is between these models.

In the expert model the professionals view themselves as very much in charge because of their expertise, responsibility, and therefore decision making. The client is relatively passive as a recipient of advice, "prescriptions" about health or behavior, or possibly therapy of one kind or another. At the other extreme clients, for example the parents, are viewed very much as consumers of the professionals' services, with the right to select what *they* believe is most appropriate to their needs. Decision making is ultimately in the parents' control; professionals act as consultants and teachers. Negotiation and discussion play a large part in the professional relationships.

In the transplant or what might be called the partnership model, professionals perceive themselves as having expertise but sharing it and imparting it to parents and other non- or paraprofessionals so that they mediate or facilitate much of the training or therapy of the child and parents.

Not all models suit all problems. What is important is that a worker should know what his or her assumptions are. The authors referred to previously help you to uncover your orientation to problems of children and their families with the following questions:

- Have I met the family?
- Do I consider the child in the context of his/her family?
- Do I have regular, two-way communication with the family?
- Do I respect and value the child as a person?
- Do I respect and value the family?
- Do I feel the family has strengths to help the child?
- Have I identified the parents' abilities and resources?
- Do I always act as honestly as possible?
- Do I give them choices about what to do?
- Do I listen to them?
- Have I identified their aims?

- Do I negotiate with them?
- Do I adjust according to the joint conclusions?
- Do I assume they have some responsibility for what I do for their child?
- Do I assume I have to earn their respect?
- Do I make the assumption that we might disagree about what is important?
- Do I believe they can change?
- Have I tried to identify the parents' perceptions of their child?

A high proportion of "yes" responses suggests the generalized use of a consumer model; many "no" responses indicate an expert model.

The model you adopt will be determined not only by the agency you work in, the clients who seek help at that agency, but also *your* view of human nature. The way you construe problems and the solutions to them reflects your beliefs about families, their problems, and their strength to make progress and change.

Problem Parenting

I referred earlier to the difficulty for the worker of deciding when a problem can truly be considered to be serious. When should we begin to worry because behavior, whether it is a child's or adult's, goes beyond the bounds and can be said to be abnormal or dysfunctional. In other words, when is a problem really a problem?

There is no simple answer to this question. One would be hard pressed to find absolute distinctions between the characteristics of parents who come to be diagnosed or assessed as problematic by psychiatrists or social workers and those of other unselected parents. The judgment of what is abnormal (that is, a deviation away from a norm of standard) is essentially a social one. Certain adults fail to meet particular expectations on the part of society for what constitutes appropriate parental behavior. Unfortunately, terms like "normal" and "abnormal" are commonly applied to parents as if they are mutually exclusive categories. The point is that the attributes and actions

8

which society judges in its evaluation of good and ba
and abnormal parenting are ones that in some degree ს.
are manifested by most adults (see Figure 1a).

This figure demonstrates how a wide range of parental
behaviors can be reduced to two major dimensions that can
be described as Love–Hostility and Autonomy–Control. Thus
we have parental transactions that are warm and loving at one
extreme and rejecting and hostile at the other, and then again
activities that are restrictive and controlling versus ones that are
permissive and promote autonomy. According to this model an
antagonistic parent is one who combines hostility and restric-
tiveness, while a protective parent is one who is both loving
and restrictive.

Figure 1a. The range of parental behavior types within two major
dimensions: autonomy–control/hostility–warmth.

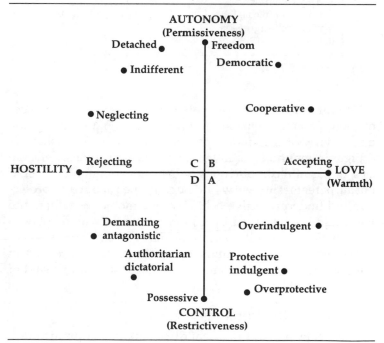

(From E.S. Schafer, 1959.)

9

Figure 1b. Details of children's behavior as influenced by the two major parental dimensions: restrictive parenting and permissive parenting.

		Restrictiveness		Permissiveness
Warmth	A	Submissive, dependent, polite, neat, obedient Minimal aggression Maximum rule enforcement (boys) Dependent, not friendly, not creative Maximal compliance	B	Active, socially outgoing, creative, successfully aggressive Minimal rule enforcement (boys) Facilitates adult role taking Minimal self-aggression (boys) Independent, friendly, creative, low projective hostility
Hostility	D	"Neurotic" problems More quarrelling and shyness with peers Socially withdrawn Low in adult role taking Maximal self-aggression (boys)	C	Delinquency Noncompliance Maximal aggression

(Adapted from W.C. Becker, 1964.)

You can also see how the potential long-term consequences of these parental behaviors—illustrated in Figure 1b—guide us to a view of the kind of parenting which entails risks.

Signs of abnormal parenting involve exaggerations, deficiencies, or harmful combinations of behavior common to most, if not all, parents. Thus we would be concerned about overprotective and underprotective behavior by a mother or father, and we would be concerned by a punitive parent who displays a combination of hostility and poor self-control.

The differences are mainly quantitative; differences *not* in kind but in degree. The same (as we shall see) can be said of children's problems.

Children With Problems

Parents' enjoyment of their children is likely to diminish rapidly and give way to anxious concern, and perhaps anger and resentment, when they show signs of abnormal or deviant behavior and emotion. Parents and teachers begin to worry about children when their actions persist in being:

- **Not understandable**, that is, when their moods, attitudes, or behaviors defy good sense and lack reason or meaning;
- **Unpredictable**, such that there is a Jekyll-and-Hyde-like quality of changeability, disconcerting switches in mood, friendliness, and cooperation;
- **Rebellious** and uncontrollable in the sense that adults are unable to impose their authority and/or their children seem unwilling or unable to control their own behavior.

Few parents or teachers have not observed undesirable forms of behavior in a particular child or adolescent, at one time or another, and tend to be resigned about such manifestations. "Well, that's what you'd expect, isn't it, of a toddler or teenager." It is when such actions are *frequent* and *intense* that real concern is felt; in other words, it is a matter of degree.

At what point is it inappropriate to be philosophical about your client's difficulties? When should your mental "alarm bells" begin to ring; when do you cease saying to clients, "Ah well, she'll grow out of it"?

At the most-general level you might ask yourself:

- What are the consequences of the child's actions, benign or unfavorable?
- Does the child's style of life prevent her from leading a contented life in which she is able to enjoy social relationships, and play and learn effectively?
- Does the child's behavior, in terms of his development toward maturity, represent a retrogressive trend, that is, does he resort to thumb-sucking and temper tantrums as a way of deflecting mother's attention from the rival baby sister?

By the way, you could substitute *parents* for *child* in most of these questions to assess the seriousness of their problems. Every stage of development is marked by certain life tasks—physical, psychological, and social skills and challenges that have to be mastered by the child, the adolescent, and eventually, the adult. Some of the more important of these tasks can be indicated in chart form (see Table 1).

Table 1. Life Tasks

Life stage	Life tasks—it is important to:
Infancy (birth–2)	• Feel attached to one or more people • Know that people and objects still exist even when they can't be seen • Develop ideas through handling objects • Develop movement skills
Early Childhood (2–4)	• Begin to develop self-control • Begin to develop language • Explore and pretend in play • Develop further movement skills
Middle Childhood (5–7)	• Develop ideas about being male/female • Begin to think about right and wrong • Develop ideas of numbers, etc., through practical experiences • Play cooperatively
Late Childhood (8–12)	• Develop cooperative skills • Be a member of a team • Begin to think about yourself • Develop academic, artistic, craft, and athletic skills
Early Adolescence (13–17)	• Become accustomed to a mature body • Learn to use abstract ideas • Gain support from same-age friends • Try out sexual activities
Late Adolescence (18–22)	• Become independent and competent • Make first decisions about work • Set own behavior limits • Make close, intimate relationships • Freely choose own values
Early Adulthood (23–30)	• Develop patterns of family living • Begin to be a parent • Develop work plans • Actively choose lifestyle • Give to local community
Pre-Middle Age (30–35)	• Look anew at what's worth spending time on • Be sensitive to the "looking anew" done by people important to you • Be the parent of an older child
Early Middle Age (36–50)	• Review commitments in midlife • Cope with children leaving home • Develop relationships with partner • Take an active part in community life

Table 1. Life Tasks (*continued*)

Life stage	Life tasks—it is important to:
Late Middle Age (51–65)	• Develop community involvement • Complete or wind down working life • Acknowledge the prospect of death
Old Age (65–death)	• Negotiate increasing dependence on others • Evaluate one's own life • Deal with the deaths of close friends and relatives • Come to terms with one's own death

(*From Open University Course Organizers, 1982.*)

Look at Table 1 and make some notes about the life tasks which most concern your clients at the moment. Ask them about their present priorities and preoccupations. The topic of family life map (chapter 3) will examine how one individual's life tasks and those of other members of the family are interconnected.

The newborn infant needs to develop a sense of trust and, later, a growing autonomy. A lasting sense of trust, security, confidence, or optimism (as opposed to distrust, insecurity, inadequacy, or pessimism) is thought to be based upon affection, a degree of continuity of care giving, and the reasonably prompt satisfaction of the infant's needs (Erikson 1985). Some parents may be too immature or preoccupied by personal problems to do this. The major hazards to the development of a perception of a benign, trustworthy, and predictable world in which children initiate independence-seeking and perceive their own actions as having meaningful consequences are neglect, abuse, and indifference. Extreme inconsistency and other social and physical conditions interfere with the child's sense of personal adequacy or hinder the acquisition of skills. Such influences are likely to produce a child who behaves in a troublesome manner. Incidentally, physically handicapped children are massively over-represented in the population of youngsters with behavior problems. If such children can be helped to become more competent, then they may have less recourse to problem behavior.

Two-Way Traffic: Parent-to-Child; Child-to-Parent

In many ways children's behavior can have as much effect on their parents' actions as their behavior has on them. So when parents meet certain extremely difficult or temperamental factors from a very tender age, they can be overwhelmed for a time and change the direction and manner in which they intended to bring up their child. These individual characteristics may show themselves in moodiness, overactivity, defiance, oversensitivity, unpredictability, biological irregularity, and unadaptability to changes in routine. The impact may be greater on adoptive parents because they may ascribe the difficult behavior to deprivation experiences, rejection of themselves by the adopted child, or even "bad blood."

What is important is that you assess the way clients construe situations and attribute meaning to what is happening to them.

The Case of Avril Hayes

This is what one mother told us about her child at the Leicester University Center for Behavioural Work With Families (U.K.). Names have been changed and aspects of the case disguised for purposes of confidentiality:

> *From the first day that I saw my daughter Avril, I realized that she was more lively than her sister Stella and wouldn't be content to be in a room by herself. She would scream and I went through endless months wondering if I was feeding her incorrectly, whether she had a pain or was unhappy, but finally came to the conclusion that she just wanted company ... but on her own terms. I wasn't allowed to make a fuss of her but she didn't want to be alone. Meanwhile, other problems were emerging. She would never sleep during the day like other babies and eventually wouldn't sleep much at night either. When I went to cuddle her she would scream, bite, or kick, and this showed itself particularly at bathtime and changing time. Guilt was my first emotional feeling towards my baby. Pure unadulterated guilt. Guilt because no one really wanted her; guilt because I had foisted a child upon my family (I was the only one who welcomed the pregnancy) who was proving to be every parent's*

Figure 2. Perceived self-efficacy

(*From M. Herbert, 1987.*)

nightmare. Protectiveness came very quicky after guilt. I would protect her against the world if necessary. But love was hardly noticeable except in my fierce protective instinct. How can you love a baby who alternately screams and cries for 18 hours out of every 24, who won't feed without an all-out battle, who shows no response when you pick her up, cuddle her, talk to her, play with her, or just try to love her? Avril caused violent quarrels between my husband and myself (things unknown previously) and arguments between relatives on how to deal with her. I did so try to show my love for her, but she just didn't appear to want it.

By the time Mrs. Hayes came to us at the Center she had lost all confidence in herself (a loss of what psychologists call self-efficacy). She was thoroughly depressed and demoralized and doubted whether anyone could help her. The case of Avril and her family is continued in the following chapters as an example of working with a family having difficulty.

Perceived Self-Efficacy

An eminent theorist, Albert Bandura (1976) is of the opinion that human behavior is subject to two major categories of influence: efficacy expectations and outcome expectations, represented in schematic form in Figure 2.

These are the constituent parts of *perceived self-efficacy*. They are distinguished because a parent may believe that a particular reward or discipline will produce certain outcomes such as improvement in a child's behavior. However, the parent may have serious misgivings as to whether she has the patience and consistency to bring about such a desirable outcome. All psychological procedures designed to bring about change, whatever their type, are thought by some professionals to depend on beliefs about the level of skill required to bring about an outcome and the likely end result of a course of action. *Efficacy expectations* are thought to be the most important component. The main effect on outcome expectations is through the strengthening of efficacy expectations, for example, the self-expectation that "I *am* able to do it!" In their approach, successful helping depends on the degree to which the interventions create or strengthen the client's expectations of personal efficacy. It appears that verbal persuasion has only relatively weak and short-lived effects on such expectations. *Performance accomplishments,* on the other hand, are very potent: hence the success of techniques like behavior rehearsal and modeling. In rehearsal or modeling, clients practice skills have been demonstrated to them.

Fortunately most parents, with little or no training, rear their children, with the help of other socializing agents, into socially acceptable and broadly rule-abiding adults who respect societal norms around them. Despite variations in family pattern and style of parenting, all societies seem to be successful in transforming helpless, self-centered infants into more or less self-supporting, responsible members of their particular community. In other words, they become socialized. Indeed, there is a basic preparedness on the part of most infants to be trained, albeit, an in-built bias toward all things social.

Summary and Comment

This chapter has been concerned with the individual and his or her relationships; also with what goes wrong with them. We have seen that abnormalities of parenting and childhood behavior vary greatly. Problems represent, most often, exaggerations, deficiencies, or handicapping combinations of behaviors, emotions, or attitudes common to all people. You are very likely to have to deal with, or refer elsewhere, the following categories of problems:

1. *Excessive behaviors* that require reduction or elimination (e.g. dangerous actions, self-injurious behavior, aggression, phobic avoidance, etc.).

2. *Appropriate behaviors* that occur in the wrong context: for example, cooperation with delinquent enterprises; honesty that hurts—Q: "How do I look?" A: "Awful." These problems require training in determining when to do what.

3. *Deficits* that need to be made good, for example, incontinence, selective or elective mutism, poor self-control, etc.

Applying similar criteria to pinpoint deviant parental behavior, we have physical abuse or overprotectiveness as an example of excessive behavior, the continual provision to help when help is no longer required by the child as an exemplar of inappropriate behavior, and unresponsive parenting as typical of the deficit type of parenting response.

We judge the seriousness of problems in terms of their disabling and/or distressing consequences for the individual and for others. Parents will often come to you with their self-confidence, their morale, and self-esteem in tatters. Give them back their dignity by the manner in which you talk to them, treat them as "experts" with regard to aspects of their own children, and appropriately involve them as partners in the helping endeavor. In boosting perceived self-efficacy, deeds speak louder than words. In the chapters that follow, you will find interventions and techniques for helping families and find solutions and coping skills for problems they seek to resolve.

CHAPTER 2

Approaching Assessment: Step-by-Step

Children are usually a source of great pleasure and endless wonder to their parents. These joys are sometimes tempered by the concern and heavy sense of responsibility that also accompany parenthood: the pleasure may be transformed into anxiety and the wonder into puzzlement when the child begins to behave in a peculiar or erratic manner. Children who have not, at some stage of their development, been the cause of quite serious worry to their mothers and fathers are unique.

Familes, like individuals, also have their ups and downs and go through stages—some more difficult than others. Family life can be the source of tensions and problems for its individual members in their various roles: as parents, grandparents, step-parents, substitute parents, children, and teenagers.

This book concerns itself with problems that arise within families, particularly between parents and children or caretakers and children. The research literature on parent/child relationships is pervaded by the belief that optimal care and training of children during the impressionable years of life will prepare them for present and future problems and even prevent many problems in their lives (Crain, 1985; Kagan, 1984). When one considers the intimate, protracted, and highly influential nature of parents' relationships with their children, it seems self-evident that the quality of such relationships must have a vital bearing on the development of the child's personality and general adaptation. This large responsibility for which many parents are poorly prepared creates stress and feelings of inadequacy among some parents and even guilt for others.

It is worth noting that although society delegates its most crucial functions to the family, there is little formal education or training offered to prospective parents; even the informal learning and experience once offered to older children caring for younger siblings in large families, or the help from the experienced members of the extended family and from relatives living nearby, may not be available to the relatively small and often isolated family whether it be biological, step, adoptive, or single parent.

The Family as a System

Systems theory helps explain interactions within the system as it adjusts and changes and defines its boundaries (Janzen and Harris, 1997). The family is a basic social system, a social organization, or individuals defined in the literature as two or more individuals who share space, have emotional ties, establish relationships, share commitment, have established roles and tasks to accomplish functions of the family. The family system negotiates intimacy and is the basic system for socialization where children learn family rituals and social and cultural values in the context of family life. Systems theory is not a theory about behavior or intervention but an approach to understanding various organizations of people and institutions and offers a way of organizing information from multidisciplinary approaches to behavior (Longres, 1995).

Consistent with systems theory, families are comprised of subsystems such as parents and sibling subsystems which make up the whole system. Families establish boundaries that define the family and its subsystems. Permeable boundaries allow exchanges of energy and information to occur internally among the family's subsystems and between the family and its external environment (Anderson and Carter, 1990; Germain, 1991; Zastrow and Kirst-Ashmann, 1997). The social environment which the family interacts with includes a variety of other systems such as communities, organizations like schools, jails, hospitals, and the variety of organizations that employ family members and support physical and social needs of individual members. The family changes and evolves as differentiation occurs for the members and for the family as a whole in response to adaptation to pressures from internal and external environments. Families change over time and seek balance within and around family boundaries (Becvar and Becvar, 1996; Nichols and Schwartz, 1991).

Ecological systems is a framework for approaching systems and their ecological environment and is useful in understanding interactions within the family system as it adjusts and changes and defines its boundaries (Janzen and Harris, 1997). Ecological systems perspective is a subset of general systems and focuses on adaptations and accommodations that occur as systems change and evolve in relation to their environment (Kilpatrick and Holland, 1995). According to Kilpatrick and Holland (1995), six major concepts from Germain and Gitterman (1987) are essential to working with families. First, families have reciprocal exchanges with the environment as transactions flow into and out from the family system. Second, demands for exchanges and changes are defined as life stresses that produce negotiation of relationships within and between systems. Third, coping occurs as systems adjust, or as families make accommodations and adjustments in response to internal and external stresses. Fourth, habitats or settings of physical and social contexts define realities of systems such as families. For example, communities, cultures, and basic resources support functioning for family members and for the family as a whole. Fifth, a niche includes the statuses, rights, resources, opportunities, and deficits that define physical and social realities for families. Sixth, relatedness or connectedness evolves as systems such as families establish their particular place in community and environmental networks. These concepts help define the family as a system and provide points for intervention in the system.

Intervening in the family system and in its interaction with the environment is informed from an ecological systems approach. This perspective informs understanding adaptation of families and provides for intervention in various life transitions including interactions within and outside the family in its exchange with the environment.

Family systems include more than simple exchanges with the environment. From a systems perspective, the individual family members are seen as the elements or subunits. Whatever happens to one or more of its elements such as mental illness in the mother or father, the death of a sibling, or serious marital disharmony can affect the entire system. The heightened emotional intimacy and interdependence of the members of our small, intimate contemporary families are thought to place a great burden on parent(s) and children. Parent(s) are the crucial and therefore potentially weak link in the chain of rearing children where socialization occurs.

In an ecological systems perspective, children are influenced by the rules, culture, and activities of their family system. Families, parents, schools, and neighborhoods are immediate systems in the individual experiences of childhood (Fraser, 1997). Taking care of young children is likely to be more stressful for some parents than others, especially in situations of poverty, poor housing, abuse, neglect, death of a family member, and other crises. An old and popular aphorism is that "there are no problem children, only problem parents." In the context of the practices and case example that follow, we shall see that this is an oversimplification.

Reviews of the literature repeatedly point to the conclusion that there is little evidence of a connection between specific parenting practices and later characteristics of the child (Crain, 1985; Garbarino and Benn, 1992; Kagan, 1984). Available evidence suggests that what is important in child rearing is the general social climate in the home, for example, the attitudes and feelings of the parents, which form a background to the application of specific methods and interactions of child rearing. For example, the mother does best who does, with a sense of confidence, what she and the community to which she belongs believe is right for the child. Feeding and potty training and the like are important elements of the child's daily activities; but it is the social interactions they mediate, the manner in which parents undertake these tasks, that give them significance. It is how the young child is looked after that is crucial, and it is the social and psychological context of the care that matters rather than its chronology and mechanics.

The implication of all this is that a good deal of the worker's attention is focused on the present rather than the past. This is not to say that you should neglect the client family's history. The important thing is to get the balance right, a matter I shall return to. Another implication concerns the manner and form in which you get to talk to the members of the family. There may be disagreements about the formal arrangements and theories about how best to achieve change, but there is likely to be a consensus that all members should be interviewed.

The Interview

The interview is an essential method for gaining access to parents' and children's problems. It sounds deceptively simple and straightforward to say, "I am going to interview the Smith family to find out what lies behind the referral." But you need to be clear about the answers to several questions before you intrude on the privacy of a home and its family.

- Do I have the right and the family's permission to conduct this and subsequent interviews? This can be a significant problem for social workers who frequently have to wear *two* hats called "care" and "control," and whose intervention may be unwelcome, especially for involuntary clients such as those in child abuse and/or custody referrals.
- What do I wish to find out (what are my objectives) in the interview?
- Whom do I need to speak to in order to fulfill my objectives? (All the family members, parents only, the child alone, his/her brothers and sisters?)
- Do I invite them to meet me as a full family group? Do I speak to the mother first? Both parents together? Should the child be present initially?
- How do I begin the interview?
- How do I best express some quite complex and potentially threatening ideas?
- How do I reassure them about confidentiality?
- What is the best way of eliciting reliable and relevant information? How do I deal with their tendency to digress or to set an agenda which avoids key issues?
- Indeed, what *is* relevant information?

- How do I terminate the interview without leaving clients feeling "up in the air" or threatened?

These questions raise ethical concerns of clients' rights and have a bearing on intervention concerns such as the development of rapport with clients; using communication; summarizing and memory skills; obtaining accurate, relevant, and meaningful information; maintaining a good working relationship; conducting one's business in a professional and ethical manner; and so on.

Communication. Working with all members of the family in conjoint family sessions requires broad communication skills. Interviewing children demands skill, patience, and respect for children. Young children tend to be talkative but are limited in their ability to reflect insightfully their experiences; adolescents are often introspective and have a way of becoming monosyllabic when asked personal questions.

Children are not always very good at expressing their fears, frustrations, or uncertainties. They cannot always tell their parents, let alone a comparative stranger, how they feel, but they have a language that adults can learn to translate—the language of behavior and fantasy. What they do in everyday life and what they say indirectly through play or story-telling can be most revealing.

Projective techniques. There are advantages to using projective techniques for assessment including: play, puppets, dramatic creations, completing stories or sentences. These techniques permit an almost unlimited variety of responses. The client has to fall back on his or her own resources rather than stereotyped, socially desirable answers. These techniques have their critics but are invaluable if used cautiously as aids to communicating with children. The caution refers to interpreting the protocols— the made-up stories about pictured events, or the posted "letters" containing statements about feelings and attitudes to various members of the family. It is thought that children identify with the central characters in their stories; project their own feelings, especially unacceptable or difficult-to-acknowledge impulses or attitudes, onto the fantasy figures; and attribute various motives and ideas that are essentially their own, into the play or other creative situations and plots. Gil (1991) and Moon (1990) provide examples of working with children and youth in play and art therapies, respectively.

When the child is too loyal, too frightened or ashamed, or too inarticulate to speak about feelings or painful events in the family, it may be possible to express these things in the evolving story. Stories can be constructed, leaving spaces for the child to fill in about a boy or girl of similar age. Thus you begin, "Once upon a time there was a boy/girl. What did he/she most like doing?" .... "What did he/she not like doing?" .... You gradually introduce, among neutral themes, topics such as secrets, fears, worries, preoccupations, family tensions, parental behaviors, and so on.

Sentence completions are useful:

"I like to .... "
"What I most dislike .... "
"My best friend .... "
"I wish .... "
"My dad .... "
"My mom .... "
"If only .... "
"In my home the nicest thing is .... "
"The worst thing is .... "

With stories told as a response to pictures, you need to be cautious about your interpretation. There is a tendency for us to project our own "psyches" into our interpretations or to superimpose our "theories" onto the projective protocols.

Nevertheless, play, drama with puppets or miniatures, or stories are undoubtedly an invaluable adjunct to work with children. You would do well to have a store of miniatures, anatomically correct dolls, drawing materials, and pictures available for use with families and children who come to you.

Beginning Your Assessment

We have looked at various conceptual issues and methods which set the stage for the actual assessment. In Flow Chart 1,

24

we describe in summary form the ten steps you might take in seeking answers to the *what* and *why* questions.

Flow Chart 1

INITIAL SCREENING		PHASE I
	Step 1.	Explain how you intend to work. Foster a good working relationship.
	Step 2.	Obtain a general statement of the problem(s).
	Step 3.	Specify the problem(s) more precisely.
	Step 4.	Elicit the desired outcome(s).
	Step 5.	Construct a problem profile.
	Step 6.	Introduce the idea of behavior sequences by looking at your client(s) typical day(s).
	Step 7.	Establish problem priorities.
FURTHER ASSESSMENT		PHASE II
	Step 8.	Work out a family life map.
	Step 9.	Make an estimate of your client's assets.
	Step 10.	Ask your adult clients about their goals, e.g., for their children. Ask the child about his or her wishes and requirements.
		PHASE III
		Collect more detailed "baseline" data. Give clients homework tasks, e.g., keeping diaries, frequency charts, etc., of daily life, behaviors, or whatever data are relevant.
		PHASE I
		(One or possibly two interviews)
Step 1.		**Foster a good working (therapeutic) relationship.**
		(*a*) Explain who you are and how you expect to work.
		(*b*) Establish a warm, friendly, and professional relationship, i.e., work systematically.

Step 2.	**Provide the client(s) with an opportunity to state the problem *as they see it*.** (*These questions can be adapted and directed toward the child.*) (*a*) Begin with an open-ended question. "Tell me in your own words what is causing you concern . . . Take your time." (*b*) Summarize at intervals that are not intrusive to clients. "May we pause for a moment to see if I have understood correctly what you have said? I want to be sure that I get things right. As I understand it you are concerned about. . . ." Allow sufficient time for the clients to express themselves. Supplementary questions (probes) can be useful at this stage. "What is going well in the situation you are concerned about at present with regard to _____ (say the child)?"; "How does _____ contribute to family life?"; "Has anyone else expressed concern about _____?"; "Is there anyone—a teacher, friend, or whoever—who does not see this worrying side to _____, because he/she is different when in their presence?"
Step 3.	**Begin to specify the problem(s) more precisely.** (*a*) Ask for *examples*—preferably recent ones—which will illustrate the problem situation(s). "Tell me, in detail, what happens so that I can see it in my mind's eye." "What leads up to the confrontation or problem? Who says what . . . to whom, who does what . . . to whom, with what consequences?" "How does an episode usually end up?" The use of role-play may be helpful. (*b*) Find out *when, how often*, with what *intensity*, and in what particular circumstances (what people, places, situations) the problems occur. (*c*) Discover the details surrounding the *onset* of the problem(s). "How long has this been happening?"; "Are there any particular circumstances—life events—that

	may have been of significance because they occurred at the time that the problems made their appearance?" (d) "How have you tried to deal with the problems up to now. .... With what result?" (e) "Who helps you cope with the problems?" "Does anyone hinder you, as you see it?" (f) "You probably have some ideas, perhaps a theory, as to why this is happening. Would you like to try it out on me?"
Step 4.	**Find out about desired outcomes.** "I am going to ask some questions to help us clarify what you and I should work toward. If, as is likely, other members of the family are involved, we will need to consult them." Note that families in conjoint sessions can respond to the question of what they want help with.
Step 5.	**Draw up a problem profile.** Take account of the complaints and desired outcomes of all the members of the family.

Let us take time off for the moment to look again at Avril and her family. They were referred to our Center for Avril's problem. But it wasn't that simple.

Avril, aged four, demanded an inordinate amount of individual attention, monopolizing her mother's time wherever she was and whatever she was doing. She clung to her and followed her everywhere, even to the toilet, refusing to let her out of her sight, even for a few moments. Avril would not play with other children, including her sister who had no real problems. By the time she was referred to us, her behavior problems, including aggression, self-centeredness of an extreme kind, and other antisocial actions, were rampant and having serious implications for herself and her family. The problems were real enough, but there were other issues which required attention (see Table 2).

A glance at this problem profile tells us why those who call themselves systems theorists are agreed in focusing not on the individual but on the system of relationships in which they

Table 2. Problem Profile (The Hayes family)

Problem as defined	Who complains	Who manifests the problem/to whom?
Disobedience	Mother and Father	Avril/Mother (mainly) Avril/Father
Demanding	Mother	Avril/Mother
Aggression	Mother/Sister	Avril/Mother Avril/Sister
Rudeness	Father	Avril/Father
Not playing his part/"opting out"	Mother	Father/Mother
Depression	Father	Mother
Infantilizing	Avril	Parents/Avril
Rejection/ favoritism	Sister	Parents/Avril

Examples of problem	Settings	Desired outcome
Mother asks Avril to go up to bed. Avril ignores; if mother insists she says "No."	Bedtime, supermarket visiting	Avril should comply more readily
Avril demands attention or some task of mother, nags at her until she complies; tantrums if mother refuses her command or does not "obey" immediately.	Home, supermarket (especially when mother is busy)	Ask nicely, wait patiently, be more reasonable
Avril pinches, pulls hair, hits. Is also rude. When mother is driving car/attending to others (when sister teases).	In the car/home/ almost anywhere when thwarted	Develop self-control, tolerance of frustration
Makes contemptuous remarks about/to father (e.g., "You're fat"; "You're stupid").	Home	Learn to be polite and respectful
Father opts out of confronting Avril; rushes off to work in the morning apologizing to mother for leaving her to manage Avril's tempers. Obviously pleased to be "escaping."	Home. Tells mother she is best at dealing with Avril	Father to play his proper parental role
His wife is always weepy, miserable, and lethargic. She doesn't enjoy life or sex anymore.	Everywhere	Be her old cheery affectionate self
"They treat me like a baby."	Home/playgroup	Treat me like my sister
"They spoil Avril"; "She gets away with things I get punished for."	Everywhere	Treat us the same

(*Adapted from M. Herbert, 1987.*)

interact. We are not describing family therapy in minute detail in this book, but there is some overlap between home-based behavioral psychotherapy work and family therapy. After all, the latter is not so much a school of therapy as a basic redefinition of the therapeutic task itself. A systems approach places the emphasis on the individual as a member of various social systems of which the most important is usually (especially for children), but not always, the family. Therapists attempt to conceptualize the problem in a more horizontal (rather than vertical-historical) manner, viewing the client as part of a family group in which the relationship of the members, each with the other, has a bearing on his or her present predicament. The older treatment model tended to point to the identified patient as the focus of attention, for example, the child referred to the child guidance clinic. Diagnostic thinking has since been considerably influenced by what are called interactional frames of references consistent with systems thinking. The family as a system should always be considered in terms of its interaction with other community systems such as the neighborhood, school, and social and health service agencies.

The value of this open-ended approach is (a) it does not assume that the family is "the problem"; nor (b) does it jump to the conclusion that the child has "the problem." Rather it helps you to tease out, by careful and systematic assessment, the many possible problem areas for intervention. Salvador Minuchin (1974), the eminent family therapist, gives the example of the treatment of anorexic patients and their families: taking the child into the hospital; encouraging her to eat through a behavioral program; initiating family "lunch" sessions; providing individual therapy for the child; and marital work for the parents. These interventions are, nevertheless, only separate moves in the direction of changing patterns of behavior in the family system which he sees as maintaining the problem manifested by the child.

Group Processes

Increased understanding of the effects of group influences on individual behavior has also modified views of what should be taken into account in assessment, and it has become necessary to consider whether behavior on the part of an individual is to be seen primarily in individual terms or is more readily explicable in terms of group processes. In a residential context, group processes assume particular significance and may themselves, rather than the individual, constitute the unit of attention (Johnson & Johnson, 1987).

It is a small wonder when we look at the history of Avril that we had a complex case on our hands: a depressed mother, an unhappy child, a discontented sister, a frustrated and confused father, and a generally miserable, tense family life.

Avril, from early in life, had been a difficult and hyperactive child. From the day of her birth Avril would cry day and night. The nights were particularly difficult. Mrs. Hayes spent most of them nursing her to allow the rest of the family to have some sleep. There were also serious feeding problems. The parents were worried that Avril would starve herself, so forced feeding was necessary for several months. It could take up to three hours to feed the baby. Indeed, she was an unusual child in other ways. She was difficult to amuse, taking only the most fleeting interest in toys. She seldom smiled. Her moods were volatile. When she didn't appear to be depressed and withdrawn she was often screaming for attention. Her mother and father found it impossible to enjoy their youngest child as she was so difficult to rear. She hated any change in routine and was predictable only in her unpredictability. Mrs. Hayes felt guilty for having the child when she had been advised not to and would fiercely protect Avril, even though she might secretly agree with the criticism. Finally, because of the marital tension and lack of her husband's support when dealing with Avril's behavior, Mrs. Hayes reached a low point of depression, involving physical and nervous exhaustion; all this further minimized consistent and effective mothering of her child.

Thinking in "ABC" Terms

At this point, we shall begin to think in "ABC" terms—Antecedents, Behaviors, Consequences. This basic learning equation brings us to the next step in assessment. We shall return to Avril as we progress throughout this book.

Step 6.	**Teach your clients to think in terms of behavioral sequences.** This will provide us with an understanding of some of the significant influences that trigger and maintain unhappy interactions within the family. Provide the client with materials to collect information and set homework tasks.
Antecedent events .... ↓ Behavior/interaction ... ↓ Consequence	What happens? What events precede, lead up to, set the stage for the problematic behaviors/interactions being complained of; and what happens after the event? What social (or other) outcomes flow from the problematic interaction?

This is the basic learning equation; the ABC analysis or functional analysis. It provides a helpful description of the key elements of an interpersonal situation and their interrelationships.

The records in Figures 3a, b, and c elicit information about the behavior of the child and on the antecedent and consequent behaviors by members of the family. You might collect the information by means of (a) a handout such as that illustrated opposite by Avril's chart, which, incidentally, incorporates a parallel measure (b) of the mother's reactions, or (c) a simple diary record with the kind of headings illustrated there.

You will have to ask, observe, and possibly role play, over a series of interviews and home visits in order to know which events tend to follow which, in what circumstances.

You might ask parents to describe a "typical day" in the life of the family: who does what, when, how . . . to whom or with whom . . . with what consequences. (Chapter 5 contains an example of a questionnaire/rating scale dealing with family functioning and family difficulties.) The typical day tends to highlight particular times and situations in which there is family friction.

Figure 3(a). Handout ABC Chart

CHART: *Avril's* DATE: *4/7* WEEK: *2*

OBSERVER: *Mother* CODE:

BEHAVIOR: <u>*Defiance*</u> = *defined by situations when Avril refuses to obey (despite warning) a request/command : (i) to do something*
(ii) not to do something Ⓓ

<u>*Tantrum*</u> = *Avril screams / kicks / shouts* Ⓣ

ANTECEDENT EVENTS (BEFORE)	BEHAVIOR	CONSEQUENT EVENTS (AFTER)
Avril asked for a chocolate at the checkout counter; I said "No." She grabbed one. I put it back. She snatched it. I put it back.	Ⓓ	*Avril ran away and climbed on a display counter (see below). She only came down when a shop assistant offered her a chocolate.*
I told her off when we got home.	Ⓣ	*I went to the bathroom with a magazine. The noise subsided.*

33

Figure 3(b). *Mrs. Hayes's Rating Scale:* My anxiety level when Avril defies me in front of other people

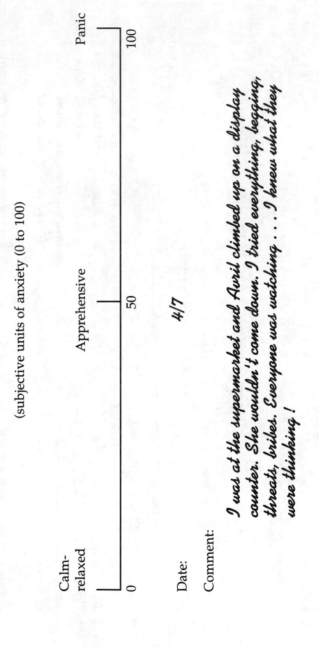

(subjective units of anxiety (0 to 100)

Calm-
relaxed

Apprehensive

Panic

0

50

100

Date: 4/7

Comment:

I was at the supermarket and Avril climbed up on a display counter. She wouldn't come down. I tried everything, begging, threats, bribes. Everyone was watching . . . I knew what they were thinking!

34

Figure 3(c). ABC Diary

Time	Antecedent: What happens beforehand?	Client Behavior	Consequences: What happens next?
9 p.m.	Mother asks Avril to put her toys away.	Avril takes no notice.	Mother tidies them up.
9:30 p.m.	Father tells Avril to go to bed.	Avril says "I don't want to, just give me a little while more."	There is a debate. 1. Father tells her it is late (she ignores). 2. Mother pleads. Avril argues. There is a heated exchange. 1. Mother scolds. 2. Father shouts. Avril is given 10 more minutes.

35

Step 7.	**Establish problem priorities.**

Those workers with mandatory obligations will doubtless have their own guidelines on priorities. But do ask clients what their greatest worry is, what their top priorities are for bringing about change.

Your and their hierarchy of tasks might be influenced by the following considerations with regard to the problem(s):

- Their annoyance value
- Their actual/potential dangerousness
- Their interference with the life of the family or its individual members
- Their accessibility to change (improvement) and an intervention
- Their frequency, intensity, and magnitude
- Their disabling implications
- The "costs" of change in terms of resources (time, money, etc.) and other people's well-being
- The ethical acceptability of the desired outcome
- The availability of the necessary skills resources on your part or the part of your agency—to provide help

Summary and Comment

In this chapter we have asked the vital "what" question that is the beginning point of any assessment of a family and its problems. The first seven steps of this process were set out. This phase of your investigation should take two or three interviews/observation sessions. The need to be specific and precise was emphasized.

Start where the client *is*. Without necessarily accepting his or her (or their) assumptions, allow them the opportunity to describe the problem in their own terms. The client may see the difficulties as being the child's alone. Don't challenge this view immediately. Wait until you have your data, then extend the agenda to include parental and other factors.

Working with families requires a particular perspective or *systems* approach. It is essential to take account of the interdependence of family members and the fact that what happens to one person is likely to affect the others. This focus on the family as a system requires an understanding of group processes as well as individual influences for the assessment of child and family problems.

CHAPTER 3

Taking Account of the Family

By this stage you should have enough information from your initial assessment and data gathering to know whether the problems are sufficiently salient and serious for you to continue the assessment. In working with children and their families, important and early action toward an immediate problem solution needs to be offered if possible. For example, in situations of needed resources, can those resources such as income or free access to child care, be found? The child could be out of school because the family has not provided or allowed necessary immunization for school admission. If problems troubling families are readily resolvable from a professional perspective, referral and education for obtaining needed services and resources are valuable intervention activities on your part. If intervention is not so immediate and the problem so readily solvable, has your assessment thus far helped determine if the family is willing to agree, or establish a contract, to continue in treatment and work toward problem resolution? Finally, is intervention, based on your assessment, within your range of expertise? Are there alternative treatment resources that would be more helpful to your client? Your professional, ethical judgment enters the decision of "where to from here" based upon your encountering the family and assessing the problems they are troubled by.

Families, not unlike the members within them, experience evolution and change throughout the various stages, or cycles of family life. It is important to always bear in mind that movement, change, and transition are quintessential to the development of children, and, indeed, adults; the same can be said of family life. Both individuals and families have their life cycles and life tasks in their development through the life cycles of families and their members (Carter and McGoldrick, 1989; Janzen and Harris, 1997).

The birth of a first child to a couple makes parents of them and transforms their partnership into a family. While their children are growing up and changing, parents too are facing shifts in their own personal development, from youthful maturity to early middle-age. We cannot consider children or adolescents and their problems without considering the manner in which they interact with their parents, who are not without their own preoccupations and anxieties. Let us take an example of parents who are thirty years old and upward when their first child reaches puberty. Insensitive offspring would call this middle-age. Delayed child bearing provides young adults an extended time for career preparation and for establishing their lives as a couple before including a child in their family. For couples who delay having children into their thirties, their children will reach their "teens" when they are in their forties or fifties. These couples may view their middle years as the "prime of life." But what do the teenagers make of them in their thirties, forties, or fifties? For some, their parents' generation seems to have lost its zest for living or to be boring; while for others, the distance between generations seems to have little bearing.

On the other hand, children born of teen parent(s) will likely be reared, at least in their early years, by parents who struggle to work, pay bills, find better jobs, and enroll in various degree and training programs. Life circumstances of families affect children whether it be age of parenthood, income, employment, rural versus urban lifestyles, extended family relationships, physical and mental illness or disabilities, or marital changes such as divorce or remarriage (Helton and Jackson, 1997; Mason, Skolnick, and Sugarman, 1998).

The point of all this is that a "family life map" constructed by you and your client family can illuminate interesting connections. It may indicate why confrontations occur between members of the family who face different life tasks (see chapter 1) and life events. A decision by one to make a change in his or her lifestyle can affect the entire family. Just as a family responds and adjusts to life events and decisions for change by

39

its members, it also must respond to unexpected events or crises that may be so powerful as to cause the family to need help with finding new ways of coping or of identifying alternative ways of functioning, particularly in the face of great losses such as death, job loss, debilitating illnesses, and even catastrophic national and community disasters. There are many major life events that frequently cause families to seek help. The following list identifies some of the major, yet common, life events that occur in families.

Life-Event Information

Common and often overwhelming life events confronting families call for careful assessment and information gathering. These events are potentially disruptive and stress producing and can have long-term impact on a family's approach to problem solving, coping, and communication. It is important to identify major events that impinge at present or that had a potentially disruptive influence in the past on the lives of your client family and its members. Such major events include:

- Death of a spouse
- Divorce
- Marital separation
- Detention in jail or other institution
- Death of a close family member
- Major personal injury or illness
- Marriage
- Marital reconciliation
- Retirement from work
- Major change in the health or behavior of a family member
- Pregnancy
- Sexual difficulties
- Gaining a new family member (e.g., through birth, adoption)
- Major change in responsibilities at work (e.g., promotion, demotion, lateral transfer)
- Son or daughter leaving home (e.g., marriage, attending college, etc.)
- In-law troubles

- Outstanding personal achievement
- Parent(s) beginning or ceasing to work outside the home
- Beginning or ceasing formal schooling
- Major change in living conditions
- Trouble with the boss
- Major change in working hours or conditions
- Change in residence
- Changing to a new school
- Major change in usual type and/or amount of recreation
- Major change in church activities (e.g., a lot more or a lot less than usual)
- Major change in social activities

Families with teenagers frequently seek help as each seeks to accomplish life tasks appropriate for his or her age and development. It is these mature families struggling with adjustments and conflicts rather than stress related to unexpected crises or devastating life events that sometimes challenge even experienced professionals.

Parents sometimes create their own problems by trying to live through their children, relying mainly on vicarious satisfactions. In this context, it is commonly asserted that middle age is a more difficult phase of life for women than men. The changes in her life are in many ways more obvious. The children are becoming less dependent, if not totally independent, of her; and until this period of her life her maternal interests may have been uppermost in her life. Although her concern continues, her direct role as a mother is coming to an end. But we must not exaggerate the "empty nest" phenomenon. Among middle-aged people whose younger child is about to leave high school, most women do mention the approaching departure of the youngest child as a forthcoming change but do *not* consciously believe that it will be a difficult time for them. Most men ignore the imminent event in their conversations with researchers, their attention being already directed to their own retirement in the future.

Marriages are likely to be undergoing greater *strain* at this juncture then at any time since the initial impact of the intimacy of living together when the couple first set up home. This is *not* to say the relationship is necessarily poor or terminal; but there may be special marital stresses. Coping with turbulent youngsters is difficult especially if a person is not getting full support from his or her partner. Difficulties in the marriage may become more exposed, more abrasive, if offspring are rebelling, getting into serious trouble, or playing one parent off against the other.

This age group has been referred to as the "middle generation" because their own parents are usually alive, and they are likely to feel obligations to the younger generation *and* the older one. Some parents feel trapped by the needs of aging parents and demanding teenagers and wonder where those chances of "doing their own thing" have vanished.

All or part of these life events may or may not be present for some or all of your client family members. One of the strengths of a good assessment is that not only is the presence or absence of these life events determined for your client family members, the "worry index," the degree to which these events were and/or continue to be a source of stress and worry, is identified. For example, in one family situation sexual impotence, which caused great stress for the parents at one time, is now a source of a certain amount of humor once the problem was identified and an eye medication changed to one with fewer side effects. Families can identify those stressors they cannot change, those they can change, and those that are becoming less stressful without action on their part. It is important to identify life events and life tasks for families so that expectations are developmentally appropriate for the members as well as the family as a whole.

Step 8.	**Work out a family life map.**
	Your client's family life map will be constructed with the family and will include data mapping accomplishments, or lack thereof, for life tasks and life events for each member of the family. Your client's family map might look something like Figure 4.

Figure 4. A family life map: Transitional stages of life

TIM: 22 months	ANNE: age 10 years	PETER: age 14	MOTHER: age 38	FATHER: age 45	GRANNY: age 66
LIFE TASKS	*LIFE TASKS*	*LIFE TASKS*	*LIFE TASKS*	*LIFE TASKS*	*LIFE TASKS*
• Develop motor skills	• Cope with academic demands at school (underachieving)	• Adjust to physical changes of puberty	• Review her life and commitments	• Review her commitments in mid-life	• Deal with increasing dependence on others
• Develop self-control	• Developing her sense of self	• Adjust to sexual awareness	• Adjust to loss of youth and (in her perception) "looks"	• Develop new phase in relationship with wife	• Come to terms with old age/death
• Elaborate vocabulary	• Learn to be part of a team	• Cope with the opposite sex (shyness)	• Cope with an adolescent as a patient and caring parent	• Face physical changes—some limitations on athletic/sexual activity	• Cope with loss of peers
• Explore his world—make "discoveries"		• Deepen friendships (intimacy)			
LIFE EVENTS	*LIFE EVENTS*	*LIFE EVENTS*	*LIFE EVENTS*	*LIFE EVENTS*	*LIFE EVENTS*
• Parents insist on obedience now	• Afraid to go to school (cannot manage math)	• Worried about his skin (acne) and size of his penis	• Coping with late child—an active toddler	• Threat of being laid off	• Poor health
• Adjust to temporary separations when mother works	• Bullied by a girl in her class	• Has a girlfriend—his first	• Has taken part-time job to relieve feeling trapped	• High blood pressure	• Gave up home when bereaved (may have made a mistake!)
• Not the center of attention and "uncritical" deference	• Jealous of attention Tim gets (calls him a spoiled brat)	• Upset by his parents'quarrels	• Feels guilty	• Worried about drifting apart from his wife	• Enjoys the little one, but
	• Worried about father's health	• Complains that his mother is always watching him	• Bouts of depression	• Had a brief affair	• Feels "claustrophobic" with all the activity/squabbles
			• No longer enjoys sex	• Feels unattractive	
TODDLERHOOD	PREPUBESCENCE	ADOLESCENCE	← MIDLIFE	MIDLIFE →	RETIREMENT

43

The Family as a Dynamic Organization

The family is a dynamic institution, that is to say susceptible to change in several ways. The family is more than the sum of its parts, more than the static aggregate of the individual personalities who make up its membership. It has, in a sense, a life of its own. The members interact in many subtle ways that give a particular "feel" or atmosphere to a family; they have different and *changing* roles that in turn change the "personality" of the family as time goes by; they have their successes and failures that reflect on the family; alliances form, dissolve, and reform. The family thus has its own life cycle from "infancy" to "old age" with associated changes in its size, "shape," and function. It also has its pool of skills. The all-important transmission of culture cannot be inflexible as would be a genetic code determining our physical equipment. But nor can it be left to chance. The welfare of the individual and the continuity of the culture depend upon there being a satisfactory means of socializing the new generation into society's mores, attitudes, and skills, and to ensure that they, in turn, will satisfactorily transmit the culture. The family plays a major role in this important socialization process, thus preparing children to transmit cultural traditions and societal mores to future generations.

Theories of Family Life

Defining interactions and development of families is approached from a variety of perspectives, and each perspective informs its intervention. In other words, what we believe about families shapes how we work with families. Selected and widely used models of family therapy vary in the theoretical framework embraced and interventions applied. Working with family members conjointly, that is, together, fostered the movement toward intervention in family systems as we know it today. Satir (1983) focused on the interaction of family members and involved the entire family in assessment and treatment. Salvador Minuchin based structural family therapy on family systems, their transactions and changes, and intervened

44

through changing transactions and reorganizing relationships of members in the family with respect to the strengths and contributions of each member and of the family as a system. Individual, subsystem, and family boundaries are important in the realigning and joining techniques of this approach (Minuchin, 1974; Minuchin and Fishman, 1981).

A widely used approach to understanding and helping families in the strategic family approach focuses on the world view or the conceptual frames of reference of families and their members in terms of how they see themselves and alternatives in the context of their lives. Strategic family therapists see dysfunctional behaviors and coping efforts as symptoms in response to the context of families' lives. The question of "why" is not as important as "what" is going on in the hierarchy of the family, in their systems of power and control, and in how the family is organized and can be restructured. Strategic family therapy is directive and teaches clients to take control of behavior including violent and angry behaviors and to forgive themselves and others close to them (Haley, 1987; Madanes, 1981, 1984, 1990).

Solution-focused family treatment focuses on solutions, not problems. Problems are defined and viewed as experiences that have a purpose and then goals for new solutions are defined. Clients are helped to value and explore experiences, take action toward solutions, and explore ideas and beliefs through their own language and stories of themselves and their experiences. There is no singular right solution but a range of solutions around which action and anticipation of future success can occur (O'Hanlon, 1993; O'Hanlon and Weiner-Davis, 1989). Berg (1994) applies solution-focused intervention to families and children who are clients of child welfare services. Intervention is relatively brief, recognizes change in families and individuals in families, and is directive in helping families find solutions and create new solutions for those that work less well.

Having its roots in behavioral theory, the social learning model is a useful approach to understanding how families function and to helping families change behaviors (Horne, 1991; Horne and Saygre, 1990; Janzen and Harris, 1997). Learn-

45

ing occurs in the environment families create for themselves. There, behaviors occur and are accepted, reinforced and established, are ignored, or are unaccepted and sometimes punished. This process shapes and reinforces behaviors within the culture of the family and its process of development. As such, this learning process occurs in response to interactions and relationships in the family and is not generally a planned nor consistent process. Family members establish functional and dysfunctional behaviors in their relationships as they interact and cope in their daily lives.

Behaviors that trouble families are often the impetus that serve to cause families to seek help with family functioning. When they do seek help, generally the behavior of a family member is presented as the problem to be treated. For example, families seek help with problem behaviors such as alcoholism of a family member, hyperactive or aggressive behavior of a child, eating disorder of a member, delinquent behavior of an adolescent, or conflict with a marital partner. The family therapist intervenes to establish the frequency and extent of the problem behavior and provides a therapeutic environment where the family can learn to restructure behaviors. In the social learning model, behaviors are approached as learned through cognitive processes involving satisfaction and reinforcement. In this model, dysfunctional behaviors can be understood and diminished and new functional behaviors can be learned. The social learning approach extends beyond behavioral therapy as it recognizes the social context of behaviors, relationships that reward behaviors, and the cognitive and problem-solving capacities that enable families to normalize problems and set about structuring their environment to successfully change behaviors and alleviate problems in family functioning. The social learning approach offers structures in working with families so that opportunities for relearning can be identified, affirmed, and practiced. (Goldenberg and Goldenberg, 1991).

The systems perspective provides a framework for understanding family functioning and relationships within the family system and community and social systems in the family's environment. Unhappiness within families produces unhappy members, all of whom are affected and involved in the particular problem, and all of whom need to be involved in improving the unhappiness or problem. It is within the functioning and life cycle of families that children develop; experience stages of their biological, social, and emotional development; and are greatly impacted by their experiences in their families. From infancy through young adulthood, children learn to behave, develop an image of themselves, and establish the map for their world view as adults. Throughout life cycles of families, children, and adults, systems and systems constructs play a major role in individual development and understanding human relationships (Carter and McGoldrick, 1989).

Major theories of family functioning and human behavior are reviewed by Vetere and Gale (1987) and Zastrow and Kirst-Ashman (1997). Some concepts important in working with children and their family system you will need to understand and perhaps explore in the literature include:

- *Cohesion,* which reflects the transactions—the emotional attachments of members—and their individual autonomy. It is at its highest in *enmeshed* (closely interrelated, mutually involved) families and at its lowest in *disengaged* (unattached) families.
- *Boundaries,* which delineate the components belonging to the system and those belonging to the environment; they are defined by *rules* which specify individual's roles, what subsystem he or she belongs to, and the appropriate behavior which such membership entails. Boundaries can be *clear* (easily recognized and acceptable rules), *diffuse* (ambiguous and chaotic because rules are unstable or absent), or *rigid* (inflexible, unadaptable).
- *Adaptability,* which indicates that a family can modify its roles and relationships in response to influence for change.
- *Homeostasis,* which is a term that describes the "steady state" of the "organism" (for our purposes the family)— indicating that the various subsystems are in balance and the whole system is in harmony with the environment. To achieve and maintain homeostasis in the face of change and stress, a system must be open.

- *Open*, which means that family members have a high level of exchange with the outside community, as compared with systems that are closed and take in little new information or energy.
- *Closed*, which have very little exchange with the community outside its boundaries.
- *Feedback* processes are believed to characterize social systems and reflect the ability of the family to "recognize" its own output as input at some later stage. For example, the family that is functioning well is capable of monitoring its progress toward family goals and correcting or modifying its actions to bring itself back on track, if necessary.

All families are different in their own ways; nevertheless, certain dynamics and problem areas occur in the lives of many families. Families in need of professional help often have the commonality of similar problem areas. In the life of a professional, rarely will a client family seek help to celebrate their successes. Instead, it is the configurations of problems and stress that cause stress in the lives of families and their members for which professional intervention is necessary. Let us look at the all too common problem of family violence, a problem area where family cohesion is often minimal and boundaries are marked by either extreme rigidity or excessive diffuseness. Victims of family violence are usually those members most unable to protect themselves—sometimes the elderly member, the mother, and all too frequently, the children.

Family Violence

The cozy image of the family as a nurturant organization and a haven of safety is shattered more often than we care to think, when it erupts with violence. The point has been made by experienced workers that people are more likely to be killed, physically assaulted, hit, beaten, or slapped in their own homes by other family members than anywhere else, or by anyone else, in our society. Three groups of people are particularly vulnerable: children, women, and the elderly. It is not good enough to categorize the perpetrators of such awful deeds as degenerates, drunks, psychopaths, or mental cases. Such categorization simply applies known labels to unacceptable behavior. Some labels even excuse violent action by implying that the perpetrator is not accountable for uncontrollable behavior.

The evidence suggests that many diverse factors, including social and psychological factors, contribute to family violence. We consider these in chapter 4. Various forms of physical abuse are obvious and easily assessed or diagnosed if seen by a physician. Other forms, equally disabling for the victim, include psychological and emotional abuse and neglect. Children seen with unexplained injuries and old and healed cuts and fractures that have gone untreated are likely victims of physical abuse. Abuse is willful and harmful action toward the victim while neglect is more likely to be a lack of care and a problem of omission. Although the problems of abuse and neglect may both go on over time, neglect is likely to go undetected and unreported much longer. Abuse and neglect of children are commonly referred to as child maltreatment, a problem that occurs in the social, cultural, and family context of the lives of children. Having a multicasual origin, child maltreatment is a serious problem in the lives of families and has long-term consequences for victims. Common categories of abuse and neglect are presented by Faller, Bowden, Jones, and Wildebrandt (1981) and Tower (1996).

Abuse

- Physical abuse is the infliction of a range of physical injuries to a child and can include bruises, cuts, burns, scalds, injuries to bones and joints including fractures, and serious internal injuries to various organs of the body, head, and brain. Failure to thrive, particularly when food and water are withheld, is physical abuse.
- Emotional abuse is the infliction of psychological and emotional assault, including threats of serious physical or sexual harm, scapegoating, confinement, disregard, yelling, and punitive communication. Emotionally abused children often present symptoms such as bed-wetting, aggres-

sive or bizarre behavior, difficulty in forming relationships, poor self-esteem, and problems in school.

- Sexual abuse is the sexual assault and misuse of children by adults, siblings, or parents and is sometimes difficult to diagnose but may include genital infections, bruises and lacerations, pregnancy, and bloody or infectious discharges. Children exposed to sexual abuse are often more familiar with sexual and physical information than typical for their age and development, display excessive masturbation, and sometimes are involved in sexual behaviors as the perpetrator. Exploitation of children for personal satisfaction or for monetary gain, such as pornographic literature or movies with sexually explicit content involving children, is sexual abuse.

Neglect

- Physical neglect is the failure to provide a safe and nurturing home for a child and may include a failure to feed, shelter, clothe, and protect from harm. Failure to thrive may be due to physical and/or emotional neglect.
- Emotional neglect is the failure to nurture the psychological, social, and emotional aspects of a child's life and may involve an absence of love, affection, attention, intellectual and emotional stimulation, social interaction, and warmth related to a lack of cuddling and demonstration of love and affection.
- Supervisory neglect is the failure to provide supervision to assure safety including: protection, not being left alone for periods of time inappropriate for age and development, and not being abandoned.
- Medical neglect is the failure to provide medical care including immediate and appropriate care for critical injuries or illnesses, immunizations, and medical treatment when needed.
- Educational neglect is the failure to provide school enrollment and attendance on a regular and timely basis so that the child is appropriately on time, in school when not ill, and provided with necessary clothing and materials for school.

Conflict in Families

Other family problems or family dysfunctions which professionals are likely to be called upon to deal with include the following:

- *Chaotic* family organization; little or no organization, which makes the management of change or coping with stress extremely difficult;
- Overly *rigid* organization, which inhibits change when change is necessary or leads to a stereotyped and therefore inappropriate reaction to events;
- Too great a *distance* between members of the family leading potentially to emotional isolation and physical deprivation;
- Excessive *closeness* between members of the family leading potentially to overidentification and loss of individuality;
- An inability to work through *conflicts*, solve problems, or make decisions;
- An inability on the part of parents to form a *coalition* and to work together, with detrimental effects on the marriage and/or the children;
- An *alliance* across the generations disrupting family life as when a grandparent interferes with the mother's child-rearing plans and actions;
- Poor *communication* between members;
- A failure to respond appropriately to each other's *feelings*.

Some of the ways in which a child may contribute to a family's inability to cope with conflict have been described by psychiatrists and family therapists:

- *Parent-child coalition,* where one parent attacks the other, using one of the children as an ally;
- *Triangulation,* where both parents attempt to induce a child to take *their* side;
- *Go-between,* where a child is used to transmit messages and feelings;
- *Whipping boy,* where one parent, instead of making a direct attack on the other, uses their child as a scapegoat;
- *Child as weapon,* where one parent attacks the other using the child as a weapon;

- *Sibling transfer*, where the children agree to divert the parents from arguing;
- *Pacification*, where one child acts as a peacemaker;
- *Detour through illness*, where children learn that disagreements between parents may be reduced when they are ill.

Changing unwanted behaviors, or developing skills of interacting and relating, where skills are faulty or absent, usually requires the participation, and the willingness to change, of parents and, sometimes, the entire family. To this end one might say that every family makes use of its combined store of skills so that members can usefully share and learn from each other. Broadly speaking these skills fall into seven categories: relationship, social, communication, problem solving, coping, study, and work skills.

Parenting skills include several of these categories (see chapter 9); deficits in parental abilities can lead to problems in the offspring—your analysis is by this time beginning to move toward a formulation of why things are going wrong for this family. The *what* question merges into a *why* question, the answers to which are the subject of the next step.

Step 9.	Make an assessment of your client's skills (incentives, resources).

Parenting is a complex series of skills, part commonsense, part intuition, and part empathy, that is, the ability to see things from another's point of view.

Parents *can* be trained in many of the necessary skills of child care and behavior management; the latter is a major theme of this book. Although not so easy, those attachments and feelings that come so readily to most parents and children, but which are absent or distorted in some, can be encouraged.

Ask your client to go through the skills listed in Table 3 with you. He or she may be pleasantly surprised at how many they can claim. Unless your clients know that they possess certain skills they may not be able to make the most constructive use of them. It is important not to demoralize clients with this exercise; not all of them are pertinent for the particular individ-

Table 3.   A List of Parenting Skills

I and my child	*I and significant others*
Skills I need to relate effectively to him/her	Skills I need to relate effectively to others (e.g. my partner, teachers, friends) involved with my child
• How to communicate clearly	• How to be reasonably objective about others
• How to "listen" carefully so as to understand	• How not to be possessive
• How to develop my relationship	• How to be assertive (without being intrusive or bossy)
• How to give help and care and protection without "going over the top"	• How to influence crucial people and systems (e.g. school)
• How to teach and discipline	• How to work in groups (e.g. parents' groups, pressure groups)
• How to show and receive affection	• How to express my feelings clearly and constructively
• How to manage/resolve conflict	• How to inspire confidence and strength in others
• How to give and receive feedback	• How to see my child's friends from his/her point of view
• How to maintain a balance between extremes (e.g. loving without being possessive)	• How to resist/cope with jealousy
• How to negotiate sensible compromises	
• How to set limits—reasonables ones, and stick to them	

(*Adapted from B. Hopson and M. Scully 1980.*)

ual. There may have been little or no opportunity to develop some of them.

Now do something similar for the child or teenager. Look for positives in the child's situation: what is going well in the situation you are concerned about at present with regard to the child or teenager? How does this young person contribute to your family life? What are his/her good points? You might draw up a balance sheet for attributes perceived by parents as on the *credit* or *debit* side. You may find it useful to ask the youngster to carry out the same exercise with regard to himself/herself.

CREDIT	DEBIT
Sally has a nice sense of humor.	*She's moody and unpredictable.*
She is clever.	*She has to argue over every little thing.*
Etc.	*She tells lies.*
	Etc.

Step 10(a).	**Ask your clients (parents) what their goals (ambitions, plans) are for their child.**

In the case of children, *change* and *development* must have some point—a destination and thus a direction. Only parents and children can decide on their goals and aspirations although your counsel, based on professional knowledge and experience, should play a part.

Step 10(b).	**Ask your clients what their goals are for themselves; in other words, their self-orientated goals.**

54

We have been discussing goals which involve children and the interactions between parents and children. But what of goals involving adults in their own right, where you may have to counsel them? A mother may wish to increase her self-confidence and banish her recurrent bouts of depression. A father may ask for help in controlling his temper and reducing his irritability. A teenage brother or sister may desire to play a greater part in their family's decision-making.

We have now reached Phase III of the Flow Chart (chapter 2); it is good practice to have a preintervention record of the extensiveness of the client's problems based upon a week or two of observations and self-reports. This baseline allows you to evaluate any changes that occur before and after intervention. Baseline data provide the standard against which to measure the effect of your intervention.

Baseline Data Collection (further one or two interviews, preferably including home visit[s]).

From this baseline you collect information about the extent and precise circumstances of the problematic interactions. You show your client(s) how to observe behavior so that, in a sense, you can observe things through their eyes during the time you cannot be with them.

Until now the main source of information has been the interview—a systematic approach to obtaining information about the problem, its nature, frequency, antecedents, consequences, etc. It may have been conducted at the office or in the client's home. Next, the baseline data collected by interview are checked, supplemented, and quantified by:

- Direct observation of the client in natural settings, for example, home, school, youth clubs;
- Direct observation in other settings, for example, office, reception center, and so forth;
- Self-recordings by the client (diaries, activity charts, self-ratings) in his/her day-to-day life or special situations;
- Use of questionnaires, rating scales, and the like, completed by the client or others; use of audio or video cassette recordings

55

Summary and Comment

We have carried forward the analysis of the dynamic interactions within the family in this chapter. By the end of Phase II of the assessment you should be in a position to decide whether the problems are sufficiently serious to continue on to the collection of baseline data. If not, you need to advise parents why you do not regard a further assessment or intervention as necessary. Perhaps the child's problems are normal for his/her age and situation. Perhaps parents have exaggerated because of their personal anxieties or ignorance of child development. Of course, you cannot simply dismiss parents with a philosophical "Don't worry" statement. They may require information about child behavior and development, or some understanding on how to manage the child's not unusual but worrying fears or tantrums or bed-wetting. Knowledge of age-appropriate behavior is obviously vital for the professional and information necessary for parents.

We have seen that many of the problems affecting parents and their children are the problem of the family, *as a family*, and need to be construed as such. Problems within the family with which you are likely to deal are those involving relationships (e.g., sibling rivalry and jealousy, parental overprotection, marital discord); lack of knowledge (e.g., ignorance of what to expect of children at different ages); disagreements over the sharing of finite resources (such as money, time, attention); conflict (over policies such as rules, discipline, routines). Helping parents to resolve conflicts with adolescents is a valuable contribution to happier family life, as is the reduction of aggravation brought about by planning of "around the clock" rules and routines for the toddler who needs help with activities such as dressing, meals, visiting, shopping, and going to bed.

Among the most serious problems you might be called on to deal with is violence within the family. Physical and emotional abuse are described, together with a range of family dysfunctions.

CHAPTER 4

Assessing the "Why" Question

Some parents (and, indeed, professionals) dwell on the past when they look for the why's and wherefore's of their off-spring's difficulties. It is important to maintain a balance between past and present when trying to find reasons or causes for current behavior. The past cannot be changed, although you might "liberate" some from the past by resolving or changing present unhealthy attitudes which are *rooted* there. In any event, it is only in rare instances that current problems can be traced to specific past experiences with any degree of confidence.

Yet when things go wrong, our society gets an irresistible urge to find something or someone to blame. And when they go wrong with children, or the relationships between parents and their children, the finger is often pointed at the mother. The literature on childhood psychological problems is full of overprotective, dominating, or rejecting mothers.

But is it really all so one-sided? What are fathers doing during these early years of their children's lives? The cynic might think that fathers were remote figures because it is mothers who generally bring the children to the office or clinic and are interviewed.

More surprising is the relatively neglected role of the child in all these unhappy events. Is it just a one-way process, with awful or stupid things being done to a passive infant? Certainly by encouraging some activities and discouraging others, parents influence their children's behavior and personality. But in all sorts of subtle ways, their behavior is also shaped by the child. In the crucial business of growing up, there is a two-way traffic in the relationship between parents and child.

Most current theories about the problems of, for example, child abuse place the sole emphasis on parental and, in particular, maternal psychopathology and environmental factors. The role the child can unwittingly play in his or her tragic predicament is usually overlooked. Yet research suggests that there are children who, from birth, show characteristics that make them not only difficult to rear but also difficult to love.

It is commonly known that among all the allegedly harmful factors blamed for this or that problem, whether adverse parental characteristics, family conflicts, or the like, it is possible to identify significant number of children who developed without serious problems, despite being subjected to these influences. Those practitioners who are behaviorally oriented will lose little sleep over the doubts and uncertainties about the precursors of psychological problems—the tenuousness of the link between conditions of the child's life including home and school circumstances far removed in time from present manifestations of troublesome behavior. This is because human actions, whether simple or elaborate, normal or abnormal, are brought about by *many* influences rather than a single factor. And whatever the influence of personality traits, attitudes, and ideas, shaped over years of learning and development, the young person's day-to-day actions are powerfully controlled by current events, such as opportunities and temptations and the favorable outcomes, for example, reinforcements, to which these actions give rise.

Such observations give rise to a critical issue concerning the way you work: the theoretical perspective you adopt, or the particular model of human behavior that informs your practice. In order to help parents and their children effectively, you need to be clear about your underlying assumptions, as to how and why such individuals behave in the way they do. In what way do *you* make sense of your clients and predict or anticipate how they are likely to respond to your intervention?

Formulation of Causes in the Case of Avril Hayes

You will soon detect the predominant model underlying our *formulation* of the causes of Avril's and her parents' difficulties. We had looked for patterns of antecedent and consequent stimuli which might be precipitating and maintaining the problem behavior. We also examined other situations in which the child's behavior differed from that in the "problematic" situations, for example, evidence of prosocial behavior and the settings in which it took place.

The case of Avril was thought to be one largely but by no means the whole story of faulty training and learning. For complex reasons that reach back to Avril's conception and birth, Mrs. Hayes had become trapped in a pattern of behavior in which she unwittingly "encouraged" the very behaviors she wished to eliminate in the child's repertoire. Avril's demands, with few exceptions, for being waited on, attention, and so on, were acceded to following her display of tantrums and disruptive behaviors. The invariable outcome in the case of defiant actions was to increase the interaction between Avril and her mother. The resulting attention was reinforcing these noncompliant actions. It was quite straightforward to identify favorable consequences. To take but one example, she was being allowed to veto activities she did not like. Conversely, in all examples of misbehavior, there were no really negative or unfavorable consequences which might serve to diminish the behaviors.

With regard to the cues for the performance of problem behaviors, the most significant of these were the presence and actions of Mrs. Hayes. The currency of her commands and threats had been debased; Avril did not trust her words. She had learned that her wishes for her mother's undivided attention, and "obedience" to her commands, were likely to be met if she persisted long enough or escalated her coercive behaviors.

Essentially she had learned that certain antisocial behaviors were guaranteed to produce "payoffs." This lesson, applied in the school situation, could have aversive consequences for her and reduce her ability to learn. It was our opinion that they had affected her social development adversely—her manner was babyish and frustrating. From the point of view of other members of the family, Avril's egocentric, monopolistic, and immature behavior was undoubtedly undermining their well-being. Her sister was beginning to imitate some of her behaviors. As her parents saw things, they had endeavored to provide the best that they could for Avril, and yet they were faced with a situation in which they no longer enjoyed their child. They increasingly quarreled over how to deal with the situation. These considerations, among others, contributed to the decision that an intervention was required.

She was certainly receiving a large amount of attention including physical proximity and verbal exchanges, but much of it took a negative form. It was precisely because of the endless rounds of disputations between parents and child that Avril was precluded from much of the usual range of symbolic rewards or social reinforcers which belong to happy and meaningful family communications. Avril, as a volatile, demanding child, had made constant assaults on Mrs. Hayes' self-doubts. This is how her mother described the situation:

> *As time went by, Avril had developed into a despot. She shows a general aggression, a degree of willfulness, and various other unacceptable behaviors. She whines, clings like a limpet, is insecure, and worst of all for me, incessantly disobedient. . . . The situation over the years has deteriorated, compounded by an increasing tiredness on my part. This gradually deepened into general depression for which my doctor prescribed drugs. They didn't help; in fact feeling slightly drunk and rudderless made coping even more difficult. I was tearful, tense, often unreasonably angry, erratic and emotional, and then silent and withdrawn in turns. The tension in the house was painful. All the time her behavior has gotten worse. We were trapped in a vicious circle. Life was so miserable for me at this time that when I think back I can still feel the emptiness inside, the feeling of isolation, the constant fear that I would totally lose control and hurt her. I was really desperate. It was an effort to go out, even to go shopping. I looked awful, felt awful. Sometimes the loathing for Avril spilled over and I would find myself wanting to tell her, "Go away out of my life, I hate you. You've ruined my life." Sometimes I would start then have to bite back the words, remembering that I did love her. Afterwards I would feel consumed with guilt that I could even think of these things. And overall was this dreadful sense of failure. Failure as a mother and failure as a wife, even failure as a woman. I have never been so close to a total breakdown.*

As Mrs. Hayes appeared to bear the brunt of most of Avril's misbehavior, it might be concluded that her father was able to exercise control over her. This was not so; in fact, Mr. Hayes' small part in this analysis of the problem situation reflects his minimizing of the contact he had with Avril—much to his wife's annoyance.

Having attempted to identify the conditions controlling the problem behavior, the next task was to try to explain their origins. The importance of this is not so much to help the client achieve insight, although awareness may facilitate change, but rather to discover to what extent the original "causal" factors continue to influence the current controlling conditions. Avril's developmental history was analyzed in order to seek any possible contribution to the problem by somatic or other factors. Physical conditions might produce problem behavior directly or might contribute to it indirectly through the reaction of children and/or their parents to any disability.

You may remember that Avril, from early in life, had been a difficult and overactive child, and that from the day of her birth she would cry day and night. The nights were particularly difficult. Mrs. Hayes spent most of them nursing her. Being of such a commanding temperament, Avril learned from early on the strategy of how to gain attention from her mother and the rest of the family. The parents always intervened when she was crying, shouting, screaming; when she was frustrated, disobedient, and aggressive, they often obeyed her commands for the sake of peace, to save time, or to avoid embarrassment. A variety of situations and settings became cues for verbal disputes and other forms of coercion by Avril. Her difficult behaviors escalated at supermarkets, friends' homes, car drives, and the like. Here the parents were constrained even more than usual in responding to her oppositional behavior. Here is a summary:

Avril appeared to be a child who displayed a range of surplus behaviors almost from birth; these have been shown to be closely linked with the development of maladaptive behaviors at a later age. In addition, her mother's ability to cope had been considerably reduced in a number of ways. First, Mrs. Hayes had been handicapped by her fatigue and depression and in particular by the fiercely protective and even defensive attitude she had toward this "unwanted" child who had turned out to be so difficult. This, together with a philosophy of child rearing which was a reaction to her parents' methods, had considerably limited her choice of disciplinary procedures.

Clearly, the number of times the word "learning" appears in the formulation is numerous. The social learning model will be drawn on as a theoretical model to understand and intervene with Avril and with the Hayes family as a unit.

Theoretical Approaches to Understanding Behavior

Social Learning Model

It is hypothesized that a major proportion of a child's behavior is learned, maintained, and regulated by its effects upon the natural environment and the feedback received with regard to these consequences. Behavior does not occur in a vacuum; nor is it a passive process. It is a result of a complex transaction between the individual, with his or her inborn strengths and weaknesses, acting and reacting with an environment that sometimes encourages and sometimes discourages certain actions.

An important feature of the social learning model is the acknowledgment of the *active* role of cognitive variables, such as, complex interpretive, thinking processes, in the way we learn. The part played by *understanding* in learning is significant. Not all learning, for example, to walk, to ride a bike, involves understanding, but much learning involves knowing rather than simply doing. Stimuli have meaning to the learner, who acquires knowledge of the situation which can be used in adapting to it. The emphasis, therefore, is on *awareness* in learning (Goldenburg and Goldenburg, 1991; Horne, 1991).

Many problems in adults as well as children, are the consequences of failures or distortions of learning. The laws of learning that apply to the acquisition and change of normal socially approved behavior are assumed to be relevant to the understanding of self-defeating and/or socially disapproved actions. More specifically, the behavior problems of childhood are in large part due to the child's learning inappropriate responses; they are also the consequences of the child's failure to learn the appropriate behavior.

With all forms of learning the very processes which help the child adapt to life can, under certain circumstances, contribute to maladaptation. An immature child who learns by imitating an adult (observational learning) will not necessarily comprehend when it is undesirable (deviant) behavior that is being modeled. Mrs. Hayes is a good example of a parent who does not always realize that she is reinforcing unwanted behavior by attending to it (instrumental or operant conditioning). If the consequences of a behavior are rewarding or favorable to a child, that behavior is likely to increase in strength. For example, it may become more frequent. Put another way: if Pat does something, and as a result of his action something pleasant happens to him, then he is more likely to do the same thing in similar circumstances in the future. When psychologists refer to this pleasant outcome as the positive reinforcement of behavior, they have in mind several kinds of reinforcers: tangible rewards, for example, sweets, treats, pocket money; social rewards, such as, attention, a smile, a pat on the back, a word of encouragement; and self-reinforcers, that is, the ones that come from within and which are nontangible: self-praise, self-approval, a sense of pleasure.

Behaving in a manner that avoids an unpleasant outcome leads to the reinforcement of behavior, thus making it more likely to recur in similar circumstances. If a young girl does something her parents do not like, such as losing her temper too easily, they may increase her ability to think first and hold her temper by penalizing her consistently for failing to do so. In this way they are providing what is called negative reinforcement. She avoids punishment by appropriate actions. They may not have to apply the penalty if she believes their threat because of their record of keeping their word. Consistency and persistence are watchwords in early learning, especially with certain volatile children, particularly children who display hyperactivity.

The reason we look at the "A" term (antecedents to problem

behavior/confrontation) in the "ABC" sequence, referred to in chapter 2, is that it seems that the antecedents of a behavior, its cues or triggers, are very important. If you think about and watch the settings of your client's behavior, it may be that the child behaves in a noncompliant way, or has a tantrum on some occasions but not on others; that is, some situations seem to act as cues to behave in a particular way (see Figure 5).

People tend to tailor their behavior to the particular places and the different persons with whom they find themselves. In the case of children, this chameleon capacity often leads to misunderstandings between home and school with each blaming the other when more often than not they are difficult in the one setting but not the other.

The so-called operant conditioning rule is of great significance in social development. Fortunately, as we have seen already, there *is* a basic "preparedness" on the part of most infants to be trained—that is, a bias toward all things social. The baby *responds* to the mother's friendly (baby talk) overtures in a sociable manner that produces in her a happy and sociable reaction. The baby also initiates social encounters with vocalizations or smiles directed to the mother which cause her in turn to smile back and to talk, tickle, or touch. In this way she elicits further responses from the baby. A chain of mutually rewarding interactions is thus initiated on many occasions. Parents and child learn about and nurture each other in the course of these interactions.

Learning to be skillful and social. Learning is the key to our understanding of the process of socialization. Parents and teachers teach children skills and guide them toward prosocial actions and away from antisocial activities. There seems to be a fair amount of latitude in learning conditions for those children with intact central nervous systems, healthy bodies, and relatively unvolcanic temperaments. They acquire an understanding of and willingness to abide by society's conventions, despite parental inconsistency, contradictory demands or double-binds, and ambiguous rules. For them, parental inexperience or poor judgment seems no more than a minor hindrance in the business of growing up.

Figure 5. Layout for a preliminary analysis of a problematic classroom situation.

1. *Antecedent Events*

   Peter is asked to do something or to stop doing it. Or he is asked to answer a question about the work, or about his lateness.

   2. *Behavior*

   (i) Noncompliance. He pays no attention; if Miss Smith insists, he resorts to

   (ii) Verbal abuse. He makes rude comments, criticizes, occasionally swears and shouts.

   3. *Consequences*

   Miss Smith shouts at him, scolds him, or discusses what he has done with him.

   Sends him out of the classroom.

   All classroom work comes to a stop; all the pupils watch the confrontation.

   The original cause of the confrontation is forgotten.

Persons: He's rude and disobedient mainly with Miss Smith; occasionally to other teachers; never with Mrs. Simpson or Mr. Jackson.

Places: Classroom only, never in the playground.

Times: Mondays in particular – usually at the beginning of teaching periods.

Situations: Mainly when asked to do something or when challenged over being late or without his equipment. Particularly when questioned about, or criticized for, his work.

(from Herbert, 1987, with permission.)

65

The welfare of the individual and the continuity of the culture depend upon society's having a satisfactory means of indoctrinating the new generation into its mores, attitudes, and skills and to ensure that they, in turn, will satisfactorily transmit the culture. The family plays a major role in indoctrinating and training the child for life. All parents are informal learning theorists and all are in the business of changing behavior.

They use various techniques to teach, influence, and change the child in their care. Among those used are material and psychological rewards, praise and encouragement, giving or withholding approval, and other psychological punishments such as reproof or disapproval. At its simplest level this process is as follows:

Acceptable behavior	+ Reinforcement	=	More acceptable behavior
Acceptable behavior	+ No reinforcement	=	Less acceptable behavior
Unacceptable behavior	+ Reinforcement	=	More unacceptable behavior
Unacceptable behavior	+ No reinforcement	=	Less unacceptable behavior

Of course parents also give direct instructions, set an example or model desired actions, and provide explanations of rules, that is, inductive methods. When the family fails in providing appropriate and consistent socialization experiences the child seems to be particularly vulnerable to the development of antisocial conduct and delinquent disorders (see chapter 6). Typically children with persistent antisocial problems come from families where there is discord and quarreling; where affection is lacking; where discipline is inconsistent, ineffective, and either extremely severe or lax.

Relationships. Many relationships can be understood in part in terms of social learning principles. Adults initiate and prolong relationships of intimacy in close friendships, courtship, mar-

riage, and cohabitation as long as those relationships are reasonably satisfactory with regard to what are called their
"rewards" and "costs." It may seem crass to think of human
relationships in terms of what are reminiscent of economic
exchanges and bargains. Nevertheless, for example, in marital
interaction a *social exchange* model not only helps us to assess
what is going wrong with a partnership, but also to do something about it.

In this model, marital discord is thought of as a function of
prevailing rates of reinforcement (satisfaction) and punishment
(dissatisfaction). Individuals, it is assumed, try to maximize
satisfaction or positive rewards arising from the partnership
while minimizing the dissatisfaction or the negatives generated
by the marriage. We shall return to the use of notations of
behavior exhange to bring about behavior change in adults and
young people, in chapter 11.

The social learning approach is certainly one approach to
working with Avril and her family and is the preferred
approach for this particular case in the practice experience and
expertise of the authors. Nevertheless, there are a variety of
approaches that offer explanations and interventions for working with children and their families. These various approaches
or theories provide a way to view the situation in terms of
explanations and possible solutions. It is important to consider
a range of theories and to be able to evaluate the utility and
application of various theoretical perspectives for their use in
working with particular cases or problems. Being able to select
and apply the theoretical framework most appropriate in a
particular practice context requires familiarity with the theory,
the research supporting it, its application, and the outcomes
expected from such application. More than one theoretical
approach to working with Avril is appropriate and it is the
responsibility of the practitioner to make an informal and ethical decision on how to proceed with intervention based upon
information gathered from assessing the problem presented.
Several theoretical frameworks are briefly presented for the
purpose of broadening the scope of potential interventions in
this case.

Medical Model

The medical model provides explanations of human problems in terms of disease or other physical processes. Such explanations have been questioned by social workers and clinical psychologists. But a critical exercise that rightly rejects pathological explanations of actions and feelings (where inappropriate) has been taken to an extreme and is often neglected in cases where it is essential to consider the contributory influence of physical factors, for example, in cases of bed-wetting and soiling. The tendency to "throw the baby out with the bath water" is sadly a common one in the helping professions. The medical model addresses a problem to be treated and, therefore, fails to treat the whole person (Payne, 1991).

Physical or medical explanations may encompass, for example, infections, that is, as they affect bladder incontinence, and physical disabilities in so far as they affect learning, and thus achievement and self-esteem. The concept of brain damage is a popular explanatory notion for hyperactive, conduct-disordered patterns of behavior. And it is a good example of the misuse of a medical explanation. Being tautologies or renaming in most instances, they tell us very little about the child and only too often are therapeutically pessimistic. For example, parents and teachers are sometimes told that a particular child's difficulties at home and at school are a result of brain damage, suffered perhaps as early as at birth. This is no more helpful than for a general practitioner to tell a mother her child is physically ill when she takes him along for a diagnosis of a bodily malaise. Certainly no program of rehabilitation, either remedial teaching or treatment, could be planned on the basis of such a vague diagnosis as brain damage. What is needed, in describing children, is not a meaningless label but precise information about their specific physical and intellectual problems, and also about any emotional and social difficulties that have a bearing on their ability to learn (*Diagnostic and Statistical Manual of Mental Disorders*, 1994).

Psychometric Model

This model places a person high or low or somewhere in between on what is called an intelligence quotient (IQ). The average is 100. Avril's IQ is extremely high. Her score is equaled or bettered by only one or two percent of children of her age. By the way, this important information came as a shock to her parents who had now to reconstrue their somehow "subnormal" child.

One of the drawbacks of the psychometric model and the medical model is the tendency to classify individuals in terms of what they *cannot* do or what they do not have. Negative assumptions and conclusions can become recipes for pessimistic inaction.

Personal Construct Model

Personal Construct Theory has a particular bearing on practice theories. Even the most proudly theoretical social worker has attitudes. These attitudes (or theories) have *inter alia*, a knowledge function that gives meaning to the world we live in. They provide a frame of reference with which people can make interpretations of life, and they are an economical way of putting together a variety of facts and creating a model for action. The fact is that all individuals are concerned to anticipate or predict what happens to them and around them. If you are able to make sense of your world you can then make the necessary adaptations to changing circumstances. To this end each and every individual *constructs* in his or her thought processes a model of events. This model is like a figurative set of goggles through which the individual *construes* life and its events and inhabitants. On the basis of this construing or interpreting, he or she is able to take appropriate or inappropriate actions. Inappropriate actions are generally in response to one's faulty constructs.

The theorist of this model, George Kelly (1955), uses the metaphor "man the scientist" to illustrate his contention that individuals are constantly trying to understand and predict or anticipate events. The term "personal construct system" illustrates an important dimension of his theory. The term "personal" underlines the fact that every individual lives in a unique world. People may resemble one another in their construing processes, but essentially no one is a carbon copy of another. Every person lives in a world that is unique to him

69

or her because it is idiosyncratically interpreted and experienced. For example, the way thought-disordered schizophrenic people see their world depends on the way they have arranged their hierarchy of constructs and the importance they attach to them.

Thus, Kelly provides one answer to the age-old question of why two people react very differently to the same situation; the two people are *not* in the same situation, it only looks the same from the perspective of a third observer. The situation may be very dissimilar from the point of view of each individual's construing system. Each may be reacting meaningfully in terms of his/her own situation as he/she interprets it. Psychological constructs guide behavior we observe; thus, changed or new constructs bring new behaviors as well (Payne, 1991).

A "construct" is the basic unit of this theory, and the term is differentiated from the term "concept" in order to stress that it is a hypothesis rather than a category. A construct is also a discrimination of a bipolar kind. Thus, "good" is not just a category of events, but specifically contrasts events which are "good" with those that are "bad," and others which are neither good nor bad. Constructs have a limited range of convenience; thus good or bad is applied to people but not to birds. A mother might construe her child as bad. One might find that the construct "bad" is linked or associated in her mind most particularly with the dishonest pole of the honest–dishonest construct. The associations between constructs (construct-systems) are complex, often unconscious; some are shared, others are idiosyncratic.

Parents evolve a construct system to make sense of the world of children and family life. Parents bring constructs from their family of origin and elaborate with more recent experiences of actual parenting. These constructs give meanings to their offspring's behavior and facilitate mutually satisfactory interactions. Sadly some construct systems lead or mislead parents into confrontations with their babies. If the crying of a very young baby is construed as *willful naughtiness* and smacking is construed as an *appropriate training method or punishment* for dealing with naughtiness, a problematic and potentially dangerous situation might arise.

70

The child, too, actively seeks to make sense of his or her world. It is an important part of your assessment to tease out how the child views those parts of the world that are salient to your quest for understanding. There are techniques such as repertory grids for identifying child and adult construct systems. (See Figure 6.)

There are also active role-play methods for helping clients to test out the way they perceive their world. Role play is helpful in identifying positive and useful perceptions and behaviors as well as self-defeating and misconstrued perceptions and behaviors. They are useful for those who have low self-esteem and feel persecuted and socially isolated (see the case of Avril's mother, chapter 8). These are the steps you take:

- The person is encouraged to try out or explore patterns of behavior contrasted to his/her own. This is based on a carefully scripted role sketch worked out with clients and derived from a compromise between what they are actually like and what they would like to be like.
- They are invited to practice these patterns in everyday life.
- They gain some experience from practice of how the environment can differ in appearance and "feel" and how it reacts when they behave in a different manner.
- Practice generates new and more effective skills that can be supplemented by novel experience from the feedback they have received.
- The expectation is that by receiving new and helpful forms of feedback from the environment they will change the self-defeating attitudes that control their behavior.

There have been several developments in the measurement of personal constructs by means of Repertory Grid Techniques (Kelly, 1955). In its original form the client was asked to name twenty people he or she knew, according to different role titles. Thus we might get "father," "wife," "person you admire," "teacher you disliked," and so on. These are called *elements*. Constructs were then elicited by selecting three of the elements at a time, and asking the client: "In what important way are two—any two—of the people alike and thereby different from

Assessing the "Why" Question

Figure 6. An example of a completed Role Construct Repertory Test.

CONSTRUCTS

SORT NO.	EMERGENT POLE	IMPLICIT POLE
1	Don't believe in God	Very religious
2	Same sort of education	Completely different education
3	Not athletic	Athletic
4	Both girls	A boy
5	Parents	Ideas different
6	Understand me better	Don't understand at all
7	Teach the right thing	Teach the wrong thing
8	Achieved a lot	Hasn't achieved a lot
9	Higher education	No education
10	Don't like other people	Like other people
11	More religious	Not religious
12	Believe in higher education	Not believing in too much education
13	More sociable	Not sociable
14	Both girls	Not girls
15	Both girls	Not girls
16	Both have high morals	Low morals
17	Think alike	Think differently
18	Same age	Different ages
19	Believe the same about me	Believe differently about me
20	Both friends	Not friends
21	More understanding	Less understanding
22	Both appreciate music	Don't understand music

Figures (roles), with SORT NO.:

AUTHORITIES — VALUES: 19 ethical person, 18 happy person, 17 successful person; 16 boss, 15 rejected teacher, 14 accepted teacher

VALENCES: 13 attractive person, 12 threatening person, 11 pitied person, 10 rejecting person

INTIMATES: 6 ex-pal, 8 pal, 7 ex-flame, 9 spouce

FAMILY: 5 sister, 4 brother, 3 father, 2 mother, 1 self

(From Kelly, 1955.)

72

the third?" The repetition of this exercise produced constructs that gave some insight into the way the person construed his or her interpersonal environment.

The role titles were written along the top of a grid from left to right and the elicited constructs down the side from top to bottom. Kelly illustrates the recording or constructs (see completed example, Figure 6) in the following manner:

- When a decision has been made whether two of the three people indicated by circles (17, 18, and 19 in the grid) in the first row are "alike in some important way that distinguishes them from the third person," the client puts an X in the two circles corresponding to the two people who are alike but nothing in the third circle.
- Next she/he is asked to write a word or short descriptive phrase under "emergent pole" (the "construct"), indicating in what way the two are alike.
- The opposite of the characteristic is then written down under "implicit pole" (or "contrast").
- Next she/he places a "√" (check) under every other person who has this important characteristic.
- The second row is now considered—this time marking circles of a different triad (circles 14, 15, and 16 in Kelly's illustrative grid). Other people in line 2 who have this characteristic are given a "√" also.
- The rest of the grid is completed in this way.

Kelly's analysis proceeds as follows:

- He first looks at the grid without any statistical analysis to see something of what the person is telling one directly.
- Next it is possible to obtain matching scores between any pair of rows. Take a piece of paper and place it beneath the first row of checks and blanks and mark each check or cross on your piece of paper. Now move your paper one row down. You can count up the number of times blanks and checks/crosses correspond in rows 1 and 2 (or any other row).
- The probability of actual matching scores (or lack of them) can be calculated statistically to see how significantly the

constructs relate one to another. (Chance matching in this case would be half the possible total—nineteen.)

- The same method can be used for the columns to find how the person sees the people in his/her life compared with one another.
- A matrix of matching scores would show (for example) which construct is more highly matched with all other constructs and which element is most highly matched with all other elements.

Few individuals require more than twenty or thirty rows to express their repertory of constructs. One might ask the client to construe important *experiences* (e.g., wedding, first serious quarrel with partner, first major disappointments with child, etc.); *situations* (e.g., caring for children, being a housewife, doing housework) and so on. In other words you are not limited to persons. This and subsequent forms of repertory technique are designed so that statistical tests can be applied to the set of comparisons every individual has made. It is assumed that the *psychological* relationships between any two constructs, for a given person, are reflected in the statistical association between them when they are used as judgmental categories.

Problems in the statistical analysis of the matrix have given rise to procedures in which grids are analyzed by asking people to *rank order* their elements (e.g., nicest to nastiest, most loving to least loving, etc.) or rating them on seven-point scales.

Exercise. Try out an exercise in eliciting constructs on yourself.

1. Elicit constructs using members of your family as elements: mother, father, husband/wife, yourself, child 1, child 2, . . ., grandparents, aunts, uncles, and so on. Tease out the way you construe family relationships and family members by putting the name of each person on a card, taking three at a time, and going through the formula: "In what important way are my father and my husband alike and thereby different from Uncle Joe?", and so on.
2. Elicit constructs using your *clients* as elements. This could be interesting! What are the important ways in which you construe the people you help?

3. Elicit constructs using the people *who help you* as elements, for example, grandparent, friend, mother, neighbor, etc. Add in, as elements, the persons who you feel are hostile or unhelpful in your life.

Psychodynamic Model

Psychoanalysis is one of the most controversial systems introduced to professional social work practice. Many psychologists, psychiatrists, and social workers are now questioning the place of psychoanalysis in these helping professions. There is no questioning of the status of Sigmund Freud (1974), the founder of psychoanalysis. Freud's thinking has been more pervasive than that of almost any other researcher; many of his discoveries are today's "clichés."

From psychoanalysis comes an accent on the one-to-one (dyadic) helping situation, on long-term intensive casework, and a choice of methods involving the development of insight. What have come to be called psychoanalytically or, more popularly, psychodynamically based theories represent a significant ideological strand in social work.

Many social workers describe their orientation as being psychodynamic. The term encompasses theories of personality and therapies which assume the existence of unconscious mental processes, which concern themselves with the elucidation of motives, and which assume the significance of transference relationships, such as, the transfer on to the therapist of attitudes and feelings attaching to significant others. It is the *verstehende* (understanding) aspect of psychoanalytically based theories rather than the application of analytic treatment techniques which has contributed to social work practice.

It is sometimes argued that the interpretive-insight approach promotes excessive self-absorption and diverts attention from groups and structures as causes and remedies for psychosocial problems. Still, a psychodynamic perspective on psychosocial issues might be essential in social work because it is one of many ways by which meanings in exceedingly complex situations can be grasped.

A good example of this is the psychodynamic theory of ego defense mechanisms. The construct ego or self is seen by contemporary psychodynamic theorists as the central integrating aspect of the person, and any threat to its valuation and function is a vital threat to the very being of the individual. As a result, a variety of "devices or coping mechanisms" are gradually accumulated by the self so as to soften anxieties and failures and protect the integrity of the ego by increasing the feeling of personal worth (Arlow, 1995). There is evidence that all of us learn to use strategies such as these. It is when we use them inappropriately or to excess, with too great intensity, or too inflexibly that they become maladaptive. The trouble is that they involve a certain amount of self-deception and distortion of reality and may prevent, by a sort of short-circuiting, the realistic and painstaking solution of problems.

To a very great extent we are unaware or unconscious of our use of these strategies. One of the purposes of adopting particular strategies is to reduce tension. The minimizing of immediate discomfort reinforces their use. An individual makes choices and carries out actions which will reduce and, if possible, avoid anxiety, pain, or any other distress.

Let us look at some of our psychological strategies:

Emotional insulation (isolation, dissociation). In all these defensive strategies the individual reduces the tensions of need and anxiety by withdrawing into a shell of numbness and passivity, also by lowering expectations, by remaining emotionally uninvolved and detached. Apathy and defeated resignation may be the extreme reactions to stress and frustration of long duration. Cynicism is often adopted, particularly by adolescents, as a means of protection from the pain of seeing idealistic hopes disillusioned.

Displacement. Displacement is a defensive strategy that involves a shift of emotions or of an intended action from the person toward whom it was originally intended onto another person or object. An example could be a child who is a nuisance because she pinches, bites, and scratches her playmates at school and harasses the teacher in a variety of ingenious ways. Investigation might reveal that the fault lies in part in the playground situation at school but also has its roots in the home situation.

76

Projection. When feelings arising from within ourselves are unjustifiably attributed to others, such behavior is called projection. It helps us to avoid conflict over our own barely conscious or acknowledged feelings and impulses by finding scapegoats and ascribing these obnoxious, intolerable, and therefore unacceptable ideas to them. By disowning these tendencies we protect ourselves from anxiety. Thus the individual who feels hateful jealously and hostility to his wife may deny feelings to himself but complain bitterly that his wife is unpleasant to him and rejects him.

Rationalization. Rationalization is a technique that helps us to justify what we do and to accept the disappointments arising from unattainable goals. The "ego" uses rationalization to modify otherwise unacceptable impulses, needs, feelings, and motives into ones that are consciously tolerable and acceptable. Rationalization helps to reduce cognitive dissonance. In simple terms, this means that when there is a discrepancy between behaviors and thoughts (cognition), psychological distress is caused. This distress will persist until the behaviors and cognition are made harmonious again.

Take the case of the professional who takes great pride in his or her skill with family problems but is making no progress. The sense of failure and ineffectiveness is rationalized away be describing the family as chaotic and the members as immature and therefore unsuitable for treatment. By this rationalization, the gap between the estimation of oneself and one's performance disappears. Thought and behavior are made congruent. This tactic makes the repugnant more acceptable and the incompatible compatible.

Common rationalizations explain away the unacceptable and sometimes make the incompatible bittersweet. In the former we justify failure to obtain something that is desirable on the grounds that it was not really worthwhile after all. In the attitude we mollify ourselves for an undesirable outcome by saying that it was for our own good.

Fantasy. Fantasy is one of the favorite tactics of children. In order to cope with stressful circumstances we not only deny unpleasant reality, but we create the sort of world of fantasy we would like to inhabit. Incidentally, fantasy also provides children with the opportunity to rehearse in imagination the solutions to their problems without entailing the risks of the real situation. Fantasy can be productive in such cases. Nonproductive fantasy is the too-persistent indulgence in a wish-fulfilling kind of mental activity. It compensates for lack of achievement. "Walter Mitty" fantasies allow a person to be the conquering hero he or she would like to be. People may also explain away their failures and inadequacies by what are called "suffering hero" fantasies—seeing themselves as misunderstood, "put-upon," but nobly courageous victims. In this way the individual retains his or her self-esteem. Fantasy solutions gloss over unpleasant reality. Children who daydream a lot are frequently trying to compensate for or escape from unacceptable environmental realities.

Reaction formation. Reaction formation is a method of defense whereby individuals suppress their desires and then adopt conscious attitudes and behavior patterns that are quite opposed to the unconscious wishes. Reaction formation is extreme and intolerant in its manifestations. Those who devote all their time to the obsessive condemnation of sexual license in others may well be having trouble in coping with their own sexual inclinations. In children, a "don't care" independent attitude may well mask a craving for nurturance and a need for dependency.

Escapism. Escapism is a technique for denying and avoiding reality. Clients may evade disagreeable facts of life by refusing to see them. Escapism is a method for denying unpleasant circumstances. They may simply withdraw from competitive situations if they feel at a disadvantage and may fail. They may tend to be indecisive and procrastinate in times of stress, putting off the actions that have to be faced realistically.

Defensive strategies or defense mechanisms are not without some experimental confirmation. The mention of psychoanalytic or psychodynamic theory is a reminder to us that its tenets are not wholly antagonistic to behavioral theory, although many would claim that they are. The psychodynamic approach to problem development stresses the "understanding" and historical element more than does the behavioral approach, which emphasizes explanations of behavior in the here and now. Nevertheless, the specification of reinforcers, the "C" term in the ABC analysis, is one in which some theorists would see a potentially useful borrowing from Freudian ideas. ·

Human beings old enough to have acquired even a rudimentary self-image demonstrate a need to perceive themselves in at least a moderately favorable light. A reasonable agreement between the self-concept ("myself as I am") and the concept of the ideal self ("myself as I would like to be") is one of the most important conditions for personal happiness and for satisfaction in life. Marked discrepancies arouse anxiety and can be indicative of psychological problems.

You might ask the client to write an account (or talk it out) on the theme "Myself as I am" and another entitled "Myself as I would like to be." Compare them and discuss the points of mismatch with the client. It could be a help in setting realistic and meaningful goals.

There are sometimes heated debates about the status and, indeed, viability, of psychoanalysis. There is wide disagreement among distinguished thinkers as to whether it is a science, a myth, a theory, a therapy, or a premature synthesis.

Some theorists argue that it is perfectly possible for psychoanalytic investigations to be termed scientific, unless the word science is understood in a very rigid and narrow sense. Freud himself regarded psychoanalysis as a science.

Charles Rycroft, an eminent psychoanalyst, believes that the controversy between psychoanalysts and critics like Hans Eysenck is not a meaningful one. Freud's work was really semantic, but owing to his scientific training and allegiance he formulated his findings in the inappropriate conceptual framework of the physical sciences. As Rycroft puts it:

If psychoanalysis is recognized as a semantic theory not a causal one, its theory can start where its practice does—in the consulting room, where a patient who is suffering from something in himself which he does not understand confronts an analyst with some kind of knowledge of the unconscious—i.e. who knows something of the way in which repudiated wishes, thoughts, feelings, and memories can translate themselves into symptoms, fantasies, and dreams, and who knows as it were, the grammar and syntax of such translations and is therefore in a position to interpret them again into the communal language of consciousness. It seems to me that it makes better sense to say that the analyst makes excursions into historical research in order to understand something which is interfering with his present communications with the patient (in the same way as a translator might turn to history to elucidate an obscure text) than to say that he makes contact with the patient in order to gain access to biographical data (Lee and Herbert, 1970).

If evaluated carefully and critically, the writings of psychoanalysts can open "mental doors" for social workers to dimensions of experience that are not readily accessible to ordinary common sense. It is assumed that this insight will give them greater control over their behavior. Many of our motives are unconscious, and it is impossible to come to terms with an "invisible enemy." The therapist tries to make the invisible visible, the unconscious conscious, so that reality can be grappled with.

It would be mostly safe to say that all insight therapies are "talking" therapies. The patient or client does a lot of talking about his or her personal life, early history, personal relationships, work, ambitions, fears, and worries. The psychotherapist, to a greater or lesser extent, also verbally offers interpretations of the patient's conflicts and problems, reassurance, and sometimes advice in order to direct the person's thoughts and actions into potentially fruitful channels. If the child is very young, conventional psychotherapy is inappropriate. Children are not always able to put their anxieties into words. They are not always interested in exploring their past life. They are too close to the episodes that are thought by psychoanalysts to be crucial in the development of dysfunctional behaviors to enjoy talking about them. They will not always free-associate. The main problem is that the motivation to participate in analysis is missing because children are often brought for therapy against their will.

Play as communication. Play makes use of children's families and natural mode of expression—play with dolls, miniatures, puppets, paint, water, and sand—in a special playroom. This provides a background for the therapist to discuss their problems with them (Webb, 1991).

Theories of the importance of play in childhood go a long way back. The first person to advocate studying the play of children in order to understand and educate them was Jean Jacques Rousseau. There have been several theories put forward to explain the meaning and utility of play in childhood; they generally emphasize its function as a means of preparation for the future, as a natural process of learning, and as a means of release from tensions and of excess physical energies. In many ways play, for children, is life itself. They use it in order to develop their personality and their ability to get on with other children.

Sigmund Freud's daughter, Anna Freud, used children's play in a manner analogous to the use of dreams with adults. Play was analyzed so as to uncover unconscious conflicts. This involved the interpretation of the symbolic meanings, the unconscious motivation underlying drawing, painting, games, and other forms of imaginative play. She transposed classical psychoanalytic theory into a system of child analysis.

There have been several offshoots of psychoanalytical play therapy and also systems of play therapy which are not in this mold at all. The active forms of play therapy have much in common with the desensitization techniques used in behavior therapy. Other forms of play therapy—relationship therapy and nondirective therapy—have evolved and continue to be used. We return to this topic in chapter 9.

Family Process Model

The family process prospective, exemplified by the model of intervention known as family therapy, shifts the focus for understanding problems and dealing with them from the individual's behavior to his/her relationships with the family. In this view, many problems have their source in family behavior patterns that are faulty or self-defeating, that is, dysfunctional in different ways.

Family therapy and family-oriented behavioral work are commonly but certainly not exclusively used when children present problems. Like other psychological therapies, these approaches are made up of several variations on a theme—the theme here being that the family is more than the sum of its parts and vital to work with in its own right. Some of the many techniques focus specifically on presenting problems, dealing with *current events*, while others grapple with the question of how the *family history* has influenced the family unit.

The process model of working with families calls for joining the therapist and the family together in the process of change and focusing on interactions and transactions. The intent of the process model is to utilize these interactions and transactions to move toward healthier exchanges, thus increasing processes characteristic of wellness versus those processes reflective of dysfunctions and problems in the family system (Satir, 1982). Satir calls for the therapist to lead and facilitate but to avoid "taking charge" or directing family members. The process model calls for all members of a family system to be involved in the treatment process, including significant others who are intrinsic parts of the family system.

Psychological, physical, and emotional systems of each member and of the family as a unit intertwine in interactions and transactions that occur between and among members who live in family systems overtime. Family communication and interactions are a key to understanding demands and accommodations that family members make to please, aggravate, gain power, generate warmth, insure belonging, elicit responses to love and caring, and to shape and reshape their family system. Exploration of these interactions provide families a way of understanding and changing interactions that cause pain and disruption. Therapeutic processes include exploring new ways of sharing positive feelings and emotions through healthier processes in family transactions. Family members develop new perspectives of themselves and their family system as they experience risk taking and sharing of meaningful interactions and feelings through the process of therapy. Techniques include interventions such as family sculpting, visualizations, empty chair, role playing, hugging, apologizing, forgiving, and expressing feedback from emotions experienced (Bowen, 1978; Minuchin and Fishman, 1981; Satir, 1982).

Empirical Research Model

A typical approach to the understanding of family problems is the accumulation of data on the basis of studies—clinical and experimental research—of particular topics. A matter of particular concern to us is family violence, initially presented in chapter 3. This illustrates the value of the empirical research model, especially where no theoretical model fits neatly.

The various forms of family violence—physical, sexual, and emotional abuse—perpetrated on children, spouses, or the elderly, have been the subject of much research but remain poorly understood and certainly cannot be fit into any simple theoretical model. Certain characteristics of *those who abuse* seem to apply to all types of family violence. The research literature points to similarities in the following areas (Faller, Bowden, Jones, and Hildebrandt, 1981; Tower, 1996).

- Poor or low self-esteem
- A sense of incompetence (low self-efficacy)
- Social isolation
- A sense of being unsupported/helpless
- Depressed
- Lack of warmth and empathy
- Poor impulse/self-control
- Aggressive
- Experiencing marital difficulties
- Misperceiving the victim
- Likelihood of having been a victim of abuse in childhood

These findings represent factors that are associated with family violence. Appendix 4 contains a table describing common *family* attributes based upon empirical research. It is important to remember that a correlation does not necessarily imply causation. A correlation is sometimes found between criminality, alcoholism, drug abuse, and low intelligence and the various forms of family violence. Obviously there are many people who drink heavily or have criminal records but never abuse children, wives, or grandparents. Causation is a difficult concept; some factors may set the stage or predispose a person toward abusive behaviors. The childhood experience of being abused oneself may lead to abusive behavior to one's children or spouse. Other episodes of abuse, trauma, and personal indignities may trigger particular incidents of assault.

Multifactorial causation occurs with the problem of family violence, as in so many other areas of family dysfunction. The majority of child abusers are under 20 to 30 years of age, most wife abusers are between 20 and 30, while most abusers of the elderly are between 40 and 50 and above. Both sexes are implicated in family violence. Unemployment, low income, and extramarital problems are stresses that can contribute to family violence.

Those who are abused tend to have one or more of the following attributes:

- A poor relationship with the abuser
- A relationship of dependency
- Physically weaker than the abuser
- Emotional and social isolation
- Ill-health/disability

In some families all forms of violence take place; in others it is one category. In some homes violence is accepted as the "norm." Abusing families are particularly distinguished from non-abusing families by their lack of affectionate relationships, and by the abuse of power by the strong over the weak; for example, children, the frail elderly, and others are susceptible to being scapegoated for frustration experienced by the abuser.

Affectionate relationships within a family act as a buffer against stress; they generate supportive action for those who are distressed. Individual coping skills, self-confidence, and personal strengths also mitigate the influence of stress and make violence less rather than more likely as a response to frustration and misery.

The influence of all these psychosocial factors and the potency, for good or ill, of family relationships make it imperative that you observe all the family *together* as well as *individually* and that you tease out their perceptions of each other. Look carefully at

- Their attitudes
- Their perceptions
- Their expectations
- Their actions
- Their feelings toward each other

Check on their knowledge of child development and of aging processes. Detailed and rigorous observation and monitoring are vital where high-risk families are brought to your notice (see Appendix 3).

Summary and Comment

We have looked briefly at various models used by members of the helping profession in the quest for an understanding of their client's difficulties. The assumptions, attitudes, or constructs held by practitioners also have implications for their choice of intervention. For example, a common assumption underlying many therapeutic endeavors entails a cathartic or hydraulic view of emotion. This assumption is based on the belief that antisocial, unpleasant, and atavistic feelings can be channeled away through a figurative "overflow pipe" leaving behind the loving, cooperative, prosocial human being that exists underneath. The way in which the cathartic purging is administered varies widely, but the principle remains the same. Such an assumption can lead to quite opposite therapeutic advice or procedures in psychotherapy and behavior modification, respectively, especially with regard to aggression.

At present, aggressive children, whatever the reasons for their problems, may be subjected to therapeutic regimes that encourage them to "act out" their hostile behavior. Intervention may be in the form of regression therapy used in some residential establishments or the permissive atmosphere encouraged in some intermediate treatment approach. Or it may range to models or program that seek to inhibit such expressions and to encourage alternative prosocial actions. Adherents to regression or psychodynamic theory view the latter course of action as "symptomatic treatment"—tinkering with surface phenomena. They would expect the "real" or "underlying" causes to break out elsewhere (a phenomenon called symptom substitution) as a result of such superficial attempts at battening down emotional "safety hatches."

But the latter social learning group would see this as a self-deluding argument and would accuse the proponents of "acting out" theory of sustaining, by reinforcement, the very behavior they claim to want to remove, and of simply relabeling such problematic behavior with some technical term of doubtful validity—and then calling this the cause. In any event, the answer to such fears is to conduct a comprehensive and rigorous assessment and an ongoing evaluation (plus follow-up) of outcomes for the treated client.

PART II

Understanding Development and Change of Families and Children

The essence of life is development—hopefully, a forward momentum toward greater maturity and fulfillment—and this presupposes change. These aspects of life apply not only to individuals but also to the families within which they reside. Life is all about change—expected and unexpected, welcome and dreaded.

Change is often painful and not infrequently resisted. This tension between adapting to new circumstances (transformation) and resisting change that is a feature of the individual's attempts to maintain some equilibrium in his or her life (homeostasis) is also characteristic of family systems. General systems theory highlights the significance of the concept of system *adaptability*. Within the family, different members may be involved in adapting to very different life circumstances. While a girl is moving toward womanhood and experiencing some of the unwelcome changes of puberty and adolescence, her grandmother who lives in the same house, is adjusting, not to development, but to the *dissolution* of some of her strength, vigor, and independence. Both are in a stage of transition, and each strives in her own way to come to terms with new realities.

In the following chapters we examine some of the salient features of childhood and adolescence, as well as those involved in the adult role of parenting in its various manifestations, such as, adoption, fostering, and single parenting.

CHAPTER 5

Childhood and Adolescence

All sorts of terms or euphemisms have been used to refer to the troublesome but common behaviors and the more serious psychological difficulties displayed by children and adolescents. There is the popular expression "maladjusted," and others such as "abnormal," "nervous," "highly strung," "emotionally disturbed," "difficult," to mention but a few. They include a large and mixed bag of problems ranging from depression, anxiety, inhibition, and shyness to noncompliance, destructiveness, stealing, and aggression. In essence, these problems represent *exaggerations, deficits,* or *disabling combinations* of feelings, attitudes, and behaviors common at one time or another to many young people. Aggression, shyness, and a combination of low self-esteem and poor concentration are examples of behaviors frequently seen.

There is a distinction between those difficulties which primarily lead to emotional disturbance or distress for the young people themselves, such as, anxiety, shyness, depression, feelings of inferiority and timidity, and those which involve mainly the kinds of antisocial behavior that disrupt the well-being of others, notably those in frequent contact with the young person.

Terms like "normal" and "abnormal" are commonly applied to children as if they are mutually exclusive concepts like hard and soft; the label "abnormal" attached to particular children seems to suggest that they are deviant in some absolute and generalized sense. This is misleading; every child is unique and the most that can be said of any child is that some of his or her actions or attributes are more or less a deviation from a *norm* or social standard.

Table 4. A Child Behavior Rating Scale (for parents)

How much difficulty do you have with your child's behavior on the following items? Circle the number that best sums up your opinion: 1 = never; 2 = sometimes; 3 = often. Indicate whether it represents a problem to you.

Behavior	Never	Sometimes	Often	Do you see it as a problem?
Aggressiveness	1	2	3	Yes/No
Whining	1	2	3	Yes/No
Temper tantrums	1	2	3	Yes/No
Lying	1	2	3	Yes/No
Jealousy	1	2	3	Yes/No
Demanding attention	1	2	3	Yes/No
Disobedience	1	2	3	Yes/No
Bed-wetting	1	2	3	Yes/No
Daytime wetting	1	2	3	Yes/No
Shyness	1	2	3	Yes/No
Speech difficulties	1	2	3	Yes/No
Fears	1	2	3	Yes/No
School refusal	1	2	3	Yes/No
Soiling	1	2	3	Yes/No
Overactivity	1	2	3	Yes/No
Reading difficulty	1	2	3	Yes/No
Boredom	1	2	3	Yes/No
Apathy	1	2	3	Yes/No
Mood changes	1	2	3	Yes/No
Irritability	1	2	3	Yes/No
Wandering	1	2	3	Yes/No
Tics	1	2	3	Yes/No
Oversensitivity	1	2	3	Yes/No
Quarreling	1	2	3	Yes/No
Poor/finicky eating	1	2	3	Yes/No
Timidity	1	2	3	Yes/No

Assessment of Children

It is obviously very useful to know about the social norms and the norms of development when making an assessment. You might incorporate into the assessment steps (set out in chapter 2), some of the material included in the following pages because of their direct relevance to children's behavior problems. Thus you might ask the parent(s) to rate the child's difficulties (Table 4) and the situations in which they occur (Table 5).

Table 5. A Situational Rating Scale (for parents)

Do you have difficulty with your child at the following places or in the following circumstances? Circle the number that best sums up you opinion.

Place/Circumstance	Never	Sometimes	Often	Do you see it as a worrying problem?
Visiting friends	1	2	3	Yes/No
Shopping (e.g., supermarket)	1	2	3	Yes/No
Going on a bus	1	2	3	Yes/No
People visiting your home	1	2	3	Yes/No
Taking the child to school or nursery	1	2	3	Yes/No
	1	2	3	Yes/No
Leaving the child at play-group	1	2	3	Yes/No
Getting the child dressed	1	2	3	Yes/No
Mealtimes	1	2	3	Yes/No
Getting the child to bed	1	2	3	Yes/No
Getting the child to stay in bed	1	2	3	Yes/No
Quarreling with brothers	1	2	3	Yes/No
sisters	1	2	3	Yes/No
friends	1	2	3	Yes/No
Getting the child to go to parties (friends' homes)	1	2	3	Yes/No
Getting the child to speak to people	1	2	3	Yes/No
Taking children's toys	1	2	3	Yes/No
Getting the child to share toys	1	2	3	Yes/No
Getting the child to be polite	1	2	3	Yes/No

In the case of concern about *relationships*, whether child-child, adult-child, or child-adult, draw up a balance sheet of the positives in the relationship and the negatives. (See example in chapter 3.) At the most general level, you need to ask of the client: "What are the consequences in the short- and long-term of his or her *behaviors*?" In the case of parents, "What is their method of child management?"

There are supplementary questions (applicable to parents as well as to the child) to ask. Affirmative answers to several questions like these might well be of significance:

- Does the client get excessively miserable, embarrassed, shy, hostile, anxious, or morbidly guilty?
- Does he/she give vent to anger too easily?
- Is his/her tolerance of frustration low?
- Is he/she inflexible in the face of failure?
- Does he/she find it difficult to cope with novel or difficult situations?
- Does he/she experience difficulty in establishing affectionate, lasting relationships with adults and peers?
- Does he/she fail to learn from experience, such as, from disciplinary situations?
- Does he/she find it impossible to get on with most teachers or other adults in authority?

Your answers to these questions could be important diagnostically because problem behaviors have unfavorable consequences for the youngster and/or those in contact with him or her. Generally speaking, there is an association between intense and prolonged feelings of unhappiness and psychological disorder; there is a loss of a sense of well-being.

Typical problems of childhood. A feature of much problem behavior in childhood is its transitoriness. So mercurial are some of the changes of behavior in response to the rapid growth and the successive challenges of childhood that it is difficult to pinpoint the beginning of serious problems. Among the problems which decline in frequency with age are elimination or toilet-training problems, speech problems, fear, and thumb sucking. Problems such as insufficient appetite and lying reach a peak early and then subside. Many problems show high frequencies round about or just before school age, then decline in prevalence, and later rise again at puberty. Among these are restless sleep, disturbing dreams, physical timidity, irritability, attention demanding, overdependence, somberness, jealousy, and, in boys, food finickiness. Only one undesirable behavior generally increases systematically with age—nail biting. This habit reaches a peak and begins to subside only near the end of adolescence. Among the problems which show little or no relationship to age is oversensitiveness.

We know as a result of longitudinal studies of children over many years that, for the most part, children who suffer from emotional problems such as fears, phobias, shyness, and inhibitions, become reasonably well adjusted adults; they are almost as likely to grow up normal as children drawn at random from the general population. In a sense these difficulties are the emotional equivalent of growing pains. But that is not to deny that they sometimes persist and reach levels of intensity that cause all-round suffering.

There is another category of difficulties that declines at a rather later stage, and at a slower rate, than most others; for example, overactivity, destructiveness, and tempers. In fact, one-third of boys still have temper explosions at 13. In their *severe* forms these and other types of aggressive, antisocial behaviors constitute a constellation of problems referred to as "conduct disorders." They involve physical and verbal aggressiveness, disruptiveness, irresponsibility, noncompliance, and poor personal relationships; delinquent activities, early drug and alcohol use, and substance abuse may also feature as part of the syndrome. This behavior pattern is notable for the fundamental inability or unwillingness on the part of the youth to adhere to the rules and codes of conduct prescribed by society at its various levels: family, school, and in the community at large. The problem may become particularly troublesome (disruption in the classroom) and/or serious (delinquency) during adolescence. We deal with it in the next chapter.

It is a useful assessment skill to be able to identify the periods when children are most vulnerable to emotional problems, so as to mobilize resources to help them and their parents through a difficult period. The term "crisis intervention" has been used to describe the expert assistance needed at certain times in people's lives when they not only experience a heightened desire for help but are more susceptible than usual to the influence of others. Children also experience such periods of crisis when, for example, they go to a hospital, endure parental illness, separation or death, cope with the birth of a sibling, or learn to live with a handicapped sibling.

Developmental tasks. A developmental task arises at a certain period in the life of an individual. Successful achievement leads to happiness and success with later tasks while failure leads to unhappiness in the individual, disapproval by society, and difficulty with other tasks. The tasks might be ones such as learning to talk or to control elimination; or they may involve the development of self-control over aggressive and sexual inclinations, acquiring moral attitudes and social skills, adjusting to school life and mastering academic competencies, and becoming self-directed and self-confident. Some are vital psychosocial tasks.

Erik Erikson (1985) has put forward ideas about the interplay of "ego" and "alter" that is so critical in personality development—namely, the achievement of a balance between the poles of recognizing and accommodating the needs of others as opposed to imposing self-centered demands on other people. An extreme lack of balance in reciprocity between itself and others (in either direction) gives rise to unsatisfactory social relationships. Children demand parental support, and they try to limit the restraints parents put upon their pleasures. The balance, therefore, is about a compromise between sometimes incompatible mutual demands.

Erikson's scheme of child development and its tasks is given in Table 6.

From birth to about four years of age the child needs to develop a sense of trust and, later, a growing autonomy. The major hazards to the development of a perception of a trustworthy and predictable world, in which children initiate their independence-seeking, are social and physical conditions which interfere with their sense of personal adequacy and/or which hinder their acquisition of skills.

Even very young babies exhibit a need to be competent, to master or deal effectively with their own environment. Psychologists consider it to be related to such motives as mastery, curiosity, and achievement. The psychologist Martin Seligman (1975) has this to say:

> The infant begins a dance with his environment that will last throughout childhood. I believe it is the outcome of this dance that determines his helplessness or mastery.

Table 6. Developmental Tasks

Age period	Characteristic to be achieved	Major hazard to achievement
Birth to 1 year	Sense of trust or security.	Neglect, abuse, or deprivation of consistent and appropriate love in infancy; harsh or early weaning.
1 to 4 years	Sense of autonomy— child viewing self as an individual in his/her own right, apart from parents although dependent on them.	Conditions which interfere with the child's achieving a feeling of adequacy or the learning of skills such as talking.
4 to 5 years	Sense of initiative— period of vigorous reality testing, imagination, and imitation of adult behavior.	Overly strict discipline, internalization of rigid ethical attitudes that interfere with the child's spontaneity and reality testing.
6 to 11 years	Sense of duty and accomplishment—laying aside of fantasy and play, undertaking real tasks, developing academic and social competencies.	Excessive competition, personal limitations, or other conditions which lead to experiences of failure, resulting in feeling of inferiority and poor work habits.
12 to 15 years	Sense of identity— clarification in adolescence of who one is, and what one's role is.	Failure of society to provide clearly defined roles and standards; formation of cliques which provide clear but not always desirable roles and standards.
15 to adulthood	Sense of intimacy— ability to establish close personal relationships with members of both sexes.	Cultural and personal factors that lead to psychological isolation or to formal rather than warm personal relations.

(*Adapted from E. Erikson, 1965.*)

When he makes some response, it can either produce a change in the environment or be independent of what changes occur. At some primitive level, the infant calculates the correlation between response and outcome. If the correlation is zero, helplessness develops. If the correlation is highly positive or highly negative, this means the response is working; and the infant learns either to perform that response more frequently or to refrain from performing it, depending on whether the correlated outcome is good or bad. But over and above this, he learns that responding works, that in general there is synchrony between responses and outcomes. When there is asynchrony and he is helpless, he stops performing the response, and further, he learns that in general responding doesn't matter. Such learning has the same consequences that helplessness has in adults: lack of response initiation, negative cognitive set, and anxiety and depression. But this may be more disastrous for the infant since it is foundational.

During the next stage, from approximately four to five years, comes a sense of initiative, a period of vigorous reality testing, imitation of adult patterns of behavior and imaginative play. Overly strict discipline, interference, overprotection, and the like can disrupt the successful achievement of these attributes, making for poor spontaneity and uncertain testing and appreciation of realities.

A sense of duty and accomplishments is the next developmental task—from 6 to 11 years—when the child puts aside much of the fantasy and play-life and undertakes real tasks at school and develops academic and social skills. Excessive demands or competition and personal limitations which lead to persistent failure can make a crisis of this important stage and can result in feelings of inferiority and poor work habits.

From 12 to 15 years, children consolidate their sense of identity, clarifying who they are and what their role in life is to be. Society may make for difficulties for the early adolescent by failing to provide clearly defined or valued roles and standards for the young person.

In later adolescence, from 15 to adulthood, a sense of intimacy is desirable—an ability to establish close personal relationships with members of both sexes. The last two stages are described in more detail, in the section on adolescence.

Failure to master previous developmental tasks are thought to hinder the individual in the next psychosocial endeavor.

Underachievement. Perhaps one of the most serious consequences of emotional and behavioral problems is its deleterious effect on children's learning in the classroom and hence their achievement. Even when highly intelligent, those pupils with psychological difficulties tend to have real difficulties in school performance. The greater the number of problems manifested by the child, the poorer, on the whole, is school performance.

Friendlessness. Many of the difficulties which children have to cope with are social ones—the problems of getting along with other youngsters of the same age, with teachers, with their own parents, and also with themselves. Young people need to like themselves, to rely on themselves, and to know themselves. It was Aristotle who suggested that friendly relationships require a certain liking for oneself. Also needed is a degree of self-awareness and social sensitivity. The boy or girl's self-image plays a part in all of this; if it has been endlessly subverted by criticism or rejection they are likely to feel unworthy and inferior and display aggressive or attention-getting behavior which betray defensiveness and overanxiety.

Children who are acceptable to their peers tend to

- Demonstrate sensitivity, responsiveness, and generosity; they help others and give attention, approval, and affection to their peers;
- Be confident in their social contacts, active, and friendly;
- See things from the other youngster's point of view;
- Be good at resolving day-to-day dilemmas involving person-to-person relationships;
- Make others feel accepted and involved, promoting and planning enjoyable group activities;

97

- Demonstrate empathetic actions. Empathy involves the youngster's capacity to control his or her behavior by considering its effect on the experiences of others, particularly the potential victims of proscribed behavior.

If you are concerned about your client's inability to make or keep friends, carry out a small exercise in "accountancy." Look at things from the other person's point of view. Is your client *mature* enough to sustain the reciprocity of friendship or is he/she insensitive, too demanding, or disloyal? Is his or her company rewarding enough?

Dealing with unwanted behavior. If an intervention seems likely, encourage parents to think of positive outcomes as well as the reduction of *unwanted* behaviors. Suggest that they consider their priorities, thinking of their child's behavior as falling into three color codes: green, yellow, and red.

- *Green* is the "go-ahead" code for the type of behavior they want from their child, the actions which they facilitate by praise and encouragement; for example, sharing toys with another child or eating meals without a fuss. They should include those individual attributes of the child—aspects of his or her personality which make for their uniqueness.
- *Yellow* is for "caution" behavior, which is not encouraged but is tolerated because the child is still learning and making mistakes; for example, "decorating" the bedroom's walls with finger paints or hurling toys across the room in a moment of fury. Any sort of stress like relocation, illness, or some upset in the family may mean a temporary step backward in the child's behavior.
- *Red* is definite *stop* for behavior which needs to be curbed as soon as possible. Obviously anything that could be dangerous for the child or for others has a red code: running into the road, touching the hot iron, attacking the baby.

Any limits set should be for the child's safety, well-being, and development. Parents should be advised to keep them to essentials. It is crucial to ensure that children know exactly what they are and what is expected of them. Chapter 11 develops this theme of rules and routines.

Adolescence

To the layperson, adolescence refers to the period of transition between childhood and adulthood. It coincides roughly with the so-called "teens," but the number of years devoted to adolescent development varies from culture to culture. If the physiological changes of puberty are most commonly taken as the onset of adolescence then it is sociological phenomena such as status, duties, privileges, the end of education, the right to marry and enjoy economic independence that are most frequently taken as the termination of adolescence. During the past half-century or so, adolescence in Western societies has become a progressively longer span of years, indeed as long as ten years in duration. This reflects the mixed feelings we have about the decision as to *when*, in law or social custom, a young person is grown-up and responsible: old enough to drink in a bar, mature enough to manage a bank account, to indulge in sexual intercourse, to get married, to vote, or to be held responsible for a criminal act.

Puberty: The Gateway to Adolescence

The physical and physiological changes that take place at about the age of 12 in girls and 14 in boys are due to the action of hormones and are quite dramatic; growth in virtually all parts of the body is sharply accelerated. During so-called transitional periods like adolescence, individuals are in the marginal position of having lost an established and accustomed status and of not yet having acquired the new status toward which the factors impelling developmental change are driving them.

Self-discovery. The major task of the adolescent stage according to many contemporary psychologists is the young person's need to shape and consolidate his or her own identity as a unique and mature person. The development of self-identity refers to the core of an individual's character of personality and is thought to be a vital precursor to true intimacy and depth in personal relationships. It begins with teenagers'

99

intense concern for discovering their individual nature and ends when they have established a coherent sense of self and personal identity. This task of *becoming* a unique person is usually completed between the ages of 18 and 22.

It is important to remember (and to remind parents) that adolescents are *individuals* and they are as different one from the other in their personal qualities as are children and adults. Their tendency to conform to teenage culture and fashion may present a superficial similarity which the media find convenient to headline, especially when there is a sensational incident involving young people. Social workers and other professionals would do well to encourage parents and other adults to recognize and accept the new challenges, tasks, and needs which preoccupy these sometimes puzzling young adults who are emerging from childhood.

Individual and gender differences. Girls' development is roughly two years ahead of boys', and it tends to be so throughout the developmental timetable. There is usually no need for alarm if the child is somewhat early or late. Children vary quite markedly. The gap may be four years or more in the age at which they become pubertal. For girls, that age at which the menstrual cycle makes its first appearance can differ by several years. One may find an early-developed girl at the age of 12 or 13 who is already physically a woman, with fully developed sexual characteristics and destined to grow very little more in height. At about the same age, and therefore in the same classroom and social group, may be a later-developing girl who is just about to begin her growth spurt and who is little more than a child in her physical characteristics. The same conspicuous differences might be seen in boys of 14 or 15. It is obviously simplistic to think about teenagers as a homogeneous group.

Puberty is not just a matter of change in the size and shape of the body. Physiological developments in glandular secretion, particularly those affecting sexual function, occur. Until puberty, males and females have similar quantities of *both* sex hormones in the bloodstream, with only a slightly greater proportion of the sex-relevant hormone. Thus boys have nearly as much estrogen, the female sex hormone, as androgen. At puberty, however, there is a sharp increase in the secretion of the sex-related hormone. Hormonal changes bring, in their wake, increased sexual arousal; parents will also have to deal with their offspring's increased and, in part, hormone-driven assertiveness.

As I have mentioned earlier, adolescent self-centeredness has its basis in the immense physical change taking place at puberty. It also has its roots in the discovery of identity, but there are sometimes disconcerting swings from out-and-out self-admiration (narcissism) to self-hatred and self-deprecation.

How young people perceive themselves depends very much on how others see them; but it depends most of all on how they *think* others see them—which could, of course, be different from the way in which they are actually perceived. And most particularly children accept into their self-image what they believe to be their parents' view of them: and these views can have consequences over the long-term for their behavior. If your client believes that his or her parents' opinion is negative or critical (even if this is not really the case) they may exhibit insecurity and low self-esteem. If people believe things to be real, they are real in their consequences. This applies with force to the delicate area of a person's self-image.

The development of identity doesn't always proceed smoothly. But what evidence we have calls into question Erik Erikson's (1965) belief that adolescents usually suffer a crisis over their identity. Most teenagers actually have a positive self-image: furthermore this view of themselves tends to be fairly stable over the years.

There is a growing altruism and idealism to be seen in many young people. These different facets are gradually integrated into the adolescent personality. Self-esteem is a vital element for healthy adjustment. When there is a large gap between the teenager's self-concept ("myself as I am") and his or her idealized self ("myself as I would like to be"), there are also likely to be anxiety and oversensitiveness in close attendance.

A sheep in wolf's clothing. Parents worry about the imminence of adolescence and small wonder, given that adolescence has such a bad reputation. Clinicians tend only to see people who come to clinics. And adolescents who attend the clinics would not be there if they did not have problems. What is really required is a wide cross section of adolescents drawn in large numbers from the general population. Does such a sample present problems of sufficient seriousness or in sufficient numbers to give adolescence a "bad name"?

Adolescence, while certainly not immune from its share of pain for those growing up, is not usually the scourge of folklore. It is something of a sheep, albeit an unruly sheep, in wolf's clothing. For one thing the problems of growing up do not all arrive at one and the same time.

The more serious psychological conditions are probably more common during adolescence than during middle childhood, but the difference is not a very great one. Most adolescents do *not* manifest psychiatric disorders. Nevertheless, some 10% to 15% of adolescents *do* experience significant psychological difficulties. These difficulties, referred to by psychologists as "emotional disorders," are manifested by about 2.5% of preadolescent children. Their prevalence increases somewhat by adolescence, and we find that boys and girls are about equally prone to them. For most children (as we saw in the previous chapter) these kinds of problems manifest themselves briefly and then become minimal or disappear completely.

This is all very well, but you might well wish to know whether there are any *typical* adolescent problems, typical in the sense that they reflect stresses and strains which differ from those emerging in childhood, or indeed, adult life. There certainly are serious psychiatric disorders such as schizophrenia and anorexia or bulimia nervosa whose onset is particularly associated with the teenage years.

We can witness in the transition from childhood to adulthood an upsurge of moodiness and feelings of misery. Adolescents are often tormented by ideas which are self-critical, worries about the future, and fears about such matters as attending school or becoming involved in social activities.

It is reassuring to realize that although the *rates* of unhappy feelings and self-depreciation reach a peak during adolescence, the *majority* of teenagers seem generally to be happy and confident and are not the victims of serious depression or of other emotional disturbances. In fact, adolescence does not quite live up to its reputation. This may help those of your clients who are bracing themselves with trepidation for their child's teenage years.

Striving for independence. By the middle years of adolescence the striving for independence is no longer simply one aspect of a youngster's activities; it is, in a very real sense, an end in itself. It involves striving for psychological freedom from parents, freedom to be one's own person, to have one's own thoughts and feelings, to determine one's own values, and to plan one's own future.

It is also about the more mundane freedoms, to find the clothes, companions, and pastimes of one's own choice and to enjoy the privacy of one's own room and belongings. However, there are as many dangers in granting independence to young people by promoting too much freedom too soon as in strongly opposing all signs of it until late adolescence. There is, as seems usual in child development, a "golden mean"—a need to avoid extremes.

The reason why adolescent development is relatively unremarkable in the personal disturbance it causes is that there are many strength-giving continuities in this development. The adolescent builds on what has gone before; coping skills developed when younger are not necessarily redundant. Many of the changes of this stage of development represent pluses, not minuses. They take the form of increased capacities of various kinds. It is as well to remember these pluses when considering how much to advise parents to "let go." Cognitive skills in adolescence become more complete and more flexible as new powers of abstraction and logic make problem-solving easier than it was in childhood. Social skills increase in range and complexity.

Alienation. The public has been led to believe that "distracting" of teenagers from their parents is almost inevitable, and they may be expecting not to be able to communicate with their children when they get older. Alienation is *not*, however, a typical pattern. Most adolescents are still attached to their homes in a positive way, and they continue to depend upon the emotional support, goodwill, and approval of their parents. The family continues to be of critical importance; parental concern and supervision are vital during a phase when youngsters are experimenting with life. It does appear that rebelliousness and alienation are more likely in teenagers who, in spite of considerable maturity, remain economically or in other ways, dependent on their parents. Students in higher education are one example.

A majority of adolescents share their parents' attitudes toward moral and political issues and are mostly prepared to accept their parents' guidance on academic, career, and personal matters.

Sexuality. Teenagers enjoy the full range of sexual activities earlier than the previous generation. The number of teenage pregnancies has certainly increased markedly, despite innovations in contraception. The incidence of AIDS and sexually transmitted diseases among young people has also gone up.

Although adolescents have become more accepting in their attitudes to premarital sex, this does not imply a massive rise in casual sexual relationships. Young people, and particularly girls, continue to emphasize the importance of love and stable emotional attachment in premarital sex, although intended marriage or an engagement is not so often seen as a prerequisite of such relationships. The emphasis on a stable relationship with one sexual partner at a time is referred to as "serial monogamy." Girls do, however, display more conservative attitudes to these issues than boys.

It has been commonly thought that the first experience of sexual intercourse is usually with someone who is already experienced; the first partner is often older and, in the case of the girls, is quite often an adult. Explicit sexual information available to children via television, internet, movies, and magazines increases the level of sexually explicit information for young children. Schools, communities, counselors, and families have the responsibility to provide sex education to children, including information on sexually transmitted diseases and contraception.

It is noted that more than ever before, teenagers live in a social context that is increasingly permissive. While teen birth rates in the United States in 1994 average 38 per 1,000 teens, with about 51% of the fathers being over age 20 (*Kids Count Data Book*, 1997), it is noted that about 69% of unmarried births are to women over age 20 (Long, Wood, and Kopp, 1994). Certainly, a committed relationship has been traditionally thought to be essential for the rearing of children. Many young people today wish such a long-standing commitment to take the form of marriage, but a substantial minority reject such a view. The realities of increasing rates of divorce, single-parenthood, and teenage pregnancy reflect changing family structures as well as the likelihood that many children will be reared outside the traditional, long-lasting family structure of biological parents and children.

Problem Areas

Adolescence has its share of problems like any other stage of development but its reputation for emotional disturbance is worse than the reality. Many parents create problems for themselves and their offspring by *expecting* the worst. This is the notorious self-fulfilling prophecy. "Anticipate the worst and by behaving in certain ways you make it happen!" But there are certain problems that do occur in a sizeable minority of adolescents.

Depression. The new responsibilities of young adulthood and the difficulties of sexual adjustment bring in their wake feelings of misery and inner turmoil. These lead, in some adolescents, to more serious moods of depression—a sense of helplessness and powerlessness, of events being out of or beyond control. Some adolescents even entertain ideas about committing suicide; a small number actually do it.

The milder form of depression may show itself as a lack of physical energy and well-being. In its more severe manifestation, adolescents tend to be irritable and bad-tempered, and, when it is at its worst, they sleep poorly, lack an appetite, and are always dejected, apathetic, and lifeless. Young people who are for whatever reason depressed, feel helpless, sad, and useless and find it sometimes impossible to meet the challenge of life. They cease to strive and to use their full effectiveness in whatever sphere of activity they find themselves.

The checklist below will help you to detect signs of depression in your client:

- A demeanor of unhappiness and misery, more persistent and intense than "the blues," which we all suffer from now and then;
- A marked change in eating and/or sleeping patterns;
- A feeling of helplessness, hopelessness, and self-dislike;
- An inability to concentrate and apply oneself to anything;
- Everything (even talking and dressing) seems an effort;
- Irritating or aggressive behavior;
- A sudden change in grades or school work;
- A constant search for distractions and new activities;
- Dangerous risk taking (e.g., with drugs/alcohol, dangerous driving, delinquent actions).

Depression can be masked in adolescence and thus not easily detected. Another problem is that any item in the list above can occur normally in the adolescent without in any way indicating a depressive disorder. The questions below will help you to judge whether to seek professional psychiatric advice if the answers tend to be in the affirmative.

- Are there several of the signs (listed above) present in the teenager?
- Do they occur frequently?
- Have they persisted for a long time?
- Do they cause *extensive* suffering to him/her?
- Do they stand in the way of his/her development toward maturity?
- Do they get in the way of his/her relationships with (a) peers, (b) adults?
- Do they cause distress in others?

Anorexia nervosa. A problem particularly associated with adolescent girls (it can also occur in prepubertal children) is anorexia nervosa. The anorexic girl deliberately restricts her food intake; indeed, she does not want to eat at all, because she believes she is fat and wishes to lose weight. The word "anorexia" means loss of appetite. However, the absence of hunger or appetite is not a crucial feature of anorexia nervosa. Nevertheless, the teenager will characteristically act as if she has lost her appetite.

Anorexia nervosa is essentially about weight rather than eating. The really central feature of the disorder is a body weight which is abnormally low for the age, height, and sex of the person. There is a further crucial feature: the individual's attitude to her weight. What makes life difficult for would-be helpers is that someone with anorexia nervosa will not always be truthful about her feelings. If she is, she will say that she is ashamed and very frightened of the thoughts of being heavier. She may suffer in various ways through being thin, but compared with gaining weight it is seen as the lesser evil.

Adolescent females experience eating disorders that include anorexia where the intake of food is greatly reduced as well as bulimia, a disorder which is characterized by binges of eating and reducing caloric intake through vomiting, laxative, diuretics, and severe dieting. For these females there is typically preoccupation with images of thin feminine appearance and problems with compliance with authority and with nonassertiveness. Many experience competitive family expectations and report histories of failure to please adults in their lives, typically parents. One study of intervention reports the benefits of structure and support provided through treatment groups in which education about their disorder, management or eating behaviors, and learning new improved interpersonal skills and developing self-awareness in relation to others proved to be helpful (Harper and Shillito, 1991).

The acts of eating and fasting are loaded with meaning—personal, familial, cultural, and religious. They also carry the connotations of control and self-mastery, of nurturant love, comfort, sociability, and, indeed, sexuality. The "meaning" of the eating disorder for one anorexic teenager is likely to differ at certain points compared with another. Each must be individually assessed by professionals who are *trained* and *expert* in this potentially fatal psychological disorder. Parents need to be alerted to the signs in their teenager of incipient anorexia nervosa: a preoccupation, indeed obsession, with calorie counts, with having control over her diet, loss of weight, cessation of periods, concern over appearance, moodiness, and so on. It is advisable to seek psychiatric or clinical psychological advice early rather than late, if your mental "alarm bells" begin sounding from what you are seeing and hearing from your teenager.

Conduct disorders. It is quite likely that problems of conduct constitute the most frequent as well as the fastest growing problem area of childhood. The children manifesting these problems in severe form cause themselves and those who are close to them the utmost misery. Antisocial activities tend to disrupt and hinder the acquisition of crucial life skills. Their presence in childhood is predictive of problems of adjustments in later adolescence and adulthood. Children with more extreme forms do not necessarily "outgrow" their problem behaviors; the case histories of delinquents repeatedly indicate the onset of serious antisocial behavior when they were very young.

Delinquent behavior. A sizeable number of children with conduct problems become delinquent, as their rule breaking becomes law breaking. Delinquency is perhaps the most noteworthy of all activities as an adolescent manifestation. It reaches a peak at 15 years for boys and 14 years for girls. By their twenties most of the former offenders have gradually become broadly law-abiding members of the community. But sadly, the number of young people committing detected and adjudicated crimes in the United States and the United Kingdom has increased markedly. What was once an almost completely male preserve now includes substantial numbers of female offenders. The average age for the first court appearance of juveniles is lower, and there is a marked trend toward more violent offenses.

The term "juvenile delinquent" is merely an administrative term, not a clinical diagnosis. It has to be recognized that relatively minor delinquent activities, such as, petty thefts, vandalism, are surprisingly common in the teens. Such activities tend to be transitory. However, there is a small but hard core of adolescents who habitually break the law, thereby creating enormous social problems of punishment, prevention, and rehabilitation.

Drug abuse. The decade of the nineties has seen a rise in the use of substances by adults and youth. Families of all ages and composition are placed at greater risk of having a member who abuses substances or of being a victim of crime or injury as a result of another's substance abuse.

Use of alcohol and tobacco remain high among youth, and the use of marijuana has been documented to have increased. About 93% of youth graduating from high school report having tried alcohol with about 41% reporting that they experience binge drinking (Duncan and Petosa, 1995). Smoking, drinking, and illicit drug use have all increased among American youth. As many as 42% of high school seniors report having used illicit drugs during the 1996 academic year with marijuana being the drug most commonly used (Winters, 1998). There is concern that children at pre-teen ages are having greater access to drugs such as cocaine and heroin (Thurman, 1997). Smoking among adults decreased from 40.4% of adults to 26% between 1964 and 1990. Smoking among high school seniors remained at about 30% from 1980 to 1993 (Bonnie and Lynch, 1997).

Actual use of substances by adults is difficult to measure. According to trends identified from two studies involving sample sizes of 4,372 and 17,809 respondents, trends in lifetime usage for adults age 26 and older in 1993 averaged 37.3% who reported illicit drug use. There were 88.7% reporting alcohol use, and 76.9% reporting cigarette use during their lifetime (Substance Abuse and Mental Health Services Administration, 1994).

Due to the availability and increased use and abuse of drugs and alcohol, estimated need for substance abuse treatment in the United States is alarming. According to one estimate of The National Institute on Drug Abuse, which included not only reported frequency of usage but reported problems and symptoms, as many as 3.5 million people were reported to be in need of treatment in 1991 (Epstein and Gfroerer, 1998).

Increased usage of substances, pressure for legalization of marijuana, and continuing lack of information about indicators of causation and treatment success give rise to continuing concern. It is clear that increased substance abuse has links with delinquency, crime, arrests, and a range of conduct problems (Winters, 1998). Concerns of substance abuse during family members' lifetimes are very serious and long-range concerns for professionals who work with families across the range of assessment, intervention, and long-term evaluation in support of efforts for prevention and innovation in intervention.

The terms "drug abuse" and "drug misuse" refer to the observation that a particular form of drug taking is a harmful (abuse) and/or socially unacceptable way of using that substance (misuse). "Users" are likely to develop "tolerance" for a drug, which means that their body has adapted to the repeated presence of the drug so that higher doses are required to maintain the same effect. The body may react with "withdrawal effects" to the sudden absence of a drug to which it has adapted; they involve severe physical discomfort. When this occurs and leads to a compulsion to continue taking the drug so as to avoid these symptoms, we speak of "physical dependence." The more important and widespread problem of "psychological dependence" refers to an irresistible psychological compulsion to repeat the stimulation, pleasure or comfort provided by the drug's effects.

The key factor in drug taking is opportunity—the availability of drugs and people to tempt and "prompt." Users have generally been exposed to drugs by their peers or by people (not infrequently family members) whose values incline toward nonconformity or even deviance. Rebelliousness, low self-esteem, a poor sense of psychological well-being, depression, and low academic aspirations are among the characteristics commonly found in adolescent drug users. The boredom and hopelessness of unemployment also play their part. Substance abuse presents a similar picture. High-risk drug taking is defined as uncontrolled use, whether or not it is already demonstrably harmful. A person is also taking an unacceptable risk if he or she is a regular user, that is, taking drugs at predictable intervals.

It is most important for professional people and parents to be on the lookout for signs that may lead them to suspect drug use. It isn't easy, because some of the signs are not uncommon in adolescence generally. There is often a gradual change in the adolescent's habits and a general lethargy. Other signs include: aggression; loss of interest in school work, sports, hobbies, and friends; furtive behavior and frequent lying; bouts of drowsiness and sleeplessness; unexplained disappearances of money and belongings from the home.

Heroin addicts usually stop bothering about their appearance, their speech may become halting, and they tend to drop old friends and take up with new ones. Users of heroin may receive unexplained messages or telephone calls, followed by an immediate and unexplained departure. Spots of blood may be noticed on their clothes, and needle marks on the back of the hand and the inside of the elbow. There may also be thickened brownish cords under the skin where veins solidified as a result of the injections.

There is a tendency for the addict to be hostile to society, and therein lies part of the trouble when it comes to treatment and rehabilitation. A hospital too often epitomizes society in the mind of the addict. More informal methods are therefore required, and in most countries clinics run on "non-institutional" lines within the community are available. Community support groups and networking are services that can be found in most communities.

Multiple substances are experimented with and abused by many. Interestingly, there is no pharmaceuticals answer to drug abuse. Despite a lack of agreement about treatment, many substance abusers do recover. Dependence on cocaine is a serious, life-threatening addiction that often involves other drugs and exposure to illnesses, including HIV-AIDS. Research suggests that psychosocial treatment, including behavioral treatment, is relatively effective. Budney and Higgins (1998) report encouraging results from behavioral intervention incorporating psychosocial counseling, behavioral reinforcement utilizing coupons for merchandise in exchange for abstinence from cocaine, and a variety of interventions and follow-up activities for lifestyle management in the community environment.

Community-based and often ex-addict operated clinics are frequently successful in working with addicts. The addict who is desperate for drugs has an uncanny instinct for putting the most subtle and painful pressures on families and doctors alike. These tactics are familiar to ex-addicts who know from their own experiences the kinds of behavioral changes and lifestyle changes to be overcome for recovery to be possible.

Children and families exposed to and utilizing substances are at great risk for continuing abuse with even more substances. Early intervention and prevention of substance experimentation are important in the lives of children and families as we continue the battle against substance abuse and its harmful outcomes.

Sexual Encounters and Sexual Abuse

Almost all children encounter rather explicit sexual situations between the ages of 6 and 12. Many minor confrontations that occur seem to pass children by, and leave them practically unscathed. This is where robust and healthy attitudes to sex are so important.

Not all children get to adulthood with only minor sexual experiences to assimilate. And this is really one of the most pressing problems facing parents. How much might one traumatic sexual encounter at an early age affect a child varies from case to case. If a seven-year-old girl is coaxed into some kind of sexual play by an older male relative, what effect will it have on her chances of establishing a happy physical relationship later in her life? If a twelve-year-old boy is seduced by a homosexual older boy or a grown man, is the boy likely to be deflected from normal heterosexual interests himself? There are no ready-made answers to such questions; and, as is the case in many matters dealing with human sexuality, there is little solid evidence to produce.

Seductions/incidents. Many childhood sexual experiences of different kinds come about through sexual contact with adults. Alfred Kinsey in his innovative 1950s research into human sexuality, found that, among 4,441 women interviewed, 1,075 (or nearly one in four) recalled sexual contacts before adolescence with males at least 15 years of age, and at least five years older then themselves. In 609 cases in which the older males were identified, they were strangers in 52% of the incidents, friends or acquaintances in 32%, uncles in 9%, fathers in 4%, and brothers in 3%. In more than half the cases, the "contact" consisted of an exhibition of the male genitals to the child. In an additional 9%, the approaches were verbal only. In 32%, there was fondling without genital contact, and in 27%, there was either manipulation of the girl's genitals or manipulation of the man's genitals by the girl. Oral contacts with the male or female genitals were reported in about 20 cases (2%), and actual coitus (sexual intercourse) in about 30 cases (3%).

Little *physical* harm was ever reported from these contacts. By contrast, 80% of the women reported having felt *emotional* distress or fear. (Kinsey Institute for Sex Research, 1953). A small proportion were seriously disturbed, but in most instances, the reported fright was that children manifest when they see insects, spiders, or objects against which they have been adversely conditioned. A child whose prior development has been at least reasonably healthy is likely to withstand an early sexual experience. All the good work put in by parents during a young child's life is not likely to be swept aside by one chance encounter. If the parents have sensitized the child to negative attitudes and fears about sex, such a traumatic event may well serve to trigger a real emotional problem. Children react differently to sexual exploitation from very early in their lives. Each child's coping is different, and every child is to be valued and helped to overcome and resolve fears associated with sexual experiences in their lives. Serious problems tend to arise when sexual contacts (initiated say, by a relative) continue over a long period of time, and the child is too frightened, guilty, or emotionally involved to say anything to his/her parents or to authorities.

Child sexual assault or victimization is more common than once thought, as many as 20% to 30% of girls and slightly less for boys. Young men more than young women are reluctant to report sexual victimization according to one study (Finkelhor, 1979). The perpetrator of child sexual abuse is generally known to the child; often a relative who is more powerful threatens the child to maintain secrecy, and in long-term situations of abuse may threaten to harm the child and/or others in the family if the victimization is ever shared. Men more than women are reported abusers of children of both genders. Sexual abuse occurs through same sex seduction of young children yet less is known about treatment of young male victims. Regardless of gender of the victim and/or perpetrator, sexual abuse of children and teenagers is a violation that warrants legal action against the perpetrator and treatment for the victim.

For a more complete discussion on intervention with victims of sexual assault, see Faller (1988) and Sgroi (1982). The first responsibility of families and professionals is to protect children from victimization and thus assure safety and maximum potential for healthy social and emotional development. In situations where sexual abuse and victimization are suspected, a range of professionals including social workers, nurses, doctors, and others can provide intervention. For many, sexual victimization has lifelong implications including difficulties from intimate relationships, depression, perpetration of others, and violence. It is imperative that professionals acquaint themselves with the literature on assessing and treating child sexual abuse. Sexual abuse of children is a punishable crime and calls for intervention.

Although this emotive subject—a problem directed *toward* rather than *of* young persons—appears in the adolescent section, it is also about acts perpetrated on children, indeed very young children. The term sexual abuse includes the following acts:

- Rape
- Sexual intercourse
- Anal penetration
- Masturbation
- Digital (finger) penetration
- Fondling
- Exhibitionism or flashing
- Involvement in pornographic activity

C. Henry Kemp, the American pediatrician who made extensive studies of the problem, defined sexual abuse as "the involvement of developmentally immature children and ado-

---

Adolescence

lescents in sexual activity they do not truly comprehend, to which they are unable to give informed consent, or that violates the social taboos of family roles" (Kempe and Kempe, 1978). It is not within the scope of this book to deal adequately with such a disturbing and complex issue. However, it is important to be alert to possible warning "signs." *Do* seek experienced and expert help as many of these signs in children and adolescents are open to alternative explanations; and are thus vulnerable to *misinterpretation* as sexual abuse. Tables 7 and 8

Table 7. Physical Warning Signs of Possible Child Sexual Abuse

- Sleeplessness, nightmares, and fear of the dark
- Bruises, scratches, bite marks
- Depression/suicide attempts
- Anorexia nervosa
- Eating disorders or change in eating habits
- Difficulty in walking or sitting
- Pregnancy—particularly with reluctance to name the father
- Recurring urinary tract problems
- Vaginal infections or genital/anal damage
- Venereal disease
- Bed-wetting
- Vague pains and aches
- Itching or soreness

Table 8. Behavioral Warning Signs of Possible Child Sexual Abuse

- Lack of trust in adults
- Fear of a particular individual
- Withdrawal and introversion
- Running away from home
- Girl takes over the mothering role
- Sudden school problems, truanting, and falling grades
- Low self-esteem and low expectations of others
- Stealing
- Drug, alcohol, or solvent abuse
- Display of sexual knowledge beyond the child's years
- Sexual drawing
- Prostitution
- Vulnerability to sexual and emotional exploitation
- Revulsion toward sex
- Fear of school medical examinations

115

present (respectively) some of the physical and behavioral warning signs of possible sexual abuse.

Summary and Comment

We have attempted in this chapter to sketch in the broad developmental themes that are important for your understanding of childhood and adolescence. A framework of *normal* development is vital for your assessment of what is *not* normal, usual, "healthy," or functional, in a potential client's behavior. It is particularly difficult to pinpoint the onset of serious problems when childhood and adolescence are notable for the changes that take place, some of them very rapid indeed. So many signs of normal change look like "symptoms" of emotional disturbance. Therefore you need multiple criteria (working guidelines) for arriving at the decision that you are dealing with a problem with serious implications. Proceed cautiously and consult acknowledged experts, colleagues, or supervisors if necessary. This is a ferociously complex area fraught with value judgments, ethical issues, and technical difficulties. You will find a few of the typical problems illustrated in these pages but the topic is so vast that you should supplement your *knowledge base* from other literature, and your *experience* from workshops and supervised practice.

The advice is particularly pertinent to the issues of physical, emotional, and sexual abuse. The legal, moral, technical, and social ramifications of these problems go far beyond the scope of this kind of book. What is critical to remember is that most children can cope with traumas *if* the aftermath is sensitively dealt with by adults, parents, and/or the authorities. What is more damaging in the short- *and* longer-term is the abusive situation that goes on and on. As so many emotional, physical, and sexual incidents of an abusive kind occur in the child's home, this is precisely what tends to happen.

CHAPTER 6

Responsiveness in Parents and Children

Family groupings have been traced back to the Pleistocene period, some 500,000 years ago. This durability, and universality, of the family suggests that as an organization it has significant survival value for the individual and the species. But longevity of this order does not mean that the family is unchanging. It has been, and is, susceptible to social, economic, and historical forces. For example, the large extended family has given way in industrial societies to small nuclear units of parent(s) and offspring. There is an increasing number of single-parent families. In 1994, 26% of families with children were headed by a single parent. (*Kids Count Data Book*, 1997.) Then again, there are several variations in parental roles to take into account.

Birth parents give the child life, physical appearance, intellectual potential, and certain personality characteristics and special talents. The *legal parents* carry responsibility for the child's maintenance, safety, and security and make decisions about the child's residence and education. *Parenting parents* provide the day-to-day love, care, attention, and discipline. For many children the three components of parenting are embodied in one set of parents.

In the case of foster children there will at least be a split between birth parents who are also legal parents and the foster parents undertaking part of the parenting function. In foster care there is quite commonly a three-way split, with birth parents, parenting (foster) parents, and the local authority as legal parent with custody authority. Adoptive children are likely to have two sets of parents: the birth parents and the adoptive parents. The latter combines the legal and parenting roles.

The Egyptians, Romans, and Greeks all sanctioned adoption. In earlier periods, adoption was utilized primarily to serve adult ends—particularly to acquire heirs in order to provide continuity for a family line. Views on adoption have changed markedly over the years. Today's philosophy is unmistakably child-centered. In essence, the value of adoption in modern society is that it safeguards the child by providing a permanent family arrangement. Of course, adoptive parents—like biological parents setting out to rear an infant—are faced with the rather daunting task of transforming helpless, unsocial, and self-centered infants into more or less self-supporting and responsible members of the community.

Parental Responsiveness

With the birth or adoption of the first child the tasks of the parents, the roles they occupy, their orientation toward the future, all change profoundly. This simple step into parenthood provides a severe test for the parents. The inevitable changes in the partners will, in turn, alter their relationship and may place stress upon it until a new equilibrium can be established in their lives. In order to reestablish a degree of equanimity they rely on various coping "mechanisms" (see chapter 4). There may be reverberations in all of this for the child.

In working with parents the professional will be particularly interested in assessing the parents' responsiveness to their child because so many of the parental functions are dependent to some degree on this attribute. The needs of children who are potentially at risk if not responded to consistently are of two kinds: *survival* functions such as the need for food, shelter, and physical care; and *psychosocial* functions, including the child's requirements of love, security, attention, new experiences, acceptance, education, praise, recognition, and belongingness.

If they are to survive, infants and children must also acquire vast amounts of information about the environment they inhabit. The transmission by adults of information of various kinds from one generation to another, as we have seen, is called *socialization*. One of the main objectives of this training is the preparation of children for their future, one of the major themes of this chapter.

Problematic Parenting

The definition of problematic behavior is a difficult one because it *is* largely a relative judgment, and a social, subjective one at that. It is formulated largely in terms of its consequences for the offspring—his or her well-being. Social workers sometimes aid pediatricians and health professionals in cases where infants fail to thrive, in the absence of any organic (physical) illness. They have to explore the social and emotional context in which the child is nurtured.

The point is that maternal responsiveness is important in something as apparently basic as providing sustenance to a baby. Typically, feeding times must be adapted to the cycles of hunger and satisfaction expressed by the infant and responded to by the parent. During the feeding sessions mothers should preferably be calm and sensitive enough to respond from moment-to-moment to changes in the baby's behavior. For example, they commonly respond to pauses in the child's sucking at the breast by jiggling the baby. They will gaze back at the baby and talk to it. They will be alert to the child's changing needs for nourishment as it matures, by altering its diet.

Parental responsiveness is a complex and many-sided phenomenon, but there are at least three different elements that make for what one might assess to be *sensitive* responsiveness: the tendency to react *promptly, consistently,* and *appropriately* to their offspring. A social worker or health visitor would be concerned if parents continually failed to show these reactions in response to their child's hunger and pain, crying, or other communications and actions.

Parent–Child Attachment

The question of sensitive or insensitive responsiveness has been linked in part with the quality of the emotional "bond" or "attachment" that forms between the parent and baby. Obviously, the infant's survival depends upon a loving and long-term commitment by adult caregivers. Social workers and health professionals are on the lookout for signs of rejection, neglect, and abuse. When all goes well—and it usually does—a "bond" is cemented between a mother and her infant, a rela-

119

tionship implying unconditional love, self-sacrifice, and caring attitudes that, for the mother's part, are quite likely to last a lifetime.

What is this doctrine of mother-to-infant bonding? Put briefly, it is suggested that in some mammalian species, including our own, mothers become bonded to their infants through close contact—skin-to-skin—during a short critical period, soon after birth. This is an awesome claim, considering that no other adult human behavior, and a complex pattern of behavior and attitude at that, is explained in such "ethological" terms, that is, the language of animal behavior.

The close-contact, critical-period bonding theory is said to be justified on two grounds. One is rooted in studies of animal behavior. The other has to do with observations of human mothers, comparing those who have had little or no contact and those who have extended contact with their newborn babies.

Attachment of mother and infant has been thought to be the basic component to long-lasting security and sense of self-worth into adulthood. Studying infants in institutions and orphanages from World War II separation, Bowlby (1982) concluded that separation of mother and child resulted in serious physical, mental, and emotional damage to children. Later, recognizing that his sample was somewhat extreme and that his subjects were deprived of contact, love, and nurturance from nearly any source, he softened his conclusions but remained firm in the importance of lasting and consistent relationships in the development and nurturance of a child. The phenomenon of attachment continues to be of interest to researchers and has resulted in extensive study of early infant-caregiver studies and the impact of infant experiences on later development. Gaining security, self-image, and a sense of self are all part of the process of development in response to various sources of nurturance and relationships. Different responses of children reared in apparently similar ways continue to be of great interest to researchers (Skolnick, 1998).

The eminently realistic and humane idea of allowing a mother and her new baby to get to know one another early on, by means of frequent and intimate social interaction, becomes intrusive and unrealistic when the permissive "ought" of physical contact is transformed into an authoritarian "must"— whatever the condition of the mother or her offspring. Mothers-to-be, often exhausted and hypersensitive to potential dangers, may be undermined by the fear that if they do not have contact with their babies soon after delivery they may not fall in love with them.

This is not the place to review the complex and detailed studies of bonding; however, there seems to be no reliable evidence that skin-to-skin contact is necessary for the development of mother-love, and, what is more significant, mother-to-infant attachment does not depend on such contact occurring during a sensitive period of short duration after the birth of the baby.

We are *not* putting forward the idea that early human contact and relationships are of no consequence. Far from it. All relationships have to have a beginning; close mother–infant contact is decidedly desirable whenever possible. Mothers tend to like it, and lactation is facilitated. Where better to begin than at the very beginning, with the newborn child placed in its mother's arms? Mutual awareness and familiarity have an opportunity to develop. What we are talking about is foundational learning, learning how to relate to a stranger, a baby. It would seem that this learning comes quickly for some but for others more slowly. The range of individual differences is wide.

The period after birth, with its heightened emotional arousal and excited expectation and fulfillment of a new family member, may have tremendous significance for *all* members of the family. Remember that parental bonds and relationships have their own complex, many-sided developmental histories, stretching over many years. Among the factors that can influence the way a mother behaves and relates to her offspring are her age, her cultural and social background, her own experience of being parented, her personality, her previous experience with babies, and her experiences during pregnancy and birth.

Insensitivity to cultural values in clinical and social work practice can lead to much individual suffering if methods used are contrary to cherished cultural and/or religious beliefs. For some ethnic groups, bonding ideas, if applied insensitively by doctors and nurses, may have disturbing repercussions. In many Asian families, for instance, birth is a less personal event than in European families. An Indian baby is thought to be bonded to the family group rather than to the mother in particular. Unless hospital staff are sensitive to ethnic differences in behavior and attitudes after birth, these parents could feel intense conflict over "bonding procedures."

Understandably the hard-pressed social worker cannot afford to be as complacent as the scientist in risking what the statisticians call Type II errors, for example, denying relationships that actually exist because of a cautious attitude to evidence. After all, it has been suggested that separation of the mother and infant for several weeks immediately after birth may not only damage the subsequent mother-child relationship but additionally that such mothers are prone to child abuse. In fact, the evidence for such far-reaching claims is simply not available; these notions do not stand up to painstaking inquiry and investigation.

It is reassuring to realize that there are variations in the way that maternal feelings arise and grow. Mothers generally expect to have positive maternal feelings toward their infants at the time of birth. Indeed, some mothers *do* report an instant love toward their newborn babies. Others report that they feel nothing. However, you can reassure mothers that they do not need to worry if they feel initially detached from their babies, as this appears to be a fairly common occurrence. Some 40% of mothers of first-borns have been found to express an initial indifference to their infants, a state of mind that soon evaporates as they get to know their offspring.

When subjective and objective reports of the development of mother love are scrutinized, it becomes apparent that the growth of maternal attachment is usually a gradual process.

Allaying parents' fears. The practical advice to parents who have had an enforced separation—at whatever time—from their children is: do not spend time worrying needlessly. Adult bonding need not be impaired in the case of those separations in the maternity hospital, unless you talk yourself into a crisis.

Where the separation occurs later in life, children may be upset for a short time, but they will soon recover if parents appear their usual selves and avoid fussing over them in nervous expectation of the worst. We know that a child's separation from its caregiver *does not inevitably* result in maladjustment. Far from it. Brief separations are fairly common for all children and seem to have little adverse effect. The key issue is to provide good and stable substitute care during the absence or absences.

Paternal bonding. Paternal love puts a large question mark over the bonding doctrine, for it implies that a father's love is of a lower order and quality than the mother's. Yet it is not always the female who cares for the baby. This is so even in some animal species: male marmosets, to take just one example, carry the infant at all times except when it is feeding.

Most human fathers develop a strong love for their offspring, even if they were nowhere near the delivery room when they were born. A study of first-time fathers suggests that they began developing a bond to their newborn by the first three days after the birth and often earlier. They tended to develop a feeling of preoccupation, absorption, and interest. There are no clear indications that the early contact by the father with the newborn facilitates this paternal bonding. Nevertheless, the opportunity for father and infant to get to know one another early is important, especially as contemporary Western society is witnessing a massive increase in the number of single-parent families; and in some, it is the father who is the caregiver.

Fostering and adoption. If maternal bonding theory were correct, it would hardly be possible for foster or adoptive parents to form warm attachments to their charges, whom they may not have seen as babies at all. It could be said that it is possible to look after children satisfactorily without ever becoming attached to them, but how many adoptive or foster parents would say that they felt no bond with their child? Tragic "tug of love" cases have occurred because foster parents have grown so fond of the children in their care that it becomes unbearably hurtful to hand them back to their biological parents.

Not only is there no "blood bond" between adoptive mother and the child, but she has missed out vital weeks, months, and sometimes years of exposure to the youngster. Not surprisingly, there is nothing to suggest that adoptive parents are in any way inferior to their familial or parental roles than biological parents. A painstaking study of children who had been in care throughout their early years followed them on leaving care. One group of children was adopted, another returned to their own families. It was found that the latter did less well than the adopted children, both in the initial stages of settling in and in their subsequent progress. The reason lay primarily in the attitudes of the two sets of parents: the adoptive group "worked" harder at being parents, possibly for the very reason that the child was not their own, in a genetic sense.

The attitude of some people to adoption in this country in the 18th and early 19th centuries was very different from the one shared by most of us today. We gather from George Eliot's novel *Silas Marner* (1929) that on religious grounds it was believed that "to adopt a child, because children of your own had been denied you, was to try and choose your lot in spite of Providence: the adopted child ... would never turn out well, and would be a curse to those who had wilfully and rebelliously sought what it was clear that, for some high reason, they were better without." Adoption was only permissible and likely to succeed if it came about by chance, not intent. George Eliot, in her usual insightful manner, made the point that the "blood bond" is less important than the bonds forged by long-term tenderness and affection. And she has been shown to be correct.

Researchers provide evidence that adoption is notable for its high "success rate" both in absolute terms, and relative to other forms of substitute care. Like other parents, adopters will have their share of difficult children and will try to make sense of them. A commonly held belief which can be very worrying to adoptive parents is the notion that infants who are deprived of maternal care and love are affected adversely in their ability to form bonds of affection and also in their ability to develop a repertoire of socially appropriate attitudes and behavior.

An attitude of therapeutic pessimism was created in the minds of many social workers when considering problems in older children who were adopted, or the breakdown of fostering arrangements as a result of their belief in a link between their experience of early maternal separation/deprivation and the development of lasting difficulties in personal relationships and social/emotional functioning. An intolerable burden of anxiety about the child's future was also placed on parents who adopt older youngsters. But what is the evidence for such misgivings? It all began with studies of babies and young children in Dickensian-like institutions. The plight of these infants was linked theoretically to what happens to animals separated from their mothers.

Current concern about children who for whatever reason cannot be cared for by biological parent(s) calls for establishing a permanent family for each child. The situation of children in out-of-home care covers a broad range from the infant who is placed for adoption upon birth, to the abused two-year-old, to the 14-year-old who may have experienced several foster families and unsuccessful adoptive placements. Children placed in foster or adoptive families at older ages bring with them their histories of life experiences. Many will seek renewed relationships with biological relatives in their adult years, others will not. For about 90% of children in adoptive families, the new family becomes a permanent family for the child. For others, the adoptive family, not unlike some biological families, dissolves and the child may again return to the custody of legal authorities. Barth and Berry (1988) and McDonald, Allen, Westerfelt, and Piliavin (1996) provide extensive reporting of research studies on fostered and adoptive care respectively.

Responsiveness in Children

Examples of chicks or ducklings following a person have been seen by many people in nature films. Although normally attached to their birth mother, such infants can become attached with ease to an "adoptive" parent or (in the laboratory) to a moving inanimate object. Konrad Lorenz (1973) found that during a restricted period just after hatching that goslings instinctively follow the first large moving thing they see. These young creatures not only tend to follow this moving object but they come to prefer it to all others, and after a time will follow no others.

This type of early learning is referred to as *imprinting*. The fascinating question that arises from studies of imprinting is whether human attachments, preferences, or other behaviors are acquired during restricted periods of development on an imprinting-like basis. The most influential writings have been those of John Bowlby. His early opinion was that the child's strong attachment to its mother was necessary for normal, healthy development. Bowlby (1982) argued that the period in the infant's life when a major new relationship, for example, to the mother, was being formed was a vital one for determining the nature of that relationship.

At that time he thought the deprivation of maternal affection, or protracted maternal separation, was liable to result in maladjustment, which could show itself in a variety of ways, including delinquency. He was suggesting then that not only the presence of adverse influences such as a harsh rejecting mother but the absence of crucial stimulation disturbs, possibly irreversibly, the child's ability to make relationships with people. Fortunately more recent, painstaking reviews on the effect of maternal deprivation and other types of early experiences indicate the more optimistic conclusion that early experience if distressing *can* be remedied; dysfunctional responses can be reversed. Such early experience is no more than a link, albeit an important one, in the chain of development. Development is influential but shapes behavior less and less powerfully as age increases. What is probably crucial is that for some children some adverse aspects of their early learning are continually repeated and reinforced and long-term effects appear. We must not forget the likelihood that later problems and deviance may be the result of later adverse life experiences, for example, exposure to delinquent peers, and not only early learning experiences. Development is an ongoing process.

John Bowlby's (1982) revised view, following an examination of such research findings, was that the child's separation from its caregiver did not inevitably result in the maladjustment of the child. This is not to deny the vital importance of the comforting presence of a loving parent or parent substitute especially before the age of about five years in facilitating the child's healthy psychological development.

The idea of a critical or sensitive period implies that parents are all-powerful, all-responsible. Such an ideology places a great responsibility on parents to "get things right!" In fact, our knowledge about what parental practices are appropriate or beneficial must of necessity be tentative. That said, just what are the implications for children of differences in maternal and parental behavior?

Parental Patterns

There can be too much of a good thing, a point when mothering becomes smothering. And, of course, the same applies to fathering. There can also be too little parental input. Parental nurturance is undoubtedly a vital ingredient in the child's and adolescent's healthy development, but as with everything *moderation* is the watchword.

Parental Overprotection

Overprotective parents frequently alternate between dominating their offspring and submitting to them. There are two types of parental overprotection. The dominating form of overprotection may lead to excessively dependent, passive, and submissive behavior on the part of the child. It is thought that if youngsters are discouraged from acting independently, exploring, and experimenting, they acquire timid, awkward, and generally apprehensive behaviors.

Parental Dominance/Restriction

Children whose parents are authoritarian, give the child no voice, and use physical punishment as a means of discipline tend to be more dependent and, at the same time, rebellious adolescent offspring. Restrictive, authoritarian parents attempt to shape, control, and assess the behavior and attitudes of the child according to a set standard of conduct, usually an absolute standard, often motivated by theological considerations. Obedience is valued as a virtue, and punitive measures are used to curb self-will when the child's or teenager's actions or beliefs conflict with what parents think is correct conduct. They believe in *bullying*—as opposed to educating—their offspring into such values as respect for authority, respect for work, and respect for the preservation of traditional order. Verbal give-and-take is discouraged because the child should accept unquestioningly the parent's word for what is right.

The children of domineering parents often lack self-reliance and the ability to cope realistically with their problems; later they may fail or prove slow to accept adult responsibilities. They are apt to be submissive and obedient and to withdraw from the situations they find difficult. They also tend to be the sort of boys and girls who become many of the adults who have never left home, psychologically, and in many cases, physically as well.

Parental Rejection

There is a group of parents whose concern for their children is minimal and whose attitudes are casual, laissez-faire, lax, or even indifferent. For some, rejection means callous and indifferent neglect or positive hostility from the parents; but it may also be emotional and subtle. Children come to believe that they are worthless, that their very existence makes their parents unhappy. The term "emotional abuse" has been added to the concept of "physical abuse" and is defined in terms of the neglect of all or some of the basic needs of children. Table 9 provides a list of the physical injuries that *may* indicate that a child has been the victim of nonaccidental, abusive acts.

Emotional abuse is less tangible and even more difficult to diagnose. It is defined in terms of the neglect of all or some of the *basic needs* of children. There follows a list suggested by

Table 9. Physical Injuries in Child Abuse

- Bruises, weals, lacerations, and scars
- Burns and scalds
- Bone and joint injuries
- Brain and eye injuries
- Internal injuries

the distinguished pediatrician and analyst, Donald Winnicott (1958).

- Physical care and protection.
- Affection and approval.
- Stimulation and teaching.
- Discipline and controls that are consistent and appropriate to the child's age and development.
- Opportunity and encouragement to acquire gradual autonomy, that is, for the child to take gradual control over his or her own life

Emotional abuse is "signposted" by parental indifference. The child is ignored, and there may be inadequate physical care, stimulation, physical contact, and security. The child is thus denied emotional warmth and love as well as protection, support, and discipline. Overall negative attitudes may lead to abusive threats, constant criticism, and scapegoating. With older children this is sometimes accompanied by ridicule and denigrating all the child's efforts to please. Some apply the term emotional abuse also to severe overprotection.

The concept of emotional abuse is in danger of being overinclusive and far too vague. It is therefore an advantage to have rather more tangible indicators to pinpoint the presence of emotional abuse. In particular there are four types of damaging parental behavior.

Indicator 1 entails punishment of positive "operant" behavior such as smiling, mobility, manipulation.

Indicator 2 is behavior that results in discouragement of parent-infant bonding, for example, pushing children away every time they seek proximity, comfort, and affection.

Indicator 3 involves the punishment of self-esteem as when parents endlessly criticize their child.

Indicator 4 is parental behavior leading to punishing those interpersonal skills (for example, friendliness) that are foundational for adequate social presence and performance in environments outside the family, such as schools, peer groups, and so on.

One might say that emotional abuse consists of behavior that seriously undermines the development of the child's competence.

A rejecting or abusive parent tends not only to ignore the offspring's need for nurturance but also to punish manifestation of that need. One would expect, therefore, that more severe forms of rejection would lead the youngster to suppress such behavior. Parents who provide little attention and care, but do not actually punish dependent behavior, are likely to intensify their offspring's needs for attention and care. The more a youngster is "pushed away" physically or emotionally, the more he or she clings.

Parental Permissiveness

Permissive parents attempt to behave in a nonpunitive, accepting, and affirmative manner toward their offsprings' impulses, desires, and actions; consult with them about policy decisions and give explanations for family rules. Such parents allow young people to regulate their own activities as much as possible, avoid the excessive exercise of control, and do not encourage them to obey absolute-defined standards.

Prevention

Can parents preempt the development of antisocial attitudes and behavior? Life is too unpredictable and people too mysterious and complex in their makeup to justify our saying *yes* in an unqualified manner. Many persons other than parents have an influence on children's personality and behavior. But parents can encourage a strong "immune system" in their offspring—protection against some of the stresses and snares of growing up. Such a system would depend, in part, upon:

- Strong ties of affection and respect between themselves and their children.
- Firm social and moral demands being made on their offspring.
- The consistent use of sanctions.
- Techniques of punishment that are psychological rather than physical such as threats to withdraw approval.

- An intensive use of reasoning and explanations.
- Responsibility given to children and adolescents.

These generalizations are guidelines that you, in turn, can interpret to meet the particular values and circumstances of your clients.

Guideline 1: **Foster bonds of respect and affection.**
Such bonds tend to make all teaching endeavors much easier; the more affection there is as a foundation for disciplinary tactics, the more notice the child will take of what he or she is being told.

Guideline 2: **Make firm social and moral demands (set limits).**
This means attempting to establish and convey a reasonably coherent idea of the aims and objectives that lie behind the training and supervision of young people. Children whose parents set firm limits for them grow up with more self-esteem and confidence than those who are allowed to get away with behaving in any way they like. Supervision does not mean intrusive surveillance, but it does mean knowing where children and teenagers are, who their friends are, and so on. It is important to give the youngster a reasonable amount of freedom of choice within those limits.

Children who get their own way all the time interpret such laissez-faire permissiveness as indifference. They feel nothing they do is important enough for their parents to bother about.

Guideline 3: **Prepare children for life by developing family routines.**
Most routines are useful shortcuts to living. For example, routines help a child to master and carry out automatically such daily tasks as feeding, washing, dressing, going to bed, and helping him or her to achieve more with less effort.

Habit is taught by repetition of routine. A child feels secure if the main events of his or her day are as regular and familiar as the sunrise. If going to bed, eating, and washing always happen in more or less the same way, the child accepts them with little or no fuss. The morning ritual of preparation is a potent factor in getting a child off to school. The bedtime ritual is a particularly powerful habit; a regular routine of supper, bath, and then a story before bed make the child's world seem well-ordered, safe, and comfortable. It is not trivializing to set up these routines. Psychologists and social workers who visit chaotic homes know how disturbing the lack of routine is to young children and how unhelpful to older ones who enter the relatively orderly life demanded at school.

Guideline 4: **Teach children the family rules.**
Everyone needs some self-discipline or rules of conduct in order to adjust his or her needs and desires to those of others. Children *need* the affection and approval of people around; being self-centered and egotistical will not win this approval.

The ultimate aim is to give children the ability to discipline themselves, to compromise between what they want and what society demands of them. Once they can do this, their dealings with other people will be easier.

Guideline 5: **Choose rules carefully.**
Parents are in trouble if they proliferate the "don'ts"—make demands for the sake of the demands, rules for the sake of rules. Any limit set should be for the child's or adolescent's safety, well-being, and mature, emotional, and social development. It is crucial to ensure that children know exactly what the rules and constraints are, and what is expected of them. Rules are most effective when they are relatively uncomplicated, fair, understandable, and applied fairly and consistently so that the youngster knows what will happen if they are broken.

No one can advise parents about which rules to insist upon. Every family has different values, different interpretations of what is right and wrong. Their standards of behavior will accord with those of their community or religion, as well as their own values, lifestyles, and personalities.

Guideline 6: **Be consistent.**
When teaching your child to distinguish between appropriate and inappropriate actions, it is important to be consistent. It is confusing if he or she is punished for her behavior today and gets away with the same thing tomorrow merely because your reasoning or mood has changed. Parents are indignant if asked whether they ever break a promise to their child. Of

course not! It would undermine the child's trust and devalue the currency of their words. Yet they may be quite unaware of idle threats they make and of the impact of such threats.

Guideline 7: **Be persistent.**
Parents often stand out against rebellious, noncompliant behavior for some time, only to give in eventually. The child will soon infer that the meaning of their parents' word is ambiguous and that if he or she makes a nuisance, the parent will give way.

Guideline 8: **Give explanations/reasons.**
Parents might well say, "I wouldn't automatically obey a regulation myself unless I thought there was a good reason for it. So why not try to explain to children, and more particularly adolescents, why we have to have rules in a complicated world, and what would happen if everyone went their own way?" Children are more likely to internalize standards if they are justified in terms of their *intrinsic* value, rather than in terms of the punishment and odium that follow from their violation. They do need to know! When small, they cannot comprehend, unaided, the reasons for training. Later on, when in a position to understand explanations, they may be sidetracked; worse still, there may be no possible meaning to the demands made upon them, because what is being asked is unreasonable.

Guildeline 9: **Tell children what they should do, not only what they can't do.**
Explain clearly to children what is required of them. Emphasize the positive, not only the negative. Notice the child in good behavior, not only naughty behavior. By attending to positive actions parents make them more likely to occur.

Guideline 10: **Giving young people responsibility gives them the opportunity to practice and to be responsible.**

Guideline 11: **Encourage parents to listen carefully to what their child says.**
When children are expected to be seen and not heard, their parents suppress undesirable behavior without paying atten-

tion to the needs and messages that lie behind it. Children's communications are often in code. As professionals or as parents we need to be empathic, look at what they are saying with an ear tuned to the hidden messages. Those children who show-off in front of strangers may really be communicating their uncertainty, even their shyness.

For parents, and professional people who work with children, it is vital to be able to communicate understanding. Haim Ginott (1969) is concerned that the *two-way* nature of good communication between adults should also form the basis of conversations with children. A dialogue with a young child requires respect and skill. He advises parents to listen carefully to what children say. Messages should preserve the child's and parents' self-respect; statements of understanding should precede statements of advice or instruction. Ginott says that in this way parents provide a mirror to their children's personality; they learn about their emotional likeness (as they get to know their physical likeness) by having their feelings reflected back to them.

The child who comes home saying, "I hate school," learns that it is not *everything* about school that she dislikes when her mother says, "It's been a bad day today, hasn't it; you have physical education on Monday—are you still feeling a bit embarrassed getting changed in front of the others?" Or when Tom says, "My teacher made me stay in today," parents would do well to resist the temptation to answer: "Now what have you done?" or "I suppose you deserved it," both of which would have inflamed his feelings. Instead, they might acknowledge them by saying: "You must have felt awful . . . would you like to tell me what happened?"

Summary and Comment

The themes of parental responsiveness, including parent–child attachment and parental styles, are explored in this chapter. The effects of parenting variations and of physical and emotional abuse are described. *Guidelines* for doing preventive work with families may help facilitate prosocial behaviors and protect against antisocial behavior in children.

There is a discussion of fostering and adoption and of some of the unnecessary fears that adoptive parents have about the latter. Fortunately, it is possible to allay many of the anxieties parents have about separations and substitute care.

Responsiveness in children is another theme dealt with. The concepts of imprinting and attachment are described; and there is some reassuring evidence that adverse early experiences do not lead inevitably to psychological disturbance in maturity. Painstaking preventive work can be effective.

CHAPTER 7

Loss and Change Experienced by Children and Families

Psychologists have shown an increasing interest in the themes of change, loss, and gain that present in any major period of transition during our lifetime. We looked at adolescence in chapter 5 and the task that teenagers face in mastering massive changes in their lives. It is truly a stage of transition. They lose one identity, that of child, and don another, that of adult. Here is what it feels like according to one 15-year-old:

Lately I've been in a daze, and I can't think straight. Maybe because some of my brain cells are dying and I'm just about 16. My whole world is changing. Before I used to have a regular routine and all I was concerned with was school. But now I'm thinking of my future.

The point about this, whether it is an adolescent change or some other life crisis—such as divorce, the breakup of a family, or the constituting of a new one—is that new behaviors, different responses to changing circumstances, are required.

Stages of Transition

This is where your understanding of typical reactions to major transitional events will help you to guide your clients in their efforts to cope with the difficult changes in their lives. Here are the stages that tend to occur following disruptive life experience.

Immobilization. The individual has a sense of being overwhelmed, being unable to make plans, to understand or to reason. A kind of paralysis sets in.

Minimization. The person may cope with this state of "deep freeze" by minimizing the changes. The sorrow and pain caused by a girl's bereavement due to the separation of her mother and father are minimized in her awareness. The youngster may try to trivialize the changes brought about by his new stepmother's entry into the home ("I don't know why everyone makes such a fuss over nothing"). Some children and adults will deny that a change has occurred.

Depression. Depression is a common reaction for adolescents in response to transition and loss, particularly the physical changes of puberty. Middle life and old age represent a dramatic transition in the lives of adult men and women. Don't be surprised if there is an upsurge in feelings of misery and inner turmoil for any of these groups. Misery gives way in some vulnerable individuals to more disturbing feelings of depression. Depression can be a statement of helplessness or powerlessness over events being out of, or beyond, control. Some depressed clients entertain ideas about committing suicide.

Letting go. This is the stage of accepting reality for what it is, of figuratively "letting go" of the past, which means for the toddler, the dependency of infancy, for the adolescent the safety of childhood, of total parental nurturance of childlike irresponsibility.

Testing. The "letting go" provides a bridge to the testing phase, in which the individual may begin testing him- or herself vis-à-vis the new circumstances and of trying out new behaviors, skills, and even new lifestyles to the chagrin sometimes of family and friends. At this time there can be quite a lot of anger and irritability expressed.

Search for meaning. Following this stage of activity and self-testing, there is a more gradual movement toward a search for meaning and understanding of how things are different and why this is so.

Internalization. Eventually these new meanings are internalized, taken into the "psyche" and behavioral repertoire of the individual.

Transitions, it is important to remember, involve considerable stress. They are most distressing if they are unpredictable, involuntary, unfamiliar, and of high intensity and magnitude and if the rate and degree of changes are excessive. Professionals can help parents and parents can help their sons and daughters by warning them of the likely changes, or interpreting them, thus making them more predictable and manageable. Of course, being able to talk about personal and intimate matters to clients will depend upon a relationship of trust and good communication; in the case of parents, fostered in earlier years; in the case of professionals, nurtured over several sessions.

Childhood Bereavement

Childhood security may be shattered temporarily by the death of a loved parent or relative. The trauma can be lessened for the child through sensitive caring and explanations. The quality of the relationships as evidenced in the continuity and reassurance of loving care, matters more than the disruption of bonds as such. Where ill effects do occur, they are more likely if the mother dies when the child is very young; the father's death is more likely to have adverse effects if it occurs when the child is older.

Children are remarkable in the way in which they seem to accept the sad facts of life and get on with living. A simple, straightforward explanation of the death of a grandparent is usually sufficient, particularly if given in a calm manner.

Long-term problems are less associated with the death of a parent despite the finality of the break in an emotional attachment than it is with divorce where attachment may still be retained.

Parental Bereavement

Not all children are born and not all survive birth. Parents who experience the loss of a child prior to birth either through miscarriage or fetal death (death after the 20th week of gestation) experience psychological and emotional pain and loss. In occurrences of miscarriage in early pregnancy, the couple may experience loss and grief. The couple may progress through the stages of loss defined by Kubler-Ross (1969) in a relatively short period. For many, the anticipation of future and success-ful pregnancy lessens the pain. The stages of denial, anger, bargaining, depression, and acceptance in the grieving process are perhaps more difficult for the woman whose body must readjust. Psychologically, she may have welcomed and recog-nized the reality of early pregnancy more deeply than the father. Unfortunately, social and cultural practices do not pre-pare her for the inability of most family and friends to under-stand her feelings of loss nor to be sympathetic to her loss as rarely is the grief of a miscarriage felt deeply by others.

In situations of fetal death or stillbirth, socially or culturally prescribed customs are even more lacking. Some couples will want to see the infant, perhaps hold it, and may desire photo-graphs. There may be a funeral and burial involving close family and friends where the ritual of saying goodbye brings closure and comfort at this time of loss. For some couples, this difficult time of loss and grief is facilitated through the support they receive through this open process of recognizing the death of their infant. For others, the fetus may be disposed of at the hospital, and the couple may grieve in the absence of any healing ritual. In either situation, the loss is very painful. For the young couple experiencing perhaps death and pregnancy for the first time, depression and lasting inability to cope with the loss may require professional help. There is increasing recognition of the need for mothers to recognize the dead infant as a person and to grieve the loss (Germain, 1991). Recognizing the baby as a person and making the death public tend to aid the healing process for the mother and father.

When a child or teenager dies due to illness or an unexpected accident, the family experiences serious and deep loss and grief over the death of their loved one whose life was not lived to a mature end. Frequently, the process of loss is prolonged and painful. The family may seek counseling, experience severe depression, make public statements about their loved one, and always find a vacuum in their lives. For some, the stress of the experience of such severe loss may even result in separation and/or divorce. Loss of a child is extremely stressful to family members and is an experience that holds lasting pain. In these situations, helping the family come to some acceptance of the loss and to find ways to celebrate the life and memory of their child is important for all the members.

Divorce or Separation

If all divorces, all broken homes, led to serious psychological difficulties, society would indeed have an appalling problem. According to the U.S. Bureau of the Census (1993), about 4 out of 10 first marriages end in divorce. In other words, it is likely that young children are involved in the precipitating events and aftermath of a divorce.

Most children do not want their parents to separate, and they may feel that their father and mother have not taken *their* interests into account. A marital separation may result in children's reappraising their own relationships with their parents and, indeed questioning the nature of all social relationships. For younger children in particular, there is the painful realization that some family relationships may not last forever. Preschool children usually appear to be very sad and frightened when their parents separate, and they become very clinging and demanding. Bedtime fears and a refusal to be left alone, even for a few minutes, are not uncommon. Children attending school or nursery may become very anxious about going there and may protest strongly when left. Vivid fantasies about abandonment, death of parents, and harm are encountered. Such children often express aggression toward other children.

Many childish reactions at such a time are expressions of the fear of being abandoned by one or both parents. Such fears are likely to be most acute if contact has been lost with a parent. If, however, relationships between parents and child can remain intact, and supportive, these fears are lessened.

With somewhat older children, grief and sadness remain a prominent feature but anger becomes more marked. This is usually directed at the parents, especially the one with whom the child is living—which more often than not means the mother. Regardless of the actual events leading to the breakdown, she is likely to be blamed by the child for everything that has happened. The absent father is quite likely to be idealized, regardless of realities, while the mother is held responsible for driving him away. Children, especially in the age group seven to eight, may express very strong yearnings for their father.

Preadolescent children tend to demonstrate less of their inner hurt and distress, which is not to say that it does not exist. Covering-up is common, and they seek distractions in play and other activities. It may be difficult to get through to such children; they are loath to talk about what they are feeling because of the pain it causes them. Underneath this apparent detachment is often anger; again, they may align themselves very strongly with one parent and even refuse to see the other.

Adolescents sometimes show overt depression; they appear to "opt out" of family life and withdraw into other relationships outside the home. Worries about their own relationships, sex, and marriage may surface.

There are immediate reactions to parental separation. Usually they are seen in an acute form for a matter of months and then begin to subside. Studies of children's reaction to divorce vary but tend to find children to be resilient in response to family breakup. Wallerstein and Blakeslee (1989) reported that lasting emotional damage occurs for children of divorce as they fail to be adequately nurtured emotionally and carry their experience of unstable relationships into their adult lives. Amato and Keith (1991) found only minimal differences between children from divorced families as compared to children from families who remained together. Divorce has become common and is an event that impacts children. Issues of custody, caregiving, nurturance, presence of a consistent and loving parent, communication with the absent parent, and membership in extended families of both biological parents are all variables that intervene in the childhood of our children. Bogolub (1995) provides an extensive review of the literature and raises many concerns about the change in the standard of living experienced by women and children in situations of divorce.

Divorced and single-parent mothers are confronted not only with financial losses but constant caregiving demands along-

side employment and career tracks as they are most likely to
be the custodial parent. Many worries may deplete the last
emotional resources of the mother left alone. Young children
need special attention and care but she may have to seek
employment. Finding substitute caregivers can be expensive.
Housing, too, is a common and costly problem. Children from
broken homes may fare better than youngsters from unhappy,
unbroken homes. There is no room for complacency. Such
relatively reassuring information is not repeated in the area of
delinquency.

In situations of divorce, decreased financial resources are
experienced by children from all social classes. It has been
reported that children from upper-income families may experience the greatest drop in available resources and lifestyle (Furstenberg and Cherlin, 1991). In situations of children from low-
income families, they will likely experience poverty, particularly in situations where their mothers lack employable skills.

About half of America's children spend some time in single-
parent households, generally with their mothers who are either
divorced or never married. In situations of divorce, child support is generally awarded; however, the failure of fathers to
pay support has resulted in child support enforcement and
interstate enforcement of collection of overdue payments (*The
State of America's Children Yearbook*, 1996). The seriousness of
support for children is a major issue that can necessitate change
in their residence, lifestyle, school achievement, and educational opportunities.

Children of all ages react to divorce. Adolescents may have
been exposed to family disputes for much of their lives, yet
feel abandoned or rejected as a result of divorce in their teen
years. According to Bogolub (1995), older children may be able
to separate themselves from their parents' difficulties. On the
other hand, older children may react with anger and self-dam-
aging behaviors. Delinquency is associated with the breakup of homes where there has been a great deal of parental
disharmony; the association is not with the disruption of the
home, as such. The loss of a parent through a marital separation
is much more likely to cause long-term problems than a loss
through death.

From the professional's point of view, if called in to work with a family, it is vital to appreciate how an atmosphere of strife and turmoil in the home, prior to separation, is one of the most corrosive influences. This quarreling is something that children describe as very damaging—especially episodes of hostility between mother and father.

Of the factors that are significant to a benign outcome for children—after all the misery of a divorce—three are of the utmost significance:

- Communication about separation
- Continued good relationship with at least one parent
- Satisfaction with custody and access arrangements

Children who consider themselves most damaged are:

- Those whose parents are not able talk to them about divorce (apart from blaming their ex-spouse);
- Those who do not get on well with at least one parent after separation;
- Those who are dissatisfied with custody and access arrangements, whatever these happen to be.

Most children would like two happily married parents, but most would prefer to live with a single parent rather than two unhappily married ones. It is a natural wish on the part of workers to keep parents and children together, but there are times when "heroic" work to maintain an intact family is counter to the best interests of all concerned.

Reconstituted Families

Reconstituted families, in which one or both partners have been married before and are combining two families into one, are a very common phenomenon. In about one out of every three marriages, one or both parents have been married before. The difficulties of being a stepchild are legendary, so are the problems of being a stepparent of such families. Research studies have confirmed these "legends." There is an increased risk of psychological problems in persons whose parents remarry, especially where it is the parent of the same sex as the child who finds a new spouse.

There are, of course, many instances of stepparents who have brought great happiness and solace to the children in their new lives. The friction, jealousy, and ambivalence which are a common feature of stepchild/stepparent relationships can be overcome with empathetic handling—trying to see things from the child's point of view. For example, if the stepchild lets herself go, and calls her stepfather "daddy" and shows him affection, might she not lose the love of her real father because of her disloyalty?

The stepparent herself (or himself) is not immune from conflict. To what extent should the stepmother try to be a "mother" when X still has a mother? Should a stepfather be permitted to discipline the child?

More devastating than the fear and jealousy aroused by remarriage may be the fear of abandonment felt by a child whose parents allow a succession of romantic attachments to take priority over their relationship with their child.

The family plan (illustrated earlier) will assist you to compare the current life tasks and life events of the various members of the "reshuffled pack"—the reconstituted family. Assess whether these individual needs and problems clash, thus adversely affecting the new family's ability to get on with life.

Single-Parent Families

The number of such households is on the increase and the lone mothers and fathers tend to have a difficult time of it. The problems tend to be the same whether parents are on their own involuntarily or from choice, because of death, divorce, separation, or through being unmarried.

You are likely to meet the assumption that children from one-parent families will have more problems than children from two-parent families, but there is little hard evidence to confirm this fear. Children from one-parent homes are no more likely to become delinquents, drop-outs, vandals, or drug addicts than those from more "conventional" families. Such problems are related to social and economic conditions and to adverse parental attitudes and behaviors. It is not then a matter of being brought up by a single parent *per se* that puts children at a disadvantage, but the *poverty* that is only too often associated with single status.

The worries that single parents may consult you about are the following:

Disciplinary problems. Can I manage a teenage boy alone?

Understanding. Father: "I'm not sure I have the understanding and sensitivity of a woman, for bringing up a girl."

Interests. Mother: "I can't really work up the enthusiasm and knowledge for fishing—his great love."

Sex education. Father: "How do I explain to her the facts and practical matters to do with her periods?"

Gender identity. Mother: "Will he grow up effeminate without a father to identify with?"

None of these anticipated difficulties are of necessity real problems, or, if they are perceived by the parent as such, insuperable.

Support. The main need of a lone parent is support and then, good accurate information about children and their development in special circumstances.

The man or woman alone will need financial, practical, and personal help. They need support over their feelings. Looking over your family life map can highlight the tasks and events that arouse the strongest emotional reactions in them. Review with your client their support system. Problems arise when the parents cling to their children to make up for losing their partners, requiring them to grow up prematurely and creating a kind of emotional claustrophobia. Or they may try to support their children by overcompensating for what they are missing—waiting on them hand and foot, letting them do what they like.

Substitute care. Any working mother comes to see how inadequate the facilities for full-time day care are in most areas. As we saw in chapter 6, the need to make reliable and stable arrangements for substitute care for young children while the single parent is at work can make all the difference between a reasonable standard of living for the family and a miserable insecure existence. The choice is usually between babysitters, day care centers, and cooperative grandparents.

If you are asked for advice about childcare bear the following points in mind:

- A reliable sitter *can* provide stable and good quality care.
- Choose someone who is looking after only two or three children, thus providing a *family atmosphere* and a *personal relationship* with the child.
- Interview the sitter and preferably *observe* her at work in her home setting.

Summary and Comment

Transition and change have been the theme of this chapter. An understanding of typical reactions to major transitional events should help you to guide your clients in their attempts to cope with difficult changes and trauma in their lives. The theme of change is the charge of many of the helping professions dealing, as they do, with bereavement and the effects of separation and divorce. These issues are discussed in some detail. The chapter endeavors to explore some of the myths surrounding substitute care, single parenthood, and reconstituted families. Some of the real difficulties of rearing children alone and of stepparenting are dealt with. There is a list of the worries that single parents may consult you about, and the chapter describes the kinds of support and the range of your systems that will be useful in their endeavors to cope with difficult situations that sometimes arise. An understanding of transitional events and the characteristic reactions they generate should help you to support your client through a crisis.

PART III
You as Helper

The most important instrument in your work with parents and children is yourself. It is essential, therefore, to spend some time preparing yourself before you start work. There are several questions you need to ask yourself.

• **Why am I involved in this?** You may be involved in work with parents and children for a variety of reasons. We have all been children and adolescents, and many of us are parents. So we have our own experiences and prejudices; we will be immersed in family matters at both the personal and the professional levels. Whatever your reason for being involved, examine your personal motives and underlying assumptions. The area of child care is value laden; certain kinds of problems are particularly sensitive and even threatening to us. The issue of trying to help people change involves important personal, moral, and ethical considerations.

• **Do I have the right to intervene?** Behavior therapists (like others who set out to change people) are accused of *controlling* behavior. Such allegations imply that clients exist in a vacuum of free will before entering an intervention. Behavioral workers (for example) talk, on the one hand, of liberating clients from some of the unwanted controlling forces in their lives, but assume, on the other hand, a freedom of choice when it comes to accepting an intervention. They tend to say, as do other therapists, that if a client requires help and requests it, then help should be provided.

The difficulty with this comforting principle is that people can be *coerced* in ways subtle and unsubtle, tangible and intangible, to "seek" help. Some clients, for example, children, are not in a

147

position to ask for help or powerful enough to reject the offer of help. These matters should be thought through very carefully. Advocacy on behalf of the child will be an important part of your work. Indeed, advocacy on behalf of hard-pressed, demoralized mothers will be another.

• **What is my support system?** Working in a team provides an ideal support system. It is important to have people around you to back you up, share ideas, stimulate, and challenge you. You may require supervision from an experienced practitioner if you are learning to use a specialized approach like family therapy or behavior modification. If these caveats sound rather daunting then remember the positives: your potential to help individuals and families in distress and the support you can give to and gain from your colleagues. This support may be "moral"—when a colleague feels that he or she has failed with a client; it may be "technical"—a word of advice or a different and perhaps more objective perspective on the case.

Commitment, knowledge, and ethical practices are important therapeutic ingredients and enhance the effectiveness of the intervention. You need to believe in what you are doing. Confidence is antitherapeutic only when it becomes dogmatic certainty or impedes the professional's willingness to evaluate his or her work and change direction when a strategy is not working.

CHAPTER 8

Intervention: Preliminaries, Planning, and Implementation

Preliminaries

No one profession has all the skills with which to remedy the range of problems we have been looking at in Parts 1 and 2. Social workers are likely to be heavily engaged, often because of their statutory responsibilities. Members of primary care teams—GPs, nurses, and health visitors—are also in the front line. At times several professionals may be engaged in a family's life and problems, so it may be good practice to identify a key worker who coordinates and monitors a complex situation, which otherwise might become confused because everyone thinks someone else is doing X, Y, or Z.

Cultural Factors

Ethnocentricity in direct social work practice can lead to embarrassment and worse if ideologies and methods are in conflict with deeply held cultural and/or religious beliefs. Let us take two examples, one from Asia, another from Africa, to illustrate how the bonding doctrine—an issue we dealt with in chapter 7—if applied insensitively by doctors and nurses, can have disturbing repercussions. We should note how, in some Asian communities, mothers are considered unclean for the first three days after birth and close physical contact with the baby is avoided. The infant is handled by a close relative of the mother or father, depending on local custom. Some immigrant parents could feel intense conflict over "bonding procedures." Then again women from certain parts of Ghana are said to "lie between life and death" when in labor. The period of confinement is regarded as an anxious time because it is widely believed that a newborn baby may in fact be a spirit child and not a human child at all. If it is a spirit child, it will return to the spirits before a week is out: thus for the first seven days (in some areas, three days for a boy or four for a girl) mother and child are confined to the room in which the birth took place. If the child dies during that time it is assumed that it was a spirit child. The body is mutilated and buried in a pot to prevent its return in similar circumstances. *The parents are not allowed to mourn its loss* but should show signs of joy at being rid of such an unwelcome guest. It is possible to see the "adaptive" element in such cultural beliefs; they may help parents to come to terms with death, especially in areas where there are high infant mortality rates. This is speculative; what *is* more certain is that when it comes to making decisions about arrangement for birth, possible bereavement, and early child care, the primary consideration should be the well-being of parents and child and a sensitivity to their personal and cultural values.

What Resources Are Available?

Parents and members of the community are important resources. Other sources of support are the

- Social worker
- General practitioner
- School counselor
- Educational or clinical psychologist
- Teacher
- Psychiatrist
- Child and family guidance (psychiatric clinic)
- Probation officer
- Youth/community worker
- Priest/vicar/minister
- Marriage guidance counselor
- Psychotherapist
- Police

It is useful for workers to attend as many workshops and courses on family work as possible in order to learn and test new techniques and strategies. One advantage of working in a team is that members can pool and share their learning.

Communicating With Clients

The language you will encounter in your work could range from adult speech through teenage slang to baby talk. There is a great deal of power in language, and most parents and young people are not familiar with technical terminology. So don't put them at a disadvantage. At the same time guard against the embarrassingly artificial tone of voice and speech styles some people adopt with children (and the very elderly).

Collect your own examples and metaphors that aid clients in obtaining a vivid idea or mental picture of an important concept.

Examples:

I tell my clients to imagine that their child has an L plate on his or her back to remind them to be patient and tolerant when the child makes a mistake or forgets a lesson. They are, after all *learners* about life.

I remind them of the time they learned to ride a bike and first managed to gain balance. They continued to have a *wobble* and occasionally fell off. When we imagine a child has mastered a new skill (for example, not wetting his or her bed), there is still likely to be a failure or two—representing the "wobble" at the top of the learning curve.

Reviewing Goals

You would be wise to carry out a careful review of *goals* that have been negotiated and agreed with your clients.

As a reminder:
- Goals are the changes to be sought. The goal tells you how the "target behavior" (the focus of therapeutic attention) is to be changed: whether the aim is to increase, decrease, maintain, develop, or expand the target behaviors.
- Prior to designing a program, a goal should be translated into a set of behavioral objectives.
  A behavioral objective specifies:
  (i) The desired behavior
  (ii) The situation in which it should occur
  (iii) The criteria for deciding whether the behavioral goal has been reached.

Here is an example:

Target behavior = teasing brother.

Goal = play with brother without teasing him.

Behavioral objective = play with brother without teasing him, in the absence of mother.

Monitoring Change

Not all interventions lend themselves to the measurement of behavioral change *per se*. The goals, particularly if the intervention involves a counseling approach, may require an evaluation of a rather more subjective kind. Staff at the Center for Behavioral Work With Families have been attempting to develop methods that encompass the subtle complexities of clients' thoughts and feelings without sacrificing the requirement of rigorous monitoring of their progress.

At every session it is our practice to invite people to indicate on (for example) a −5 to +5 scale (see Figure 7) how they feel they are progressing toward the agreed goals. What we may perceive as "progress" is not always felt to be so by the client. Sometimes our own feelings of pessimism are contradicted by the client's reporting a renewed feeling of confidence and of being able to cope.

Parental involvement. The extent to which parents (or others) will be involved in the specification of behavior objectives, observing, recording, and implementing, an intervention plan will vary, according to the setting in which the difficulties most often present themselves, and with whom. A program may involve work in the consulting room, classroom or institution, the parental home, or even on the neighborhood street, and the use of specific techniques by a professional, a significant adult, or the child itself.

Planning the Intervention

The flow chart below is a general guide only to the intervention and some of the points of procedures you need to bear in mind.

Figure 7. An example of goal-setting and evaluation by the client.

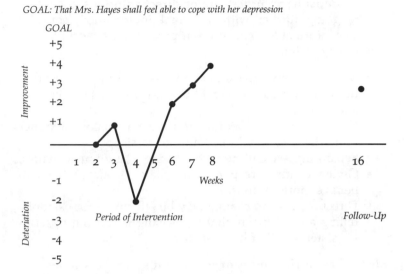

GOAL: *That Mrs. Hayes shall feel able to cope with her depression*

(*From C. Sutton, 1987, with permission.*)

Flow Chart 2: FROM PLANNING TO IMPLEMENTATION

PLANNING	PHASE I
Step 1.	Consider informal and/or direct solutions.
Step 2.	Identify client's strengths.
Step 3.	Consider the wishes of those around the client.
Step 4a.	Begin with problems where success is likely.
Step 4b.	Select relevant areas of change.
Step 5.	Choose your intervention.
Step 6.	Monitor your client's progress.

IMPLEMENTATION	PHASE II
Step 7.	Implement the intervention.
Step 8.	Review your intervention.
Step 9.	Gradually fade out the program.

FOLLOW-UP	PHASE III
Step 10.	Conduct a follow-up exercise.

PHASE I: PLANNING

Step 1: **Consider informal and/or direct solutions.**
Before going further with a formal intervention, consider whether informal and/or direct approaches are worth trying. These may include:

- Medical or physical examinations—for example, a hearing defect may result in a child being viewed as disobedient and difficult;
- Changing a child's bedtime routine may make him or her more likely to stay in bed and go to sleep;
- Separating two children who disrupt classroom activities;
- Giving children responsibility may encourage them to behave more responsibly;
- Direct requests to change may be effective—for example, telling a child firmly that his teasing is causing upset to his sister and that he *must* stop.

Step 2: **Take an inventory of your client's strengths or positive actions.**
It is important to identify or develop new behaviors/attitudes that are positive and familiar behaviors/attitudes of the client.

Step 3: **Consider the wishes of those in the client's environment.**
This is particularly important if they are suffering as a result of the behavior and have a potential part to play in a program.

Step 4a: **Begin with those problems that have a high probability of being successfully changed.**
With success, the incentive to take on more difficult or complex behaviors will be enhanced.

   b: **Select areas of change that are relevant to the individual.**
If changed, the client's new actions are likely to be encouraged and maintained.

Step 5: **Select your intervention approach (and specific methods).**

The choice is wide and confusing. Some of the options are listed in chapters 9 to 12. Whatever method you use, it is desirable to monitor your client's progress.

Step 6: **Monitor ("track") your client's progress (or lack of it).** Choose a method of measuring or assessing the behavior that reliably estimates the extent of the problem, which can be used conveniently, and which does not involve redundant information. Although there are various sophisticated procedures for assessing behavior, for most programs straightforward and simple methods are adequate.

The three main methods of assessing behavior are by rating the difficulties (see Figure 3b), recording how often the behavior occurs (known as frequency counting or event recording and illustrated in Table 10).

PHASE II: IMPLEMENTATION

Step 7: **Implement the intervention.**
Begin your intervention. Keep a close watch on what happens in the early stages to ensure that the program is being followed correctly and any unforeseen problems that arise are dealt with quickly. This may mean contact by visiting or phone with the parents every two or three days in the first week or so.

Data collection begun in the baseline period continues throughout the intervention period.

Step 8: **Review your intervention.**
In the light of the data collected relating to the target behavior(s), or any other objective information, it may be necessary to modify or change the intervention in some way. In the case of behavioral work the program is *flexible* and if the chosen target behavior is not changing after a reasonable period of time (e.g., two weeks—although there is no set time), review all aspects of the work.

One of the features of behavioral work is that it is "an approach" rather than a technique. This means that if your intervention is not working, examine most carefully the behavior of all participants and the program, and change (if neces-

Table 10. Event Recording of Parent-Child Interactions.

Visit No: _____   *Recorder:* _____   *Name of Client:* _____

Child's reactive and proactive behavior	*Often*	*Occasionally*	*Never*
1. Playing freely			
2. Laughing, smiling			
3. Running			
4. Talking freely			
5. Comes for help			
6. Comes for comfort			
7. Cuddles up to mother/father			
8. Responds to affection			
9. Responds to attention			
10. At ease with parents near him/her			
11. Joins in the activity with other children			
12. Is frightened when approached or corrected by the parent			

Mother's/Father's reactive and proactive behavior	*Often*	*Occasionally*	*Never*
1. Talking to the child			
2. Looking at the child			
3. Smiling at the child			
4. Eye contact (loving)			
5. Touching (gently)			
6. Holding (closely, lovingly)			
7. Playing			
8. Cuddling			
9. Kissing			
10 Sitting child on lap			
11 Handling child in gentle way			
12. Giving requests (as opposed to harsh commands)			
13. Helping child if in difficulties			
14. Encouraging child to participate in play and other activities			
15. Being concerned about child			
16. Responding in a nurturant manner when child cries or when hurt			
17. Answering child's questions			
18. Ignoring child's presence			
19. Even-handed with the children			

(*From Iwaniec, 1983, with permission.*)

sary) some features of the intervention. If you have the "story" about the "why's" of the case right (see chapters 11–12) any difficulties are likely to be traced to the application of the approach rather than the approach *per se*.

Ask the following questions:

(i) Are there powerful competing reinforcers or interfering factors in the client's environment operating against the program? Can these be modified?

(ii) Are the reinforcers well chosen and effective?

(iii) Is the parent working effectively and being reinforced for his or her participation?

(iv) Are the behavioral objectives realistic? Are they within the client's repertoire?

(v) Have your proceeded too quickly? Is it necessary to go back to an earlier stage in the intervention plan?

Step 9: **Phase out and terminate treatment.**
Do this with care: the durability of any improvements may depend upon it. The decision to terminate treatment should be made jointly with your client. The time for the program to end depends upon the goals established at the beginning of treatment. New or elaborated goals may emerge during the intervention.

Try to ensure natural, intermittent reinforcement in the child's different settings. A guideline is to teach only those behaviors that will continue to be rewarded after training, provided they are adaptive in the sense of contributing to the child's effectiveness and well-being and that of the community.

PHASE III: FOLLOW-UP
Contact your client(s) to check on the maintenance over time ("temporal generalization") of the improvements they made.

Step 10: **Conduct a follow-up exercise.**
You may find the following questions useful in a semistructured interview:

- When did the program end? . . . . How long did it take? . . . .
- How would you describe the situation with X now?
- What were your original "target" behaviors?

- Have any of these behaviors reoccurred (frequency)?
- How badly (intensity)?
- When, where, and how often?
- How would you describe your relationship with X now?
- Do you still worry about X?
- Do you now feel more in "control" than you did before?
- Do you spend more time playing and talking with X?
- Do you find it easier to praise X than you did before?
- Has the amount of physical contact between X and yourself changed more/less?
- Has your relationship with your other children changed?
- Have X's relationships with his/her brothers and sisters changed?
- Has X's father changed in his attitude to X?
- Has X's behavior toward his/her father changed?
- Do you feel that your relationship with your husband has changed?
- Do you think the program worked/failed?
- Who or what made it work/fail?
- How would you describe your relationship with the therapist?

An Illustration of an Intervention

We left Avril's family in chapter 4; we decided to initiate an intervention. Her mother now takes up the story.

From the beginning of the psychologist's visits my feelings were mixed! First of all there was a feeling of relief. Something was at last being done. Something concrete. I was going to be helped. For a short while I felt euphoric . . . but I was defensive as well because I knew that I must accept a certain responsibility for the way Avril was. I did not want to do that. I had had enough of failure. But I recognized I would have to face up to the truth if I went ahead with a management program. It was quite a struggle at times and my pride took quite a battering. I was very pleased that all the work in the program was going to take place in the home. It seemed natural and logical that it should.

There were problems in initiating the program as Avril's mother says:

At the beginning of Dr. H's intervention, however, I was unable to cooperate effectively. I was desperately unhappy and depressed with no clear understanding of how I came to be so. Each day I moved through a suffocating fog of failure, frustration, and guilt. Myself I saw as an unattractive and undesirable individual. I felt that my intellect had atrophied. My daily round of housework and child-rearing held no rewards, but left me bored and exhausted. Against this background a natural shyness had developed into a real fear of going out and talking to people. The fear of rejection was greater than the fact of loneliness. My home had become a prison. Because of these feelings, Dr. H. decided to work on two levels: with the family on Avril's management program and with myself—a total lack of social and personal confidence with its resulting social isolation for the child as well as myself; the accumulating anger from failing to cope with her. The angry feelings gradually eased as Avril's program progressed and I learned to express the resentment I felt when she misbehaved, but in a more controlled manner, by giving appropriate commands. We discussed my parents' way of bringing me up and how it had influenced my attitudes. The hardest problem to deal with was the self-doubt and isolation. Being depressed for several years and feeling inadequate had eroded my self-confidence and produced a profound dislike for myself. It was necessary to change that before I could look up and outwards.

Dr. H. asked me to role-play as a means of learning new ways of coping with my fears and suspicions of people. I started by writing a self-portrait. Dr. H. took each point and changed it to some extent. Where I was serious, introverted, careful, I was to be rather more spontaneous and impulsive, even a little frivolous—without "overdoing" it. I was to think and act like an attractive woman; in fact we created a different "persona" and role to my usual ones, but not too far out to make the task impossible. We went over it in great detail like a script.

The next step was not easy. What I had to do was go out and live my role daily. It was certainly very difficult at first. I felt like a second-rate actor with severe stage fright. But the remarkable thing was how it gradually became easier, and when the results were good I felt elated. I discovered casual conversa-

tions with local mothers in the park and shopping, soon unearthed common interests. I gradually developed new friendships with women in similar circumstances to myself, all with children for Avril and Stella to play with. For the first time since Avril's birth we were making regular visits outside the immediate family. Social skills are like any other; the more practice you get the better you become. As my confidence grew with each success so Avril also relaxed and she began to look forward to these visits eagerly.

Throughout this period, during which there were regularly held discussions about my own situation and problems, we also worked with Mrs.—(a social worker) on Avril's problems.

Selection of Goals for Treatment

Treatment objectives were negotiated between the therapists and the parents. The first goal was to increase adaptive behaviors in certain specified situations, as identified by the parents, with the main aim of creating opportunities for Avril to win positive reinforcement for socially appropriate behavior. There were four specified situations, one of which was putting away her toys. The second goal was to reduce the frequency of five target behaviors specified during assessment: (1) noncompliance, (2) aggression, (3) whining, (4) commanding, and (5) tantrums. All were carefully defined.

It should be noted that the introduction of the positive side of the program (rewards) was not a smooth one. There arose a series of disputations between mother or father and Avril about incentives. It was evident that we had planned a reward system that contained several loopholes as far as a perceptive and resourceful entrepreneur like Avril was concerned. As so often happens in behavior programs, we had to think again. A detailed plan was worked out with regard to the behaviors that the parents wished to encourage. A more careful contract was designed, one which specified precisely how the parents were to respond. The parents and therapist spent much time going over precisely what both parents were going to say when they issued commands to her. What came through very forcibly was that both parents tended to indulge in an internal debate when action was required (for example, the removal of Avril from the room, the technique called "time-out"). They would silently argue with themselves, "Should I?" or "Shouldn't I?" before they gave Avril a command. They were often reluctant to carry through a threatened sanction, feeling "sorry" for her or guilty afterward. My ploy in cases like this is to ask the parents if they would break a promise to give their child a treat. The inevitable denial and explanation of the importance that a child should trust one's words invites a discussion about breaking promises about punishment and the consequent debasement of the currency of words and trust.

Precise cues were suggested to the mother so that she might avoid these agonizing dilemmas and so she could act at the right time in a decisive manner. Authoritative commands, it was hoped, would nip Avril's target behaviors in the bud and prevent their unpleasant repercussions. On the consequential side, it was suggested that when she tried her delaying strategies, at the point of implementing time-out, she was to be picked up, with no eye-contact and no verbal communication, and placed in the hall (for three minutes), thus eliminating the attention she was gaining from her diversions. The response to this detailed plan was encouraging and the frequency of some of the target behavior began to diminish.

A critical point came at about the sixth week of the program. Mrs. Hayes became very despondent about the program, feeling that Avril's target behavior of aggression was not responding to her efforts. But despite the protestations, hostility, and resentment that she expressed to the therapist, she persevered. Reinforcement in the form of encouragement and praise are as important to the mediators of change in the child as to the problem child herself. After all, they are being asked to change "addictive" or reinforced habits and are in a learning situation too.

The frequency of the target behaviors decreased gradually. The record showed that from baseline frequency, noncompliance had reduced by 54%, aggression had fallen by 68%, tantrums by 95%, commanding by 94%, and whining by 100%. Whining responded most swiftly to systematic ignoring (see Figure 8).

Figure 8. A graphical record of progress in treatment

By the end of the program there was an average occurrence for both noncompliance and aggression of less than one per day. As Avril's positive behaviors increased, there were more opportunities for the parents to "enjoy" her which in themselves stimulated a high degree of mutual social reinforcement.

Termination

This phase came at the end of 12 weeks of treatment. Mrs. Hayes faded out the token reinforcement program but retained the use of positive social reinforcement (on an intermittent schedule—that is, an *occasional* basis—consistent with real life) and the occasional use of time-out as a back-up to her now generally effective verbal control. The goals that were selected for treatment were achieved to the satisfaction of both parents. This expression of satisfaction, which was confirmed by the monitoring of Avril's behaviors, constituted the main criteria for terminating the case. As a by-product of the program, Avril now gave the appearance of being a far happier child to the therapist, her parents, and their relatives. Mrs. Hayes no longer looked the harassed woman of the not too distant past. She now had a lightness in the presentation of her personality.

Follow-Up

A series of checks by telephone and visits indicated that Avril maintained her improvement for 12 months (our standard follow-up period). Mrs. Hayes felt that she had successfully reintroduced the program for short periods as and when it was necessary. She experienced a setback when she let her criteria slip and began to take the line of least resistance. A booster program was contemplated, but within a week of going back to recording, Mrs. Hayes found that she had the situation in hand, and the need for an intervention disappeared.

Summary and Comment

This chapter outlined the ten steps common to many interventions. There is no one way (or set order) for doing these things—preliminaries, planning, and initiation—but they may prove helpful to those who wish to work to a systematic plan. The importance of the key worker is stressed; as is the need for sensitivity to cultural nuances illustrated with examples from Asian and African attitudes to birth and death. Resources that are likely to be of help to you and your client are listed.

The chapter contains a case illustration that provides the reader with an insight into what it feels like to be involved in an intervention—in the mother's own words. Many of the details of therapy—the selection of goals, their monitoring, the program itself, and its termination—are provided.

CHAPTER 9

The "How" Question:
Helping People to Change

This chapter on how to help clients—the question of approaches—is written with several professions (but most particularly social work) in mind. One of the main difficulties for those who work with families is to find a reasonably clear, signposted path through the "jungle" of claims and counterclaims, contradictions and ambiguities, concerning the best way of going about things. Which approach do I use, and when? There is a bewildering array of choices including: *family therapy, behavior modification, counseling,* various brands of *psychotherapy, cognitive therapy, skills training,* and many others. The literature is not always helpful or easy to understand and incorporate in practice.

Is it best to be eclectic or is eclecticism somewhat disreputable in psychological circles? If it is, it shouldn't be; psychology has been forced to abandon general (i.e., all-encompassing) theories of human action in favor of more modest, middle-range theories dealing with *different* aspects of psychological functioning (for example, learning, cognition, personality). Even these theories tend to be fragmented and contentious. So why should practitioners eschew an *informal* eclecticism? The trouble is that eclecticism so often degenerates into a fragmented, unsystematic approach—a choice of what is fashionable, seems easy, or "feels comfortable," as opposed to what is theoretically coherent and empirically supported.

The task of helping a family can be a dauntingly broad one, encompassing (for the social worker) concerns ranging from poor housing and the need for day care for a worker, to marriage guidance and "systematic desensitization" for a phobic child. The practitioner's role might consist of being a resource-mobilizer, helper, friend, adviser, teacher, therapist, or counselor, and possessor of expert know-how of strategies for social action. Such diversification calls for a remarkably flexible response on the part of the practitioner. The scope of the analysis and level of intervention can also range widely, from the large grouping (the neighborhood or community) through the small group (the family), the couple (parents or partners) to the particular individual (child or adult).

This is not only a book about social work as such, but there is room to underline the importance in any intervention of mobilizing *human* resources—activating or reactivating helpers, friends, and social networks. There is evidence that a network of supportive persons and the quality and intimacy of the support provided can mitigate the effects of stress.

Mobilizing Human Resources

A professional can assist his or her clients by putting them in touch with people, clubs, specialized self-help groups, and other resources. Surveys have shown that one important way in which people cope with their problems is to turn to family and friends rather than to professionals for help and they, in turn, act as a buffer against some of the harmful effects of stress. As social networks, ties, and contacts promote psychological well-being, it is important for the professional to identify their presence or absence for the client. Ascertain the frequency and intimacy (the meaningfulness/emotional intimacy) of this support for your clients using the rating scale in Table 11.

Intimate or close relationships of the type provided by primary groups (those people with whom one has face-to-face interaction and a sense of commitment) are the most significant sources of support. The supportiveness of relationships is reflected by the availability of:

- Emotional support (the expression of liking, respect, etc.)
- Aid (material assistance, services, guidance, advice)
- Social companionship
- Affirmation (the expression of agreement)
- Social regulation (appropriate roles support such as mothering, fathering, partnership—husband/wife/companion, etc.)

Table 11. Sources of Support and Intimacy

	Frequency					Meaningfulness (importance)			
	Never	Hardly ever	Quite often	Often	Always (regularly)	None	A little	Quite a lot	A lot	Of great significance
A partner	0	1	2	3	4	0	1	2	3	4
Parents	0	1	2	3	4	0	1	2	3	4
Other relatives	0	1	2	3	4	0	1	2	3	4
Children	0	1	2	3	4	0	1	2	3	4
Friends	0	1	2	3	4	0	1	2	3	4
Neighbors	0	1	2	3	4	0	1	2	3	4
Colleagues/ workmates	0	1	2	3	4	0	1	2	3	4
Other parents	0	1	2	3	4	0	1	2	3	4
Acquaintances	0	1	2	3	4	0	1	2	3	4
	How often can you expect help and support from:					How meaningful/significant is the help and support you get from:				

Different kinds of support are helpful for different life crises. And the particular persons and circumstances involved in a potentially disruptive life event determine what is likely to be most effective. The support of peers and encouragement at work are positively related to well-being.

Marital Work

There has been a lot of research into the adjustments required of married couples, into the conflicts, manipulations, and changes that take place in the course of a marital relationship. The emphasis on conflict and manipulation is somewhat misleading. The evident fact is that in many ongoing marriages there is great deal of interaction which is playful, complementary, and joyous, as well as much that is hostile. The fact that most marriages survive, and are judged to be happy, indicates that the majority of adjustments are fairly satisfying.

A process of bargaining may underlie some of the similarities in marriages of long duration. It is one of the great platitudes—part of popular wisdom—that marriage is a matter of give and take. We saw, in chapter 4, that people initiate and prolong relationships of intimacy as long as those relationships are reasonably satisfactory with regard to what are called their "rewards" and "costs." In marital interactions the *social exchange* model helps us to assess (in part) what is going wrong with a partnership. For example, immature individuals are not always able to manage the give-and-take of friendship. What is called "exchange theory" gives us pointers to why this should be so; it also provides *one* method of improving people's social attractiveness and their relationships. In this theoretical model, social interactions and relationships are compared to economic bargains or the exchange of gifts. All activities carried out by one individual, to the benefit of another, are termed "rewards," while detrimental activities—hostility and anxiety—are seen as "costs."

A notable feature of a partnership that is "working" is the balance in the relationship that exists between the partners, often called "status symmetry." It concerns the mutual respect and lack of dominance and exploitation that characterize intimate and lasting relationships. In friendly or loving relationships there is an overall balance in the influence of each of the participants.

It is useful to draw up a balance sheet. On the debit side, the term "cost" is applied to deterrents that may be incurred in contacts with another person—such as criticism, neglect, hostility, anxiety, embarrassment, and the like. For attraction to another individual to occur (or to be maintained) the reward-cost outcome must be above the "comparison level," a standard against which *satisfaction* is judged.

In this model marital discord is dealt with by redistributing (with the help of a contract) prevailing rates of reinforcement (satisfaction) and punishment (dissatisfaction) within the relationship. Individuals are encouraged—following discussion, negotiation, and (hopefully) compromise—to maximize satisfaction while minimizing the dissatisfaction provoked by the couple. This is where *contracts* can be very useful, not only for marital work but for family relationships that are tense and unhappy. An example of a marital–work contract is given in Figure 9.

Figure 9. A sample contract

CONTRACT between James and Nell Small

We: (he) and (she) have decided together to improve our relationship, and with that in view we have jointly agreed to do our level best to put into practice the following rules and to monitor progress. In doing this our goal is (i) to make changes in our behaviors and attitudes, and (ii) to become more aware of our own (and our partner's) point of view. We will make the following changes:

He

1. Be more ready to say sorry,
2. Control my irritability and temper.
3. Show more interest in my wife's appearance.
4. Sit down for a chat for at least half-an-hour when I get home from work.
5. Refrain from making fun of her friends and church activities.
6. Help with jobs around the house.

She

1. Stop interfering when he corrects the child.
2. Be more relaxed about things.
3. Show more interest in my husband's work.
4. Be more ready to forgive and forget.
5. Be willing to make physical contact (e.g., not to pull away when he holds my hand, puts his arm around me).
6. Remember to check that there is gas in the car.

We do not guarantee 100% success at first, but we are committed to trying to make things work. In the case of rules being broken we agree to sit down and go over the particular disappointing incident *calmly*.

We also agree to keep a record of progress.

Signed ＿＿＿＿＿＿＿ (He)

＿＿＿＿＿＿＿ (She)

Family Therapy

Family treatment occurs in a variety of forms in child and family clinics/centers. There is no one "family therapy" but several "schools," such as *analytic, strategic, and structural* family approaches. No single theoretical perspective is center stage in treating families. Family treatment is eclectic and draws from a range of theories and interventions. For purposes of this book, we draw from several approaches, particularly the structural approach to family treatment. From this approach we consider systems, subsystems, boundaries, and rules that influence family members in their efforts to find balance in their relationships with others in the family.

In order to understand the family pattern across the generations (the extended family) and the alliances, conflicts, and attachments within the family unit, clients are encouraged to look at themselves from a fresh perspective and to try alternative solutions to their dilemmas. The *structural* approach to producing family change is associated with (among others) the name Salvador Minuchin (1974) and the Philadelphia Child Guidance Clinic. The focus of attention is very much on the developmental tasks faced by the family and its members at various stages of its (and their) life span. Day-to-day patterns of relationship—communication and interaction—between members are inferred from highly charged or repetitive sequences observed and analyzed in the therapy room. You can see from all of this that the therapeutic task is defined in far broader terms than the individual—be it parent or child. The child—brought to the clinic as the "patient" or "client" by the parents—would be viewed as one part of a complete network of personal and family relationships.

Family therapists see the total network of family transactions as greater than the sum of its parts, hence their rejection of the parents' labeling of a problem as "my son's/daughter's problem" as simplistic. The family system is viewed as the total functioning of three subsystems (spouses, parents and children, children alone)—all contained within a defined *boundary* and, in turn, operating within a social-cultural context.

The family changes continuously. For example, as children grow into adolescents they bring new elements into the family system. The peer group gains more influence. The youngster learns that friends' families work by different standards and rules. The teenage culture introduces its values with regard to sex, religion, politics, and drugs. Parents, too, are changing in what we described in chapter 3.

The structural family therapist's first step is to "join" with the family, to participate in its transactions and observe members' roles, their communications, and the boundaries within the family and between the family system and other systems. The family "organism," like the individual person, moves between two poles: one representing the security of the known, and the other being the exploration necessary for adaptation to changing conditions. When the family comes to treatment, it is in difficulty because it is stuck, trying to maintain old ways that no longer meet the needs of a changed and changing set of circumstances. The therapist takes a family (Minuchin, 1974) "along with the developmental spiral and creates a crisis that will push the family in the direction of their own evolution."

The approach involves the therapist as an energetic *intruder*. He or she works actively to restructure family organization and channels of communication by modeling, direction, and the use of "action techniques." The techniques for creating crisis or "creative turmoil" and for putting the family on to a new and harmonious path (thus enhancing the potential for growth of each of its members) are many and varied.

There is a basic sequence through which family therapy passes. Andy Treacher and John Carpenter (1984) describe it as follows:

- *The Joining Phase.* The family and the therapist are originally isolated from each other. But therapists use their skills so that they become absorbed into the family through a process of accommodation. This process creates a new system—family and therapist. It may take several sessions to create the new system, but since it is essentially a transitory one therapists carefully monitor any signs that family members are going to drop out of therapy and thus disrupt the new system.
- *The Middle Therapy Stage.* This is the phase during which the major restructuring "work" occurs. Restructuring interventions are made during sessions and consolidating homework tasks are set between sessions.

- *The Termination Stage.* This phase involves testing the family's ability to "fire" the therapist and go it alone. The "ghost" of the therapist is left behind by getting the family to simulate its ability to solve new problems and to deal with old problems if they recur.
- *The Follow-up.* A follow-up session after three months, six months, or a year enables the therapist to evaluate the impact of therapy and test whether it has been successful in achieving second-order change, which means enabling family rules and family functioning to change in such a way that the family generates effective solutions to problems.

Before looking at techniques we need to address the question of the manner in which the family members are seen—all together (on every occasion or occasionally), in differing combinations and permutations, or individually. The emphasis—some would say overemphasis—on the use of *conjoint* family therapy (i.e., seeing all the family members together) as an exclusive means of therapeutic intervention—arises from a restricted and narrow definition of the systems approach.

Treacher and Carpenter (1984), in their useful book *Using Family Therapy* (an exploration of family therapy and its various applications) criticize some family therapists for their failure to consider the significance of wider social systems. Such therapists, by their concentration on therapy with nuclear families within clinical settings, have allowed their vision of family therapy to become myopic.

The family replaces the individual as the locus of pathology; its social context is ignored, and it is "assumed that all its problems can be easily revealed to the gaze of a group of therapists who cluster behind a one-way screen." These authors maintain that such a narrow approach to understanding change within a family system cannot be defended at a theoretical level.

Change is often best effected by an intervention at another system level. For example, a worker who is attempting to produce change in a family which is experiencing many problems may be better advised to assist in the formation of a housing action group, designed to influence the housing department, than to concentrate on a more limited goal of defining boundaries between the members of a family who are crowded into a small, damp, and decaying flat at the top of a tower (p. 4).

They go on to make the important point that family therapy and individual counseling and psychotherapy have been unhelpfully polarized. The skills of working *individually* with members of a family are often indispensable to the systems approach—especially when the therapeutic task is to help an individual detach himself or herself from the family system.

Techniques

There is space for only a brief description of a few techniques of structural family therapy:

- *Enactment* is the direct illustration by the clients (as opposed to mere description) of the problems that exist between them. Clients are encouraged, where appropriate, to talk directly to one another rather than to (or through) the therapist.
- *Boundary clarification.* The creation of clarification of boundaries between family members is a feature of structural work. A mother who babies her teenager may hear with surprise her daughter's response to the question "How old do you think you mother treats you as—three or 13?"
- *Changing space.* Asking clients in the therapy room to move about can intensify an interaction or underline an interpretation being made about a relationship. For example, if a husband and wife never confront one another directly, but always use their child as a mediator or channel of communication, the therapist *blocks* that maneuver (called triangulation) by moving the child from between the parents. Here she may comment, "Let's move Sally from the middle so you can work it out together."
- *Reframing* is an important method in fulfilling the objective of helping clients in a covert—less directed—manner. It is an alteration in the emotional or conceptual viewpoint

in relation to which a situation is experienced. That experience is placed in another "frame" which fits the facts of the situation as well (or more plausibly), thereby transforming its entire meaning. Giving people different "stories" to tell themselves about themselves or about events—stories that are less self-defeating or destructive— is also a feature of behavioral work.

Improving Relationships Within the Family

All social interaction involves *mutual influence* because of human interdependence and the key role of cooperation in human societies. This influence is most potent when it has its source within a happy and cohesive family. Indeed the presence of family cohesion has a marked effect on the psychological well-being of family members.

- Members spend a fair amount of time in shared activity.
- Withdrawal, avoidance, and segregated (separate) activities are rare.
- Interactions that are warm are common, and interactions that are hostile are infrequent among members.
- There is full and accurate communication between members of the family.
- Valuations of other members of the family are generally favorable; critical judgments are rare.
- Individuals tend to perceive *other* members as having favorable views of them.
- Members are visibly affectionate.
- They show high levels of satisfaction and morale, and are optimistic about the future stability of the family group.

When these features are absent, the family members who are particularly at risk are those already vulnerable for other reasons: the young, the elderly, those coping with stress such as hospitalization, alcohol dependence, or caring for a large number of children. The list above indicates areas on which you might focus in order to encourage more cohesive activities and attitudes. Contracting—mentioned already and discussed more fully later in this chapter—could facilitate such an objective.

A Social Learning Approach to Family Violence

Concern about aggression and violence in society, both outside and within the family, has reached such a pitch that a note of despair, and sometimes hysteria, is now common in the media.

As a general principle, we can confidently claim that the maintenance of aggressive behavior is largely dependent on its consequences (and this might include "letting off steam" by a frustrated parent) and tends to be repeated, whereas those that are unrewarded or punished are generally discarded.

Coercive Families. In what have been called coercive families the cues or messages are frequently negative ones, with the "sound and fury" of criticism, nagging, crying, shouting, hitting and so on. Communication between members may not be so much aversive as impoverished or practically nonexistent. Sitting down to *negotiate* a contract with members of the family facilitates communications and introduces them to an important means of resolving interpersonal conflicts and tension of the kind that arise in the family—discussion, negotiation, compromise.

It is all very well to negotiate a contract, but what goes into it? We have to remember that coercive family systems which permit behavioral control by the use of pain are quite likely to produce children who exhibit frequent aggressive actions. Negative reinforcement is most likely to operate in certain closed social systems where the child must learn to cope with aversive stimuli such as incessant criticism. In such a family a boy will find that his violent actions (e.g., hitting) *terminate* much of the aversive stimulation—teasing, bullying, and so on—from his brothers and sisters; in addition, as many as a third of his coercive behaviors are quite likely to receive a positive payoff, such as, getting his own way.

In planning your contract or some other intervention (see Appendix 4) you must remember that people rarely show aggression in blind, indiscriminate ways. Rather aggressive (or more extremely violent) actions tend to occur at *certain times*, in *certain settings*, toward *certain individuals* (as objects), and in response to *certain forms of provocation*.

174

Assess these in terms of contemporary (i.e., current circumstances which

- *Instigate aggression (viz.* physical or verbal assaults, deprivation, frustration, conflict, exposure to aggressive models.
- *Maintain aggression (viz.* direct, vicarious, and self-reinforcement).

Your choice of approach might include the following:

- *Reduce stimuli which set the stage (so called "discriminative stimuli") for aggressive behavior.*

The absence of a supervising adult may be the signal for a child to threaten or hit another in order to take away his or her toy. This would be a rewarding consequence for the dominant child. Better organized supervision in the playground or home would be one response to this situation.

- *Reduce the exposure to aggressive models.*

If a child is mixing with a bully who is providing an example of aggressive behavior it is advisable to detach him or her from this relationship as soon as possible. If parents are modeling (sometimes unwittingly) hostile attitudes and aggressive actions, your target for intervention is as much their behavioral repertoire as that of their offspring.

- *Reduce aversive stimula.*

It is crucial to attempt to change the circumstances in which a client's aggressive behavior stems from frustrating, depriving, or provocative experiences instigated by other people or life circumstances. This is easier said than done, but a resourceful professional is often able to mitigate some of the contributory aversive "triggers."

- *Provide models of nonaggressive behavior.*

If possible, bring children into contact with children who do not adopt aggressive actions to cope with life. You might be able to demonstrate nonaggressive problem-solving by means of role-play or by video demonstrations of similar aged children using such strategies.

- *Develop relevant social skills.*

There are countless social graces and nuances that make social life easy and pleasurable for all concerned. However, there are many people—children and adults—who lack some of the crucial skills required to cope with life and to solve problems in a constructive and adaptive manner. Aggression may become part of their repertoire for "righting" perceived wrongs and for getting their own way. Social skills can to an extent, be taught; such issues are dealt with in chapter 12.

- *Apply (if appropriate) methods of desensitization, relaxation, and communication training.*

- *Discussion if it is honest and defused of rhetoric, can be a potent antidote to misunderstanding and resentment.*

In families where parents smack or beat their children for their "naughty" behavior, and often as a means of releasing their tensions, there are several things you can discuss with them (assuming that you are assured of the essential safety of the child):

- Ensure that the parents' *expectations* of the child are appropriate for his or her age and ability.
- Ascertain that their *attributions,* their theories of causation of their child's behavior (e.g., "There's a demon inside him"; "It's her bad blood"; "She does it because she hates me") are not wildly distorted.
- Check whether there are sufficient *positive interactions* (e.g., play, outings, conversation) and rewards and encouragement.

- Teach the client *cognitive self-control strategies* (e.g., self-talk).

Self-Talk

Self-talk—a sort of internal monologue—is a major preoccupation of all of us when we are beset with trials and tribulations. "I can't cope any more . . . I'm in a terrible mess . . . There's no hope . . . Oh, what am I to do?" such self-talk is accompanied by observable behavior, for example, listlessness, weepiness, sleeplessness, social withdrawal, and so on.

To help adolescents (and indeed, parents, at times) we examine and dissect some of the faulty reasoning underlying the self-talk: the exaggeration ("No one loves me ... there's *no* hope!"), the need to be all-competent, to show no weakness, to be acknowledged and loved *all* the time, to be forever right. Counseling on such illogicalities, the prompting and practicing of new self-talk ("I can manage ... I'm a good parent; "Think first, act afterward ... keep cool") may bring some relief.

A number of procedures are available for the purposes of controlling impulsive actions; they include self-management by the client of hostile feelings, together with his or her observations of the circumstances in which they occurred and their consequences. You might provide the client with positive self-statements for dealing with anger.

- *Preparing for provocation*

This is going to upset me, but I know how to deal with it. What is it that I have to do?

I can work out a plan to handle this.

I can manage the situation. I know how to regulate my anger.

If find myself getting upset, I'll know what to do.

There won't be any need for an argument.

Try not to take this too seriously.

This could be a testing situation, but I believe in myself.

Time for a few deep breaths of relaxation. Feel comfortable, relaxed, at ease.

Easy does it. Remember to keep your sense of humor.

- *Reacting during the confrontation*

Stay calm. Just continue to relax. As long as I keep my cool, I'm in control.

Just roll with the punches; don't get bent out of shape.

Think of what you want to get out of this.

You don't need to prove yourself.

There is no point in getting mad.

Don't make more out of this than you have to.

I'm not going to let him get to me.

Look for the positives. Don't assume the worst or jump to conclusions.

It's really a shame that she has to act like this.

For someone to be that irritable, he must be awfully unhappy.

If I start to get mad, I'll just be banging my head against the wall. So I might as well just relax.

There is no need to doubt myself. What he says doesn't matter.

I'm on top of this situation and it's under control.

• *Coping with arousal*

My muscles are starting to feel tight. Time to relax and slow down. Getting upset won't help.

It's just not worth it to get so angry.

I'll let him make a fool of himself.

I have a right to be annoyed, but let's keep the lid on.

Time to take a deep breath.

Let's take the issue point by point.

My anger is a signal of what I need to do. Time to instruct myself.

I'm not going to get pushed around, but I'm not going haywire either.

Try to reason it out. Treat each other with respect.

Let's try a cooperative approach. Maybe we are both right.

Negatives lead to more negatives. Work constructively.

She'd like me to get really angry. Well, I'm going to disappoint her.

I can't expect people to act the way I want them to.

(*From Novaco, 1975, with permission.*)

All the methods described above attend to the "A" term (antecedent events) in the ABC equation. The following ones are more to do with "C" term (consequent events or outcomes). Procedures based on selective reinforcement (making aggression *unrewarding* or *costly*) can reduce aggressive behavior. *Some childish aggression (e.g., temper tantrums) may be ignored* (if that is not a dangerous option) when attention has been positively reinforcing. It can be ignored when an incompatible pattern is desirable, prosocial conduct is rewarded and thus encouraged; it may be penalized by methods such as response-cost and time-out.

Contracts

Contracts draw on various ideas and concepts for their rationale. Two theories—exchange theory (which comes from social psychology) and contingency (reinforcement) theory—are most prominent, and give rise to six key concepts.

- Communication
- Negotiation (bargaining)
- Compromise
- Reciprocity
- Expectations (rules)
- Reinforcement

Social psychology tells us that groups which exist for any length of time (and we can think of the family group as a particular example) have a definite communication structure. For example, there tends to be consistency in the number of communications individuals receive, and in the number and content of communications they initiate. There is a positive correlation between the frequency of communication ("in" and "out") and the status of the individual in the group. One can imagine that a powerless member of the family is allowed or able to say very little for herself.

It is important to point out to clients that the *responses* of one individual are the *cues* for the responses of the other, which in turn become cues for the responses of the first. Shout (or whisper) and the other person is likely to shout (or whisper) back. Cues are by definition "carriers" of information; and transmission of information is the *essence* of communication. So what kind of messages do people give each other—not only in what they say (verbal cues) but what they do or the way in which they say things (nonverbal cues)?

Reciprocal contractual agreements are not unnatural to most people: they exist in families and other groupings, whether explicit or implicit. Many of the problems that arise are due to the arrangements not being reciprocal or explicit enough.

Contracts (whether written down or agreed verbally) have the effect of structuring reciprocal exchanges. They specify who is to do what, for whom and under what circumstances; reinforcement contingencies (to take one example) can be made explicit between individuals who wish behavior to change (e.g. parents, teachers, nurses) and those whose behavior is to be changed (children, students, clients).

At a time of crisis when marital partners or teenagers and their parents (or indeed brothers and sisters) are at loggerheads, angry and resentful, contracts provide an opportunity for a family to take stock and to break through vicious circles of retribution and unreason.

Contingency agreements are contracts drawn up between two or more people in which a set of mutual expectations is written down detailing reciprocal benefits and the "costs" or penalties for transgressions. The main assumptions underlying the use of formal verbal agreements or the stronger written form of contracts, are as follows:

- The publicly endorsed, unambiguous, and specific commitment to a future course of action will prove more binding, a better guarantee of compliance, than more casual "promises" or ephemeral statements of intention (think of those turned-over new leaves at the New Year).
- To obtain such results the parties concerned must not feel they have been unduly coerced into their contractual arrangements.

Applications. The following elements of contracting are important for the clients:

- Be very specific in spelling out the desired actions.
- Pay attention to the details of the privileges and conditions for both parties; they should be (a) important as opposed to trivial, (b) functional (if manifested more frequently they will increase the chances of the parties' obtaining from their environment the natural kinds of rewards which most people desire and enjoy).
- If parents wish their youngster (or adults their partner) to desist from certain actions and activities, encourage

them to express these in terms of positive change. For example, if they would like X to stop being so critical and negative they should specify the change they wish to bring about by inviting X to accentuate the positive, the pleasant, or praiseworthy. This would then have to be spelled out in terms of specific examples of behavior—words and deeds. Reciprocal requirements can be asked of parents or partner.

- Get parents (or partner) to write down five items of behavior they wish their son, daughter, or spouse would do more often.
- Don't let the parties be vague, for example, "I wish he'd be more helpful." Be concrete and specific, "I wish he'd help me set and clear the table."
- Parents may want their son to complete his homework and attend school regularly. He, on the other hand, desires more free time with his friends or more pocket money. A husband may wish his wife would be more attentive; she might like him to be sociable, and so on. Encourage discussion, negotiation, and compromise.

See the example contract in Figure 10.

Helping Your Client as an Individual

There are different levels at which you can help your client, ranging from the general (emotional support, information, advice, etc.) to the specific and technical (for example, behavior therapy). To be in a position to give effective help to your client presupposes

- Communication skills
- A good relationship
- Mutual trust and understanding
- "Therapeutic" conversational skills

Communication training. Communication training is one of the more promising of the new behavioral methods that have developed from social skills therapy and assertion training. It is valuable for training professional students in the vital skills of being clear and comprehensible in their work. At the same

Figure 10. Contract

CONTRACT between Mr. and Mrs. S—and Anne S—

Mother and father would like Anne to:

1. Let them know about her movements when she goes out at night; Anne will let them know about her movements when she goes out at night by: telling them were she is and with whom; letting them know when she'll be home.
2. Be less moody; she won't sulk for hours on end when reprimanded or thwarted.
3. Be more ready to say sorry; i.e., she will apologize when she's been in the wrong.
4. Show more concern about her school work (e.g., homework); i.e., she will put in at least an hour per night.
5. Stop being so rude to her father; i.e., walking out when he gives her advice.

Anne would like her father and mother to:

1. Stop criticizing her friends all the time; i.e., stop calling them names and saying they're no good, unless they are making a particular, constructive comment.
2. Admit when they are in the wrong; i.e., they will apologize when they have been in the wrong in their confrontations with her.
3. Give her more pocket money (a sum agreed) and review the amount every six months in the light of the rising expense and changing nature of her commitments.

All agree:

1. That the terms of the contract will not be changed except by mutual discussion and agreement.
2. That disputes will be settled by the witness (grandmother), whom all accept to be objective and fair-minded.
3. That successful execution of the contract for a month will be rewarded by a family treat (first month: an outing to a fancy (named) restaurant).
4. That failure to carry out individual terms of the contract will result in a fine on each occasion: an amount of X for Anne; and Y for Mr. and Mrs. S—respectively. The money is to go in a "penalty box" (kept by the grandmother), the proceeds of which will go to a charity of her choice.

Signed Anne ....

Mr. S— ....

Mrs. S— ....

Grandmother (witness) ....

(From Herbert, 1987, with permission.)

time it provides them with a method applicable to many of their clients-to-be. The method concentrates on the following:

- A series of exercises that puts the complete skills of communication into their component parts and teaches each of these in a carefully graded sequence to small groups of clients (or trainee social workers).
- Use of the principles, of modeling, shaping, behavioral rehearsal, and positive reinforcement (see chapter 11).
- The "teacher" seeks directly to impart communication skills, to identify blocks in communication, and to overcome these by training clients (students) in more effective methods of interaction.

The good relationship factor. Among the most frequent complaints by parents of the professionals who provide them with services are lack of concern, care, and warmth: in other words, the absence of a supportive relationship. This is a particularly sad state of affairs as it is widely held that among the most important qualities associated with "healing" properties are the therapist's understanding, respect, acceptance, genuineness, empathy, and nonpossessive warmth. These attributes are stressed in the counseling (client-centered) literature and their effect is related to aspects of the client's well-being or self-esteem.

Whether a trained professional has a monopoly of these qualities (or some unique deployment of them) is thrown into doubt, surely even for those who give most weight to the relationship factor in therapy, by the absence of significant differences in the results of professional as opposed to non- or paraprofessional helpers. The consistency of positive findings supports the potential value of nonprofessional assistance. This is good news for those social workers who believe in utilizing community resources (parents and other nonprofessionals) in the helping endeavor.

Therapeutic conversational/communications. The art of talking (therapeutic conversation or communications) is highly valued in the difficult task of encouraging change in the understanding and actions of adult and young clients. Helping people to discover insights into their mental processes and behavior is a well-known feature of therapies.

Psychotherapy. The word psychotherapy means literally "the treatment of problems of the mind." The term also implies that treatment is carried out by psychological methods rather than by the use of physical measures such as drugs. Clients do a lot of talking about their lives, their present and past, their personal relationships. Psychotherapists, to a greater or lesser extent, also talk, offering interpretations, reflecting back to the clients their feelings, and providing reassurance. Some analyze transference feelings, that is to say the client's feelings that have their origins in past experiences and relationships but are now displaced onto the person of the therapist.

It is difficult to define psychotherapy in any tidy fashion because so many different theories of personality and viewpoints about the nature of mental problems determine the approach of the particular therapist. One clinician may be a psychoanalytic psychotherapist but even then he or she could be trained in the Freudian, Jungian, or some other school. Another may be influenced by the Rogerian ideas of client-centered therapy. Typical problems dealt with by psychotherapies include

- an avoidance of situations/people/objects one should not have to avoid;
- a sense of emotional turmoil (anger, fear, anxiety, dread, guilt, depression, disgust);
- a feeling of helplessness, of not being fully in control of one's life;
- a feeling of unhappiness, distress, misery; vague feelings that life is not being lived as meaningfully, effectively, or joyfully as it should be;
- a feeling of having lost control;
- a loss of ability to make decisions;
- a loss of the ability to make choices;
- a loss of the feeling of being real, vital, committed to or enthusiastic about life;
- a sense of conflict, apathy, aimlessness;

- a sense of alienation (with self and/or society);
- a sense of being compelled to do things against one's will

These problems also lend themselves to an expert behavioral approach. It is crucial in behavioral assessment and treatment to reformulate these complaints in operational terms, that is, in overt terms of what the client says and does, and in a manner that lends itself to quantifying of the problem. Such problems are also the "bread and butter" of counselors.

An Illustration

A problem in which short-term psychotherapy utilized insight and "ventilation" (the release/expression of suppressed emotion) is the case of Jason, who acted in an extremely rebellious, disobedient, and aggressive manner his parents could not cope with. When his innermost thoughts and feelings were tapped by analyzing projective material (his stories and paintings) and by observing his repetitive games with the "family group" of dolls, it became apparent that he believed his parents had stopped loving him when his brother was born. He had been the only child for five years and had little understanding that love can be shared rather than monopolized. He had the idea that his mother and father got angry with him and punished him, not because he was being difficult and negativistic, but simply because their feeling toward him had changed and they no longer loved him. His intense jealousy of the baby was not apparent on the surface. His overzealous attention to the infant—as it appeared—covered feelings of hatred and envy. Not realizing this the parents were not able to cope with the situation. In this case the function of the treatment as it was seen by the therapist was not only to release and interpret the child's feelings, and to educate him about the inclusiveness of love rather than its exclusiveness, but also to help the mother to understand and tolerate the source of her child's anxieties and aggressions.

If the child is very young, conventional methods of psychotherapy as used with adults are not very suitable. The child is not always able to put anxieties into words. He or she is not always interested in exploring past life or attitudes. Play is a familiar mode of expression for the child and it is deployed by some child psychotherapists as a part-equivalent of "talking-therapy."

Play. Whatever the theoretical framework of a particular clinic, it is fairly common practice for children to be made to feel at ease in a playroom in which they can paint, construct things on a sand tray with miniatures, act out dramas with dolls and puppets, be aggressive with guns and choppers, and in fact, give expression to a wide range of feelings and fantasies. The skilled therapist may detect recurrent themes in the child's play, preoccupations which point to conflicts or areas of tension in the family, at school, or in some aspect of the child's life which are blocking development.

In its simplest form, play therapy is a modifying or reshaping of attitudes and feelings. But the therapist cannot simply sit down with the child and explain the self-defeating nature of his or her attitudes toward self and the environment. The child must come to see for him- or herself and to feel within that what he or she is doing is self-defeating and unnecessary. This is not usually achieved overnight. The child's attitudes need to be analyzed carefully and on a broad front and not with a superficial, facile, and "pat" formula. Genna, who had a dread of going to school (school phobia) appeared to be afraid of a harsh teacher and a bully in the school. A careful analysis of her personality and home and school background revealed that the problem was more a fear of *leaving home* rather than *going to school*. The mother, an anxious woman, whose mothering style was overprotective, was having marital problems, and the child overheard her saying to her husband that his infidelity was "killing" her. The child was afraid that her mother might die when she was not at home to keep an eye on things. There were other issues to this case and a good deal of time was required to right matters and get the child back to school.

Virginia Mae Axline (1947), in her book *Play Therapy*, describes the nondirective form of play therapy. Her approach is based upon the fact that play is the child's natural medium of self-expression. An opportunity is given to the child to "play out" feelings and problems just as, in certain types of adult therapy, an individual "talks out" his or her difficulties. Non-directive therapy with children is based upon the assumption that the individual has a growth impulse that makes mature behavior more satisfying than immature behavior. The basic principles which guide therapy are as follows. The therapist

- Endeavors to develop a warm, friendly relationship with the child.
- Accepts the child exactly as he or she is.
- Establishes a feeling of permissiveness in the relationship so that the child feels entirely free to express his or her feelings.
- Is alert to recognize the feelings expressed by children and to reflect those feelings back to them in such a manner that they gain insight into their behavior.
- Maintains a deep respect for the child's ability to solve his or her own problems if given an opportunity to do so. The responsibility for making choices and for instituting change is the child's.
- Does not attempt to hurry therapy along. It is a gradual process.
- Does not attempt to direct the child's actions or conversation in any manner. The child leads the way and the therapist follows.
- Establishes only those limitations to the child's behavior that are necessary to anchor the therapy to the world of reality and to make the child aware of his or her responsibility in the relationship.

Play therapy is an avenue to understanding children's coping and responses to crisis and may involve dolls, art, puppets, stories, and toys. Case examples of play therapy with children in crisis due to abuse, violence, foster care, divorce, illness, and other problems are available in the literature (Webb, 1991).

Talking to and Guiding Young People

Haim Ginnott (1969) is concerned that the two-way nature of good communication between adults should also form the basis of conversations with young people. A dialogue with a child or teenager requires respect and skill. Ginnott advises adults to listen carefully to what young people say. Messages should preserve their own and the youngster's self-respect.

There is a myth around that says that adolescents are beyond help. They may not be easy to help, indeed there may be an initial reaction to prickly disdain, but teenagers who experience problems *can* be helped by sharing knowledge and hard-won experience. When they face really tough decisions, most *are* open to sensitively and sensibly proffered guidance. People are most susceptible to help during periods of rapid change, and adolescence is a period of flux. At times of crisis parents are receptive to advice. Yet high on their list of complaints about professionals are failures of communication. These failures involve:

- Insufficient information
- Inaccurate information
- An overload of information at any one time
- Information that is difficult to comprehend because of technical jargon or poor presentation

Providing Information

This then is another way of helping your client by providing the factual data, or know-how about how to get access to information. That information should help them to make informed choices and decisions. You may know people who can offer objective, matter-of-fact information or guidance to your client because of their special expertise.

Within therapy, the therapist may influence the client by providing information or interpretations; by changing clients' attitudes, values, behaviors, and perceptions; by teaching problem solving and social skills; by altering the client's pattern of interests, attitudes, and understanding.

Counseling

Counseling has, as its main aim, the production of constructive behavioral and personality change. Such change emerges from a relationship of trust, one which emerges from confidential conversations between the professionally trained counselor and the client.

Carl Rogers has played a major part in developing the client-centered, nondirective approach to counseling or therapy. In the Rogerian "client-centered" approach, the goal of the intervention is to work in such a facilitative, nonintrusive manner as to remove the incongruence the individual has developed between the experiencing inner self and the self he or she presents to the outside world. In this way it is hoped to increase positive self-regard and self-direction.

Rogers's (1951), client-centered therapy, comes from an academic background in counseling and is less influenced by psychoanalytic thinking than most others in the so-called humanist-existential (or ego psychology) strand of psychological work.

Framework for counseling

- Verbal exchange is the means of influence.
- The basic assumptions about the nature of man and woman are not pessimistic (fatalistic?) like Freud's.
- Rogers has a clear notion of the wholeness of the self. The person is essentially good, rational, realistic, social, forward-looking.
- He or she may need help with their basic impulse to grow. As Rogers puts it: "It has been my experience that persons have a basically positive direction" that is "constructive, moving toward self-actualization, growing toward maturity, growing toward socialization."

The counselor should feel warm and positive toward clients, accept the experience that they are experiencing (empathy), and evince "unconditional positive regard."

The therapeutic process is akin to good education or socialization and is seen as a freeing of the "growth capacities" of the individual, which permits him or her to acquire "more mature" ways of acting and reacting one, which are less fraught with anxiety or conflict. Rogers is talking about a learning process, within a humanistic rather than behaviorist context. The attributes of the counselor that facilitate such learning are thought to be:

- *Genuineness and authenticity:* the conveying of "realness" to clients.

- *Nonpossessive warmth:* the attitude of friendly concern and caring.
- *Accurate empathy:* the capacity to see things from the clients' point of view, to "feel with" them, so that they feel they are understood.

Counseling from a client-centered perspective involves the painstaking exploration of problems. There is an attempt to clarify conflicting issues and discover alternative ways of describing them and/or of dealing with them. Counseling helps people to help themselves. This helping method (like the problem-solving approach but unlike some of the other methods) emphasizes the "self-help" element, the need to call on the inner resources of the person who is in difficulties. To this end, the counselor provides a supportive relationship that enables the individual to search for his or her *own* answers.

Nondirective counseling and therapy are based upon the assumption that the individual has, within, not only the ability to solve his or her own problems satisfactorily, but also a growth impulse that makes adult behavior more satisfying than childish behavior. This assumption puts the nondirective approach well toward the "consumer" model of service delivery described in chapter 1.

Counseling in a Crisis

In your work with children and their parents you will be called upon to disentangle what look like insuperably knotty problems. The tempo of your work is *relatively* unhurried; after all, these difficulties have been around a long time. They require a painstaking assessment and a lot of thought. But emergencies come along—acute crises—and your task is to respond quickly to alleviate the *immediate* impact of disruptive stressful events. There are many potential crises in family life that may include:

- Child diagnosed as mentally/physically handicapped
- Separation/divorce
- Loss of a member of the family (bereavement)
- An attempted suicide in the family
- Physical illness or injury

- Mental illness (e.g., schizophrenia, depression) of a member of the family
- The discovery of sexual abuse of a child/adolescent in the family
- Police involvement (a child's delinquent act) or a court appearance
- Drug abuse discovered
- Anorexia nervosa diagnosed
- Youngster runs away from home
- Truancy
- Family violence

There is no substitute in an emergency for *common sense*. All the crises described above have attracted a specialist literature. But for our purposes we shall look at a few general, common-sense responses for the professional.

- Remember that during a crisis most people (because their defenses are down) are receptive to the right sort of help.
- Do not perceive yourself in *this set of circumstances* as a long-term therapist or a specialist in an area such as bereavement counseling although such a role, or person, may become necessary if the client doesn't seem to be regaining his or her equilibrium.
- You are not there to identify or resolve *all* of the stresses and complications brought about by the crisis.
- Being aware of the *stages* of a crisis allows you to assess whether the client is "stuck" at a particular point in what theoreticians call the "crisis work," thus hindering the mastering of the emergency and delaying its final resolution. Although active crisis states vary in duration, the actual condition of intense disequilibrium is limited usually to between four and six weeks. Stages in crises of different kinds will vary, but here is one example. Colin Parkes (1972) has charted the course of grief following bereavement: it encompasses pangs of grief and pining for the lost one, also a process of searching and yearning for the departed person that may look quite irrational to the observer. Parkes also described the anger that may

flare up and the feelings of guilt that may give way to apathy and depression. Stages of loss are defined as well by Kubler-Ross (1969) in her extensive work on death and dying.

- Simply *identifying* for a person in crisis what is happening, or for concerned relatives *explaining* the normality of such events, provides untold relief and a sense of security. The *unknown*, especially the apparently irrational, bizarre happenings (to oneself or others) in times of crisis, add to the burden of the trauma itself. *Reassurance* is one of the most potent therapeutic remedies available to the emergency counselor.

- Understanding is the other remedy: providing the client with a nonjudgmental, sensitive ear and voice—listening and responding to his or her anguish. This is not the time to be coldly logical, expertly clever, or coldly objective.

Summary and Comment

We have examined several approaches—group and individual—used in the helping process. *Change* is the key word in all of this, be it facilitated by contracts, direct advice, counseling, or psychotherapy. Therapies are many and varied. Many social workers, psychologists, and psychotherapists call themselves "eclectic," drawing what they regard as the best or most valid from the various systems of therapy.

Some theorists assert that the technical claims of the diverse schools of therapy have never been adequately vindicated. Some comparative studies show little difference in the outcomes of diverse approaches even though a particular therapy, by itself, can be shown to have significant effects when compared to the absence of treatment. Such an assertion that there are insignificant differences between therapeutic approaches with regard to outcome would be hotly disputed by behavioral therapists. Nevertheless, it is just such an assumption that leads Jerome Frank (1973), author of *Persuasion and Healing*, to argue that the effective factors are the same for all therapies and they can be identified with the common components of all types of influence and healing—warmth, respect, kindness, hope, understanding, and the provision of explanations.

If it is agreed that psychotherapy is to a significant extent carried out within the framework of a "good" human relationship, questions must be put and hopefully answered about the nature of the psychotherapists's contribution over and beyond the offering of a helpful human relationship.

This chapter touched upon family violence, but the problems of emotional and physical abuse are far too complex and too technical to be dealt with adequately in a generalist text such as this one. The point to be made here is that there are specific preventive and long-term change-oriented methods to consider in addition to the *crisis procedures* adopted by a particular agency. Groupwork and behavioral methods are dealt with in the following chapter and are of proven value.

CHAPTER 10

More Methods and Techniques

The methods and client systems described in this chapter include a range of ways to work with children and parents. At the level of individual clients, there is much individual work that can be done such as that described in the case example of the Hayes family. Avril, the child, became a unit for intervention designed to change her behaviors that were distracting and disruptive for the family as well as dysfunctional for her. Mrs. Hayes, the major caretaker and the parent involved most in Avril's treatment plan, became an identified client as well. Mr. and Mrs. Hayes, a marital subsystem in the family, did not enter into intervention more as Avril's parents than as a couple exploring their own relationship. Conjoint marital treatment in this family may have been quite helpful. It is noted that conjoint family treatment, involving two or more family members, may be productive just as individual sessions with family members often are helpful. Conjoint sessions are often helpful in assessment, in situations of communication difficulties among certain members. In the case of the Hayes family, Avril's parents, together with the therapist, were able to formulate a plan for managing her behavioral problems. A word of caution: family problems reach all family members and excluding one or more family members from family treatment will likely distort the presenting problem and may well prevent common problems from being identified and resolved (Janzen and Harris, 1997).

Groupwork

At the broader level of groups, the Hayes family could have joined other couples and children in groups of families with similar problems, similar intervention needs, or simply similar learning needs. As Avril's behavior and her relationship with her mother improved, their involvement in parent-child activities, including child-care center functions, brought them into a group setting with other parents and children involved in similar activities. In this social and educational setting, they became involved in other relationships and participated in the educational setting, essentially a large group setting.

Some of the advantages of working with children and families in groups include functions such as: (1) experiential processes provide benefits of participating in a group where members learn about how others experience similar problems and often gain support for sharing, communicating, and responding to others; (2) dynamic forces of group processes, particularly in instances of treatment groups, allow the members to enter a group from a social role or from the context of the social self; however, through involvement and interaction as trust builds more of the inner self is shared as greater risk-taking occurs; (3) social functions in groups offer support, feedback, and support social behaviors such as communication skills; (4) didactic groups provide an arena for learning, information, and discussion (Garvin, 1997; Shulman, 1999).

Children and families alike belong to many groups throughout their lives and, as social beings, generally gain comfort from simple interactions with others. Many adults feel that they have failed miserably as parents, and that their child is uniquely difficult to understand and manage. Sharing experiences with other parents can be comforting, indeed reassuring. The opportunity to express feelings of apprehension, resentment, and anger in a group setting can be beneficial if handled sensitively by the group leader. Group methods of training parents may be combined with individual intervention; a marital relationship might be the subject of intervention at the same time as a program for a child's behavior problems or learning disorder is being implemented.

Discussion Groups

Comprehensive reviews of social group work, working with a variety of clients and problem areas in the context of a group setting, therapeutic groups, task groups, discussion groups, and working with groups for the purposes of social control are available in the literature (Garvin, 1997; Johnson and Johnson, 1987; Shulman, 1999). For the beginning practitioner working with families and individuals in need of information, feedback, and social contact, involving clients in discussion groups is an appropriate means of extending services that can be economical and beneficial. Discussion groups are common and economic forums for sharing information, learning experiences, and engaging in mutual problem solving. Parent training groups involve all three of these purposes.

You need to plan and organize your group carefully if it is to be effective and not degenerate into a pleasant, but essentially unproductive, "talk shop." There are several basic procedures for discussion groups. Johnson and Johnson's book *Joining Together* (1987) makes the following suggestions which we have paraphrased (giving examples from our work with parent groups; see Appendix 2).

- **Define terms and concepts.**

A group requires a shared language in order to hold a fruitful discussion. Study new terms; try to find agreement on complex, contentious, or ambiguous words, for example, words like discipline, "problem child," punishment, trust, spoiled, bribery, reinforcement, time-out. Give examples wherever possible to illustrate a word or concept's meaning.

- **Negotiate and/or establish goals.**

Clarify the objectives for every session (themes might cover child development, what to do when a child cries, discipline, sex education, adolescent risk taking). Handouts that prepare discussions for a topic, or summarize the previous meeting, are appreciated. Break down major topics into subtopics.

Spread your time over subtopics in order of importance so that items of significance are not lost. Allow time to review homework tasks if they are part of the agenda, such as, keeping records or a diary for discussion.

- **Encourage free and fair discussion.**

Encourage individuals in the free expression of ideas, feelings, attitudes, openness, reactions, information, and analysis. Do not allow (a *few* ground rules for the group could be useful here) the scapegoating or "bullying" of any one member.

- **Integrate the material.**

Relate current themes to past topics; make connections, where they exist, between issues. Fragmentary impressions from several discussion sessions are unlikely to add significantly to a parent's understanding of children and confidence in his or her parenting skills. In parents' groups (see Appendix 2) it is important to try out practical ideas such as time-out by means of role-play or homework tasks. This leads to an important point:

- **Encourage the application of the discussion material.**

Ask group members to attempt to identify the implications of the material for their own lives, the activities they engage in, and their relationships with other people. Encourage them to apply the positive things they have learned and report back to the group the "feedback" they received from this tryout.

- **Evaluate the quality of the discussion.**

Ask group members to take a critical look at their performance as a group and as individuals contributing to a group.

The Role of Course Organizer

Your coordinating or leadership role is absolutely vital if the group is to work. Here are a few more tips.

Set up the room so that all members can see and hear properly. They should be comfortable and facing each other. An approximate circle is ideal. With a family group session, it is illuminating sometimes to ask the group to arrange the room themselves to their own preferences. Stimulating material such as films, case examples, television programs, and magazines or newspaper articles can be used to initiate discussion. The discussion will "spark" if you negotiate clear themes and objectives. You can lead a group through a complete topic in a logical sequence by presenting new points to the group when necessary. It is important to "hold back" those individuals (say a father) who try to dominate the discussion. Have agreed rules for the sessions. Provide opportunities for quiet or timid members to speak; attempt to draw them out. You should ensure that everyone has the right (if they wish) to talk. Ask clarifying questions, and sum up discussion at regular intervals as well as at the conclusion.

According to the Johnsons (1987), a group intervention will be effective if it meets the following criteria:

- The group *climate* should be warm, accepting, and non-threatening—vital if people are to engage in controversy, expose their vulnerability, show their ignorance, take risks with touchy subjects.
- Learning should be conceived as a *cooperative* enterprise— impossible if the participants "come over" as hostile, competitive, ridiculing, arrogant, or judgmental.
- *Learning* should be accepted as the primary purpose of the group—a desideratum that requires painstaking and imaginative preparation of the material and sensitive but firm management of the group.
- Every member of the group should *participate* in discussion—a function, again, of a skillful, facilitative group leader.
- Such leadership functions might usefully be shared out for certain themes and/or sessions.
- Group sessions don't have to be endlessly solemn or heavy-going. They should be stimulating and thus *pleasurable,* and (at times) sheer fun.
- *Evaluation* should be viewed as an integral part of the group's activities. Group skills can be improved by constructive, critical evaluation.
- Members should *attend regularly* and come prepared—and the importance of mutual responsibility for the well-being of the group may be underlined by drawing up *contracts* with participants.

Individual Helping

There are several ways in which you can support a client through a difficult time on a one-to-one basis. Sometimes you may be able to do something *directly* on your client's behalf—

for example, acting as a mediator in a quarrel, or as an "advocate" in their pursuit of assistance from an impenetrable agency. You may be able to change the external circumstances (perhaps by improving other people's attitudes or by mitigating the aggravating circumstances) which are the cause of your client's difficulties.

If you cannot change the circumstances, you may have to rely on modifying the client's perception of or reaction to the situation. Other methods are described in the following pages. These approaches are *not* mutually exclusive; they overlap in practice and, indeed converge in the behavioral approach.

Persuasion. Persuasion rests on practical knowledge or practice wisdom. It offers reasons why the client should change his or her beliefs and/or behavior. This does not eschew the arts of persuasion. Subject to ethical constraints and the process of negotiating goals with clients, it is an important component of therapy to voice clear opinions based upon valid information and knowledge of the developmental literature and of hard-gained practice, wisdom, and experience.

Providing instruction. Teaching entails skills of "doing." The client may not be able to act without instruction, training, and monitoring. Because some actions (e.g., child-training techniques) are so ingrained in parents' repertoires, it is not usually good enough to simply *advise* parents to change. Demonstration, rehearsals, instructions, and practice may be required in order to provide clients with the equipment for change.

Providing explanation. You may be able to offer explanatory "stories" (cognitive restructuring), which help clients to reorder their beliefs about the nature of their problems. Attempting to change a person's beliefs, desires, and actions is a commonplace activity in ordinary life. The therapist is particularly interested in providing helpful explanations ("stories") or changing existing belief systems which he or she considers to generate distressing, self-defeating actions on the part of the client. Insight, then, is not rejected as a facilitative therapeutic agent.

Giving advice. Guidance is most likely to be effective if it is requested. Advice offered (you might remind parents) in a hectoring or self-righteous tone of voice, with a long-suffering or patronizing expression, or by an ill-chosen turn of phrase, can sound like a command.

Offer your *opinion* in a cool, concerned but measured way about what you consider the best course of action, in the light of what you know of the situation. Remarks indicating understanding, such as "It's a real dilemma you face, isn't it?", should (when appropriate) precede advice or opinions. You might also ask: "What do *you* see as your options/alternatives?" This approach helps to defuse anger, resentment, and irrationality from stressful situations, so that *reason* can be allowed to function.

Advise parents on how to advise their children:

- Although advice is best given when invited (even when your child may want to confirm what he or she has already decided), you can't always wait for an invitation to make a comment.
- Unsolicited advice requires particular diplomacy. Don't pull rank ("Of course, I've been around a long time, so I know best") when giving it.
- Advice can be followed, or *not* taken. If you don't see it that way, then it is a command, not advice, that you're giving.

It *is* a time to be warmly reassuring, solid, and safe. At the Center for Behavioral Work with Families, the imparting of information and advice on child development and childhood problems would be seen as an important part of our work. This might be done on a one-to-one casework basis or in a group setting. The following illustration gives you the flavor of this sort of approach when focused upon children's developmental "problems."

Individual Advice

MH (Therapist) and Mrs. Sally Smith (discussing Penny, age 7). Being left in the dark, or waking up in the dark, is not initially or necessarily an unpleasant experience for a young child. And this is precisely what puzzled Sally Smith about her daughter. "Why," she asked me, "Should Penny develop fear when she's nearly eight?"

T:	"Has Penny woken in the past and called out to you, perhaps because she felt ill or had a bad dream?"
Sally:	"Yes, funny you should ask that. About a month ago she screamed out in the night. She'd had an awful dream about death and monsters. I'm afraid she watched a monster TV film when she spent the night at her friend's home."
T:	"Did you go to her room?"
Sally:	"Yes, I went in, sat on her bed, and reassured her."
T:	"Did you put the light on?"
Sally:	"Yes, of course. Why, was that a mistake?"
T:	"It is only a possibility, of course, but a child can easily associate darkness with distress, and light with positive feelings in the form of consoling, comforting nurture—your presence in this case."
Sally:	"I hadn't thought about that."
T:	"It is preferable, in the future, to enter the room, talk to her, and reassure her in the dark. Try to ensure that there is no direct and recurrent relationship between your arrival and the light. Take her back to bed when she comes to you, and stay with her until she is calm. Don't let her stay in your bed, otherwise this will soon become a habit."
Sally:	"I'm afraid I've got so fed up with her fears of the dark and monsters and disturbed nights that I recently started to punish her. I feel bad about it, so I suppose it was a bad move."
T:	"There is no way you can punish a child out of her fear. What you might succeed in doing is punishing her into submission, so that she hides her fears from you but suffers them nevertheless. You wouldn't want that I'm sure, and it would imply a loss of confidence in you."

Sally: "So what should I do? I'm at my wit's end."

T: "You could leave the light on until Penny goes to sleep, then switch it off, and leave the door open with a light on outside so that if she does wake up she will not find herself in total darkness. To avoid sudden distress on the child's part you could explain the game to her and make sure that she knows how to switch on the light for herself should she wake up and want it on. When she is asleep, you can turn the light off again. Because the situation is under the child's control there will be no call for panic reactions. Given sufficient patience on your side, she will eventually get tired of leaving the comfort of her bed in order to switch on the light, and will decide that there is more sense in going back to sleep with the light off. The essence of the operation is that you should in no way suggest that you are putting the light off in order to punish your child. Once it becomes a contest of wills, you have defeated your original purpose of enlisting her own energies in coping with fear.

If Penny comes to your bed, insist that she goes back to her own room—and take her back yourself if necessary. Award her a star or point on her very own "bedtime chart" which is marked out in squares for every night of the week. If she doesn't come to your bedroom, give her *two* stars the next morning and lots of praise. Let her stick the stars herself. Count up the stars at the end of the week, and if they reach an agreed number exchange them for a promised special treat. Fortunately, children's fears tend to be transitory anyway; but this method should hurry along the process of clearing it up."

Settling Differences

The organizers of an Open University (1982) course entitled *Parents and Teenagers* have suggested a step-by-step approach to settling differences of opinion between parents and adolescents. Here is a parent (Mrs. Brown) working through a potentially fraught situation. She hates motorcycles and her son,

Mike, wants to buy one. She asks herself, *"Why must he have a motorcycle?"* Here is a list of answers.

- There is no public transport worth speaking of.
- He can't afford a car.
- He says his friends go on outings, and without transport he is excluded.
- He claims to be "grown-up" and therefore "responsible" and free to make choices.
- *Why should he not have a motorcycle?*
- He may have an accident . . . get hurt . . . get killed. Motorcycles are associated with rough types.

Step 1. **Working out feelings and attitudes about the situation.**
(i) I feel . . . . (e.g., resentful).
(ii) When he . . . . (e.g., keeps pestering me for a motorcycle).
(iii) Because . . . . (e.g., he know it upset me).

Step 2. **Deciding whether the particular situation is worth bothering about.**
Reasons for: High risk.
Reasons against: There'll be an awful row if I give a final no.

Step 3. **Making an approach.**
(i) Expressing one's own feelings in an unprovocative manner.
(ii) Listening carefully to the reply; clarifying one's understanding of the other's position.

Step 4. **Working out a practical agreement/compromise.**
You might provide the parents with the following guidelines.
- They should work out what is at stake. Deciding whether or not to take (or sanction) a risk depends on:
- How likely they believe the feared outcome might be.
- How important/damaging the possible outcome is.
- How much they/their teenager has to lose.

Remind them to:
- Bear in mind that risk taking is an important feature of adolescent development;
- Ensure that they and their teenager are well informed (e.g. that a potential motorcycle rider has a good machine and is well trained for driving and roadcraft);

- Discuss risk taking with their son or daughter; try to agree what he or she can do to make the experimenting relatively safe; think about what they can do to make it so;
- Try reaching a compromise or give way on one lesser risk so as to obtain their teenager's agreement to forego another one.

Role Play

Role play is an activity we have all indulged in at different stages of our lives, beginning as children playing doctors and mothers and fathers. Role play is also an educational technique that brings a specific skill and its consequences into focus. It is a vital tool for experiential learning as it allows the participants to play themselves in different or worrying situations, such as adolescents preparing for job interviews; or to play the part of another person in a known situation, such as reversing roles so that parent becomes child, child pretends to be parents. Role players do not have to be good actors. They put themselves into a *situation* that is spelled out and "acted out" on the basis of certain *assumptions* that have been carefully discussed.

By using role play as an educational technique, insights can be obtained—emotions, reactions, thoughts, behaviors, attitudes, and values can be explored. At the end of the role play, participants can reflect on the experience, and gain greater understanding of the role-played situations. Role play can be used as a vehicle for discussion; it can increase communication skills and self-esteem; it illustrates novel situations and ways of dealing with them; and it allows participants to see how others feel in a particular situation. Here are some guidelines:

- When using role play, have clear and well-defined objectives.
- Ask participants to *volunteer* for the various roles.
- Use props to identify participants in their roles if this is felt to be helpful.
- Encourage participants to identify with the role they are playing. If they are playing an unknown character, ask them to respond in the way they think that person

would. If they are playing themselves in an unknown situation, ask them to respond as honestly as possible to that situation.

- You should stage manage and direct the role play. Remind participants to come out of role at the end of the session.
- Debrief the participants. Debriefing is the period when reflection and evaluation occurs. Ensure there is sufficient time for this. As themselves, the players discuss what they learned from the experience; encourage general discussion about the relevance of the situation to their lives.

Teenagers and their parents can be helped to resolve conflict by the use of role play. The method is used to teach clients basic skills, to help them become more effective in their interactions, and to help them to become more confident when extremely anxious (for example, through enacting scenes such as using the telephone, going to an interview with an employer, or dealing with provocation).

Overcoming fear. Methods found most effective in helping young people to overcome fears include:

- Helping to develop skills by which they can cope with the feared object or situation.
- Taking them by degrees into active contact and participation with the feared object or situation.
- Giving them an opportunity gradually to become acquainted with the feared object or situation under circumstances that at the same time give them the opportunity either to inspect or to ignore it.

Exposure Training

Behavioral methods have provided the cornerstone of treatment for phobias. The aims of treatment are fourfold:

- To reduce levels of both general and situational anxiety
- To relieve disturbing physiological symptoms
- To reduce avoidance behavior
- To prevent interference in daily living

The fearful youngster may be exposed to the phobic object or situation in fantasy, in pictures, or in real life. Exposure may be graded by means of an initially easy but then increasingly difficult series of situations. This gradual mastery of fear-provoking events is also referred to as *systematic desensitization*.

Self-Control Training

Self-control procedures are designed to give the client a more effective means of manipulating the eliciting, reinforcing, and discriminative stimuli which affect behavior. The worker's role is first to carefully examine the antecedents and consequences of a piece of behavior over which the client wishes to have more control and then to suggest ways in which these events may be altered. They may be altered by either physical or cognitive changes in order that the client may achieve a greater degree of control over the behavior.

An example

Sue was heavily overweight and was anxious to control her eating behavior. She was asked to carefully record everything she ate or drank and the time at which it was consumed over a two-week period. From this data it became evident that her overeating was restricted to certain types of food and occurred during only the latter part of the day. Further investigation revealed that the sorts of food Sue ate to excess were candy, cakes, and cookies that she usually brought at a local store on her way home from work. She never overate in company, only when alone.

A self-control program was designed in order to help her resist the temptation to overeat. She was instructed to take a different route home so as to avoid the store she usually called at; if she was to be alone in the flat, she was to change immediately from her day clothes into a housecoat to help discourage her from going out to the store later in the evening. Her roommates agreed to help by not bringing any forbidden cakes or candy into the flat when Sue was around and they also made an effort to ensure that she was not left alone in the evenings. Sue was allowed to reward herself for sticking to her diet by having a favorite cake or candy at the end of each "successful" week. When tempted to cheat she was told to visualize an unpleasant and humiliating scene where a group of boys made rude and teasing remarks about her size—a hazard which she would do anything to avoid.

Stress Management

A British clinical psychologist, Reginald Beech (1985) in his book *Staying Together*, makes the point that life stresses are the enemy of personal relationships. It *is* possible to reduce the impact of stress on our lives, so his list might be useful to your client. I have paraphrased the items you might wish to put to them:

* Keep a running check on stresses in your life. Even the apparently trivial ones, when they accumulate, can become an excessive burden.
* Positive self-talk helps us to keep the stresses and strains in our lives in more reasonable proportion. (We dealt earlier with this technique.)
* Don't try too hard to solve all your problems and expect to erase them altogether. This is usually a vain hope. Concentrate, instead, on *reducing* stress. Even a small reduction in each stress can lead to a big difference in our ability to cope.
* Don't try to be all things to all people all the time. Ration yourself by taking a sensible view of your commitments, never forgetting to leave time for yourself and for some privacy.
* Don't be at the mercy of your environment. You really *can* rearrange your world—if the will is there—to fit in with what you would like to happen.
* Learn to say "No." You don't have to say "Yes" to the unreasonable or all of the reasonable tasks that are foisted on you. Examine your needs and priorities in what is being dished out and feel free to refuse sometimes.
* Cut down on the "have to." Question what you tend to take for granted; don't just go ahead and do it because you have always done so.

- Don't set out to win everything. When it really doesn't matter then take a philosophical, relaxed approach. Many so-called confrontations aren't worth the effort.
- Delegate. It doesn't always have to be *your* job. Spread the load more.
- Slow down. Don't set impossibly tiring or tedious schedules for yourself. Introduce rest pauses, moments of reflection, and pleasure into your day.
- Get some balance into your day. Find time for leisure, hobbies, social life, family life, yourself, and your work/studies.
- Curb aggression. Try to plan your way through problems. You'll end up by feeling better.
- Learn to relax. Practice makes perfect. (Relaxation training tapes are available on cassettes and are an important part of a professional's equipment these days. See Ollendick and Cerny 1981 for a training script.)
- Concentrate on staying calm. In an emergency take a deep breath rapidly but quietly; clasp your hands and press them hard against each other. If sitting, brace your leg muscles, pull in your stomach muscles, clench your jaw, and hold the muscular tension for five seconds. Now exhale slowly, feel the tension go out of you, saying the word "relax" to yourself.

  If you happen to be standing, take a deep breath, clasp your hands behind you, pressing them hard together; force your knees back to create leg muscle tension, pull in your stomach muscles, and clench your jaws. Maintain the tension for five seconds, then let it go slowly, exhaling and saying the word "relax" to yourself. Don't exaggerate the muscular tension but make sure you can feel it. Fix your gaze on something so that you appear to be preoccupied or deep in thought for a few moments, so as to conceal the stress you are controlling.

  Repeat the exercise if necessary.

Summary and Comment

The methods and techniques described in this chapter represent only a small selection of those available. It is vital that you do not rely on techniques like items in a cookbook recipe. They should come out of a clearly formulated theory of human behavior, a careful assessment, and a coherent conceptual framework for producing change.

The chapter outlines the various advantages of working in groups and provides detail of the organization and implementation of groupwork. Individual helping methods such as persuasion, instruction, the provision of explanations or insight, giving advice, settling differences, role play, stress management, and self-control training are described, with examples.

CHAPTER 11

Child Management and Behavioral Methods

Behavioral methods are very much concerned with *contingencies*, which is a technical way of referring to rules. Before we look at specific applications let us consider the perennial issue of discipline in child rearing, an issue that is concerned with rules and routines.

Rules and Routines

Why should children learn to follow rules and routines? Is it reactionary, indeed Victorian, to *insist* on obedience and conformity to rules as part of child-rearing? The answer is a resounding "No!" Setting limits *is* crucial, but the limits should not be defined too narrowly. As with all things in child development, there is a balance—a golden mean.

This is where you can help parents to work out their priorities and how to achieve them. Failure is costly for parents. Disobedience and defiance are common problems, and their consequences are frustrating, irksome, even exhausting and debilitating for parents. When they persist they can sometimes prove dangerous, particularly, in homes at risk of child abuse. There are other potentially serious consequences. Obedience is critical, if the complex processes of socialization are to work. Parents have the task of turning helpless, unsocial, and self-centered infants into sociable children and eventually into reasonable and responsible members of the community. In the early years from birth to seven or eight, or thereabouts, compliance to parental requests and instructions is vital if the child is going to learn all of the social, intellectual, and physical skills he or she will require for a reasonably smooth and contented journey toward maturity. The toddler period is particularly sensitive if social training is going to proceed smoothly.

Among the reasons for enforcing certain rules are

- The need for safety—the child has to learn to avoid dangers;
- Harmony within the family—a disobedient "brat" sets the scene for an unhappy home and disharmony between the parents;
- The social life of the family—"spoiled," noisy, aggressive, destructive children are not welcome in other people's homes and contribute to the social isolation of their parents.

Parents achieve compliance partly through example because their children love them, seek their approval, and want to be as much like them as possible. It is also achieved by consciously steering the child in the way he or she should go. A firm but loving framework of discipline helps children to develop their own guidelines and controls symbolized by what we call "conscience," so that they can look ahead to the consequences of their actions and "discipline" themselves.

You will find that most parents find discipline one of the most difficult parts of their job; so be forewarned and forearmed. They are quite likely to ask you not only awkward questions, but also for specific advice. It does not help matters to find yourself in an area, not of scientific facts, but of value judgments. *Guidelines*, rather than "formula" prescriptions, will be among the more useful aids you can provide them with. Better still, you might help them to work out their strategies for themselves, by teaching them how to solve problems.

Preparing the Child for Life

A list of guidelines has been provided in chapter 6. Here are some additional points to note in connection with Guidelines 3 and 4, the two which require broadly compliant responses from children.

The point was made there that most routines are useful shortcuts to living. Those routines, carried out on "autopilot," help a child to undertake daily tasks *around the clock* with minimum effort or fuss—once the habits are learned. In unhappy homes with a disobedient child you can predict fairly safely that one or more of the following situations will be sheer purgatory for parents, especially in single-parent families.

- Getting the child up in the morning.
- Washing self, getting dressed.
- Eating (breakfast, and later in the day, other meals).
- Getting the child off to playgroup or school.
- Obeying requests/instructions during the course of the day (e.g., "Put your toys away"; "Don't keep switching the television on and off"; "Stop teasing your sister"; "Put that chocolate back on the shelf"; "Don't go out on the road").
- Defiance of house rules (e.g., breaking rules about playing with matches, about not switching on the TV before the children's programs begin, about sitting at the table until the meal is finished, or about not taking food out of the refrigerator without permission).
- Interrupting (by pestering) mother when she is in the bathroom, on the telephone, cooking a meal, etc.
- Disrupting shopping trips by incessant "I wants," pulling items off the shelves, tantrums, and so on.
- Quarreling, fighting incessantly with brothers and/or sisters, teasing, and so on.
- Not going to bed when asked; staying there for the night.

You may be asked to suggest *practical* strategies for managing these situations. The later section of this chapter should prove helpful.

The compliance that underpins the learning of rules, routines, and good manners can be facilitated by working with parents on the following themes: ensuring that rules are clear and reasonable; that obedience or disobedience is sanctioned consistently; and that the requests and commands that give effect to rules are precise and comprehensible. If there are difficulties with the latter, model how (i.e. demonstrate and check on the client's performance) to make effective requests and commands.

Alan Hudson (1987) recommends the following steps:

- Use the child's name.
- Give a *specific* direction.

- Include a mention of time (e.g., "right now" or "when you have finished the chapter").
- Say "please."
- Get all the words together (in the form of a statement, *not* a question). Do not say: "Sandy, will you get dressed for mommy?" Do say: "Sandy, I would like you to get dressed now, please."
- Make the request standing *close* to the child; with a small child get down close to the height of the little one.
- Use a pleasant but *firm* tone of voice (no pleading, cajoling, wheedling!).
- Try to be looking at the child. It may be helpful to say: "Sandy, look at me now, please" and then give the desired command.
- If the child obeys or disobeys—ignores/refuses—follow the behavior with clear and predictable *consequences:*
  (a) Obedience is followed by positive consequences (e.g., praise).
  (b) Disobedience is followed by negative consequences (e.g., loss of privileges, time-out). Discourage parents from smacking or shouting.
- In the case of special circumstances (shopping, visiting) or places (church, restaurants), help parents to preempt problems by working out a scenario.
  (a) Explain to the child what is going to happen.
  (b) Promise a treat/privilege if the child behaves well (specify).
  (c) Engage the child in prosocial behaviors that compete with the unwanted behaviors (e.g., helping mom to pack the shopping bag rather than taking items off the shelves at the check-out counter).
  (d) Use response-cost (as a penalty) for transgressions as discussed later in this chapter.
- Do not keep repeating the request. Follow noncompliant actions with a penalty.

Behavioral methods. The preceding discussion of rules and requests has been a necessary exercise in setting the stage for a discussion of behavioral methods, many of which are potent in correcting the *extremes* of noncompliance. Of course, parents need some principles *and* practical techniques for encouraging and maintaining, not only compliant, but also other prosocial behaviors.

Here are some of the main methods couched in a form that can be presented directly to parents for use with their children. Some of the methods are illustrated by means of brief vignettes drawn from case material.

Strengthening New Patterns of Behavior

Principle 1: **Operant learning**
Those methods of intervention, based on operant conditioning, attempt to influence or control the outcome of certain behaviors through the use of positive reinforcement, such as, pleasurable consequences. Voluntary actions ("operants") that are followed by favorable outcomes for the individual are likely to be repeated.

A social worker using operant methods can analyze a family system and find out how the various members reinforce undesired behavior in some members and intentionally or unintentionally ignore or punish desired behavior. It is then possible to make beneficial alterations in such distressed systems by planning with the family systematically to rearrange the consequences of behavior so that all (or certain) members of the family receive social reinforcement for desired behaviors.

Instructions to parents. In order to improve or increase your child's performance of certain actions, arrange matters so that an immediate reward follows the correct performance of the desired behavior. You might indicate your intentions by saying, for example, *"When* you have put your toys away, *then* you can go out."* When the child has learned a behavior it is no longer necessary to give rewards regularly. Remember that words of praise and encouragement at such a stage can be very reinforcing.

Principle 2: **Modeling**
To teach a client new patterns of behaviors, give him or her the opportunity to observe a person performing the desired

actions. Social workers and others in the helping professions are very important as models in shaping behavior.

Modeling is used effectively in at least three situations:

- To acquire new or alternative patterns of behavior from the model which the client has never manifested before (e.g., social skills, self-control);
- To increase or decrease responses already in the client's repertoire through the demonstration by high prestige models of appropriate behavior (e.g., the disinhibition of a shy, withdrawn client's social interactions, or the inhibition of learned fears—e.g., avoidance of gym—or the suppression of impulsive antisocial behavior which gets in the way of social relationships); and
- To increase behaviors which the observing client has already learned and for which there are no exiting inhibitions or constraints.

Three variations of modeling—*filmed modeling, live modeling, and participant modeling*—tend to be used in clinical practice. Alan Hudson (1987) describes nine steps in the therapeutic use of modeling:

- Provide instructions to the learner (say the parent) about the relevant aspects of modeled behavior to attend to.
- Ask the learner to repeat those relevant aspects to be attended to.
- Model the behavior.
- Ask the learner to report on relevant aspects of the behavior attended to.
- Reinforce the learner for reporting.
- Repeat the modeling, reporting—reinforcing if necessary.
- Ask the learner to imitate modeled behavior.
- Reinforce the learner for imitating the modeled behavior, correcting as necessary.
- Repeat imitation and reinforcement until the behavior is displayed with 100% accuracy.

An adult example

Jenny was a quiet, shy woman in her late twenties who found it difficult to cope with her bright, forceful four-year-old daughter and was also experiencing feelings of frustration and anger about her unsatisfactory marital relationship, feelings which she had not dared to communicate openly to her husband. Assessment revealed that Jenny had almost no self-confidence and a very poor self-image, mainly due to past unhappy life experiences. Jenny was well aware of the reason for her self-deprecation and self-doubt but this insight did not seem to affect her behavior. At the Center we began an informed program involving role-playing situations in which she felt unable to assert herself. By modeling appropriate reactions and using relaxation to allay her anxiety we were able to teach her to be more assertive—behavior that reduced her feelings of helplessness and frustration and gave her confidence to make a realistic appraisal of her marriage and exert more control over her life.

Eliminating/Reducing
Inappropriate Behavior

Principle 3: **Satiation**
To get a child to desist from acting in a particular way, allow and encourage him or her to continue performing the desired act until he or she tires of it. Of course this would not be appropriate if the act was dangerous or seriously antisocial.

Principle 4: **Extinction of inappropriate actions**
To stop a child from acting in a particular way, arrange conditions so that he or she receives no rewards following the undesired acts.

Instruction to parents. Ignore minor misdemeanors such as whining, pestering, tantrums. If a child grabs toys or other goodies from his or her small brother, try to ensure the grabbing has no rewarding outcome. Return the toy to its owner. Combine training the older child that grabbing is unproductive with teaching the little one to share. Encourage them to take turns.

Withhold reinforcements such as approval, attention, and the like, which have previously and inappropriately followed undesirable behavior. Remember: your child may "work hard" to regain the lost reinforcement and thus may get "worse" before getting "better." If the problem behavior has been continuously reinforced in the past then extinction should be relatively swift; after all, it is much easier for the youngster to recognize that he or she has lost reinforcers than it is for the child on intermittent reinforcement. In the latter case, extinction tends to be slow.

Planned ignoring of behaviors includes the following:

* As soon as the misbehavior begins, turn away or work away from your child;
* Say nothing and try not to show any expression at all;
* Resist getting into any debate, argument, or discussion with your child while he or she is misbehaving;
* If you think he or she deserves an explanation for whatever is upsetting him or her, then say "When you have calmed down we will talk about it."

Example of planned ignoring

Suzy is a nine-year-old spastic girl, the only child of rather anxious and overprotective parents. They were very concerned at her difficult behavior during mealtimes when, although perfectly able to feed herself, she would refuse to eat unless fed, would throw food and utensils on the floor, and often refuse food entirely. Assessment revealed that at school lunches the child showed none of these behaviors. Nor were they displayed at home when she ate informally in front of the television in the evening. Her problem behavior was specific to family lunch at weekends and holidays, the only occasions when the whole family sat down together at the table. It appeared that this setting was providing Suzy with an audience to which she gladly reacted.

In order to combat this, her parents were instructed to ignore any "naughty" behavior and only to speak to Suzy when she was eating properly. They were not to feed her or coax her, and any food refused was to be removed without comment. Between meals snacks were forbidden and the dining room table was rearranged so that Suzy's parents were not directly looking at her. In order to help them ignore her, which they found very difficult at first, they were told to talk to each other, and thus take their minds off Suzy. Within three weekends Suzy was eating normally and has continued to do so. Her parents also used behavioral principles in encouraging self-help skills and have themselves become less overprotective.

Principle 5: **Time-out from positive reinforcement**
The well-known "time-out" procedure is intended to reduce the frequency of an undesirable behavior by ensuring that it is followed by a reduction in the opportunity to acquire reinforcement or rewards. In practice one can distinguish three forms of time-out:

- Activity time-out, where a child is simply barred from joining in an enjoyable activity but still allowed to observe it, for example, having misbehaved, he or she is made to sit out of a game.
- Room time-out, where the child is removed from an enjoyable activity, not allowed to observe this, but not totally isolated—for example, standing outside a classroom having misbehaved.
- Seclusion time-out, where he or she is socially isolated in a situation from which voluntary escape is impossible.

Time-out sometimes leads to tantrums or rebellious behaviors such as crying, screaming, and physical assaults, particularly if the child has to be taken by force to a quiet room. With older, physically resistive children the method may simply not be feasible. So the procedure and its choice require careful consideration.

When the behavior to be eliminated is an extraordinarily compelling one that all but demands attention (reinforcement) from those present, or when time-out is difficult to administer because the child is strong, the mother (i.e., a major source of reinforcement) could remove herself, together with a magazine, to the bathroom, locking herself in when the child's temper tantrums erupt and come out only when all is quiet.

Instructions to parents. The child is warned in advance about those behaviors that are considered inappropriate and the consequences that will follow from them. Time-out may last for as much as five minutes. Three minutes time is sufficient for younger children.

In practice, "activity" or "room" time-out should always be preferred before any form of "seclusion" time-out. Techniques such as time-out, which are designed to eliminate inappropriate or undesirable behavior, are unlikely to succeed unless supplemented by the reinforcement of an alternative and more appropriate behavior pattern.

A critical determination of the effectiveness of time-out is the extent to which the child actually enjoys the situation from which he or she is removed. If that situation is positively frightening, anxiety-provoking, or boring, it is possible that the time-out procedure might involve removing the child to a less aversive situation and thereby actually *increase* rather than decrease, the frequency of the inappropriate behavior.

Example of time-out

Gary was six-and-a-half years old at referral and was described as a very unlovable child. He constantly screamed and shouted abuse at his parents and had violent temper tantrums when he would indulge in physical aggression, hitting and punching people and furniture, and screaming at the top of his voice until he got his own way. He was also persistently defiant and disobedient and seemed to enjoy provoking confrontation with his parents. Observation and assessment confirmed that Gary was indeed showing all these behaviors but also revealed that they were being heavily reinforced by attention from his parents and by the fact that the shouting and temper tantrums usually resulted in Gary's getting his own way and were therefore highly functional for him.

Not surprisingly, against this background, family relationships were very strained and Gary was so unpopular that on the rare occasions when he did behave appropriately it went unnoticed and unattended to, which meant he was only getting attention for antisocial behavior.

To deal with the shouting and temper tantrums his parents removed Gary from the room as soon as he started to shout. This use of "time-out from positive reinforcement" was designed to eliminate the possibility of his receiving reinforcing attention for antisocial behavior and also insisting that he complied with the original request on his return. The parents were able to eliminate these outbursts almost entirely. At the same time great emphasis was placed on rewarding Gary for prosocial behavior with tokens which he could then exchange for privilege (such as staying up later) or a treat (such as a favorite play activity with his parents).

This program was designed to improve the relationship with Gary by providing opportunity for mutually reinforcing activities. By the end of the program Gary was much happier, showing much more prosocial behavior and getting on a good deal better with his parents.

This case illustrates how by changing behavior one can also affect attitudes. Experience at the Center is that by modifying children's more difficult behavior they become more rewarding to their parents. Mothers who have been at the stage of rejecting and even abusing their difficult children find they can see more positive sides of the child and start to enjoy the experience of being a parent as reflected in the case illustration.

Penalizing Undesirable Behavior

Principle 6: **Response-cost**
The use of *response-cost* procedures involves a penalty being invoked for failure to complete a desired response. This may involve the forfeiture of rewards currently available—as for example, when failure to complete homework results in the loss of television privileges.

Instructions to parents. To stop a child from acting in a particular way, arrange for him or her to terminate a *mildly* unpleasant situation immediately by changing the behavior in the desired direction. For example, every time he or she throws a toy in a dangerous manner the offending toy is locked away.

Example of response-cost

A hyperactive boy, Darren, was extremely disruptive and noisy. He made life miserable for his older brothers and sisters, while they read or watched television, by constantly interrupting them—making loud humming and wailing noises and also banging things. An extension of the range of rewards for therapeutic intervention is enshrined in the Premack principle or "Granny's Rule"—where a preferred behavior is made contingent on correctly performing a nonpreferred behavior. This principle worked well with Darren. A bottle of marbles representing his pocket money plus a bonus was placed on the mantelpiece. Each transgression "cost" a marble (a penny). As always, sanctions were balanced by rewards. Punishment alone tells children what not to do, not what they are expected to do. He was required to play quietly for set periods—timed with a kitchen timer and if he did this successfully he was rewarded by tokens. These tokens could then be exchanged for treats—for example, he could loudly blow his sister's trombone for five minutes: something he had always wanted to do and something he found a great incentive.

Encouraging Competing Behavior

Principle 7: **Overcorrection**

Instruction to parents. Require the child to correct the consequences of his or her misbehavior. Not only must he or she remedy the situation caused thereby, but also "overcorrect" it to an improved or better-than-normal state. In other words, you enforce the performance of a new behavior in the situation where you want it to become routine.

Get the child to practice behaviors which are physically incompatible with the inappropriate behavior.

An example

Gavin, who stole and broke another youngster's penknife, was required to save up enough money not only to replace the knife, but also to buy a small gift betokening regret. He was praised at the completion of the act of restitution. When he deliberately punctured another child's bicycle tire he not only had to repair the tire but also to oil and polish the entire vehicle.

This involves positively reinforcing a particular class of behavior that is inconsistent with, or which cannot be performed at the same time as, the undesired act. In other words, to stop a child from acting in a particular way, deliberately reinforce a competing action.

Summary and Comment

Behavior therapy (modification), unlike psychoanalysis, is increasingly being used not only by clinical psychologists but also by psychiatrists, social workers, nurses, and teachers trained in the approach.

There is a great shortage of professional people with relevant training. This can be mitigated by the fact that clinicians do not have a monopoly of helping skills or such therapeutic qualities as common sense; by providing nonprofessionals and paraprofessionals with skills to cope with future problems, behavioral work has moved the focus of therapy toward a preventive model of mental health.

This behavior modification approach has been taught to parents (see Appendix 2). Persons without a considerable amount of psychological knowledge can grasp the concepts, and many persons can be taught at one time in a relatively short training period is needed. The long-term purposes of training are to help parents to become more systematic in their own behavior, so as to be more effective in managing their children.

Parents often prefer a view of problem development that does not assume "sick" behavior based on a medical model (see chapter 1). In addition, many childhood problems consist of well-defined behaviors that are conducive of behavioral treatment. Various methods were described in the chapter.

CHAPTER 12

Using Life Skills Training

After many years of working with families with a seriously problematic child (or children) I am not surprised when I discover a socially isolated family in which parents seldom go out, the circle of friends has shrunk. For the mother who often is the primary caregiver, social isolation may result in a loss of social confidence and self-esteem. In some instances the parents were (or felt) unskilled from the beginning; in others a difficult (perhaps developmentally disabled) baby made them feel deskilled. Overall, skills which assist individuals in the many and varied "life-tasks" which become salient at different stages of life, social and problem-solving competencies are high-priority items.

The self-efficacy theory attempts to explain the interacting and mutual influence of people's self-perceptions and their behavior. You may remember that self-efficacy is a belief in oneself, a conviction that one can produce positive outcomes through effort and persistence. People high in their possession of self-efficacy are convinced of their own effectiveness. Those who are low in self-efficacy believe that their efforts are doomed to failure. Parents with a history of failure in their lives begin to believe that they cannot succeed. Their pessimism leads them to avoid the source of their fear, and avoid further handicaps for them and their children.

For example, there is no opportunity for the child to develop new social skills, let alone practice old ones, if the mother doesn't speak to people at the park, take the child to parties or friends' homes. And if unskilled patterns of behavior are allowed to continue uninterrupted, children may never learn how to cope adequately with their social environment; this leads to a sense of isolation, unhappiness, and perhaps "acting out" reactions.

The rationale for social skills assessment and training is to help children and their parents to become more flexible and socially competent, so they have less recourse to self-defeating behaviors and feelings.

In the current enthusiasm for social skills training (SST) as a "package" it is important to remember the need for an ABC analysis and *comprehensive* assessment in each case of "problematic" behavior (see chapter 2). "Cookbook" applications of SST without such individualized assessments are likely to fail, mainly because of the multicausal nature of children's problems.

A careful analysis should be made of the types of social situations that upset the child. Parental attitudes (such as over-solicitous concern about the child) can foster timidity and provide a cue for the child to behave in a dysfunctional manner when in the company of others. Parents, thus, become part of the intervention. It may be they themselves who, by excessively authoritarian discipline or excessively demanding attitudes, produce negative self-attitudes in the child. Children may feel unwilling or unable to do what is required of them by their parents, and this may transfer to social situations where they feel they are on display.

If parents themselves lack social skills and graces, they may fail to provide adequate models for their children to identify with or imitate in social situations. Again, parents who are inconsistent in their demands on their children may engender timidity in them because they never know whether what they are doing is right.

The interference model. The interpretation here is that specific skills are, in fact, present but not employed because emotional or cognitive factors interfere with the performance of their skills. The "process" of working out appropriate goals and strategies, of monitoring and setting standards, and then adjusting and controlling one's actions, may be faulty. This could result from severe anxiety, faulty self-attributions, and low self-esteem.

Social Skills Training

This approach involves a structured learning experience for developing skills for interacting with people. It aims to change specific person-to-person behaviors that influence the quality of relationships, such as:

- Assertiveness
- The ability to listen
- Conversational skills (plus greetings and partings)
- Nonverbal skills
- The ability to be rewarding
- Observational skills (reading social signals, getting information, asking questions)
- Problem-solving skills (the ability to work out solutions to novel and thorny social problems).

Even young people with poor social skills are likely to have several effective *components* of socially skilled behaviors. These can be built on, improved, and integrated smoothly, by instruction, or by feedback and prompts, during role rehearsal. Role rehearsal allows you to comment on the client's performance. It is a gradual process—building up skills by means of working out the various component tasks making up a particular skill. This "pretend" sort of rehearsal provides an intermediate step in changing behavior and developing new and more effective strategies. The end point is when the client tries out the new skill or role in real life.

To take one application: the self-effacing, timid youngster may overcome these difficulties by training in assertion. A young girl, say, practices asserting herself in an imaginary confrontation with a shopkeeper who has given the wrong change or by asking a boy to a party. The difficulty of the situation is gradually increased. The youngster then asserts herself in relatively easy real life settings, before tackling more challenging circumstances.

The basic SST technique is *role playing*. Michael Argyle and Monika Henderson (1985) describe a three-stage sequence:

- Lectures, discussions, demonstrations, videos, or films about particular aspects of the skill. The demonstration and explanation phase is most usefully conveyed by *modeling*.
- A problem situation is carefully defined, and "slooges" are introduced with whom trainees role play from 7 to 15

minutes each. The stooges are briefed about the circumstances and about which problem to introduce.

- Next there is a feedback session, consisting of verbal comments by the trainees, discussion with the other trainees, and playback of audio- and videotapes.

Sometimes a fourth session of practice is allowed for so that the trainee can rehearse the lessons he or she has learned.

This basic sequence can be expanded to include training in:

- Analysis of difficult social situations
- Conversation
- Presentation of self
- Rewardingness

Rewardingness is a vital quality in the enhancing of relationships. Intimacy and supportiveness are foundational elements in "coming over" as rewarding to others. The following indicate the manner in which people influence intimacy:

- Addressing the other person by their first name
- Showing an interest in their activities
- Sharing news of success
- Showing positive unconditional regard
- Trusting and confiding in the other person
- Acknowledging birthdays and other special occasions
- Striving to make the other person happy while in each other's company
- Inviting them to family celebrations or other intimate affairs
- Making them welcome
- Showing affection
- Open discussion of subjects such as religion or politics, sex, or death

Cognitive Approaches

If psychological treatment can boost a client's perceived self-efficacy, then the client should approach formerly dreaded situations with new confidence. Much SST training is content oriented, that is, the teaching of specific, complex skills. A cognitive approach tends to be process orientated. Children's knowledge of social exchange norms and awareness of their own special impact upon others would be seen as crucial to their ability to "read" social situations realistically and with sensitivity.

But we know that negative beliefs and unrealistic expectations may lead to disharmonious social interactions. Such matters would certainly be high among the concerns of the cognitively oriented behavior therapist. He or she would also be committed to helping the child to "unravel" knotty social situations, to analyze them, and to generate alternative solutions to the self-defeating strategies so far adopted. Those adopting a cognitive-social learning model, view effective social functioning as being dependent upon the client's

- Knowledge of specific interpersonal actions and how they fit into different kinds of person-to-person situations
- Ability to convert knowledge of social nuances into the skilled performance of social actions in various interactive contexts
- The ability to evaluate skillful and unskillful behavior accurately and to adjust one's behavior accordingly

Problem Solving

Life is full of crises, problems, and decisions, but many people do not have the appropriate skills to manage them. Much of what we think of as problematic behavior in a client can be viewed as the consequence of ineffective behavior and thinking. The individual is unable to resolve certain dilemmas in his or her life; the unproductive attempts to do so have adverse effects such as anxiety and depression, not to mention the creation of additional problems such as confrontations and interpersonal conflict. For the professional the way to decode the client's sometimes incomprehensible actions is to ask yourself what he or she is trying to "achieve"—seen from their point of view.

Often, what the client is trying to achieve is the narrowing of the *discrepancy* between his or her *actual* state of affairs and his or her *desired* (or *ideal*) state of affairs. The discrepancy *is* the problem, and the client's solutions may be making things worse. Problem solving aims to reduce or eliminate this gap with some modification—perhaps a compromise position. Most often as problem solvers we try to improve the actual state of affairs by finding an answer to a difficulty, a solution to a problem.

The process of problem solving involves you in the following activities:

- *Define the problem and its severity* as precisely as possible. This entails:
  (a) assessing the current (actual) state of affairs, and
  (b) specifying the desired (ideal) state of affairs (goals) (see Flow Chart 1).
- *Assess the nature and magnitude of the problem.* This entails:
  (a) listing the "forces" *helping* the client move toward the desired goals;
  (b) listing the "forces" *hindering* the client from moving toward this goal.

In "force field analysis," as it is called, the problem is viewed as a balance between forces pushing in opposite directions.

Current State of Affairs
(Sally's/truancy)

(a) Get your client (it may be a family group) to use brainstorming to construct a list of helping (+) and hindering (−) forces.

Helping Forces	Hindering Forces
The family's behind her.	Perhaps we put too much pressure on her.
Sally wants to return to school.	She gets panicky when she tries.
The teacher is sympathetic.	Her schoolmates tease her when she appears.
	There is a bully in her classroom.

(b) Rank the forces in order of their significance in influencing the present situation. Rate the importance of forces according to the relative ease with which they can be resolved. Do not waste time on unrealistic ideas.

- *Formulate alternative strategies.* This entails working out the various means of moving the client (individual or group) from the actual to the desired state of affairs. Creative and divergent (unconventional) thinking, inventiveness, and critical ability are all helpful at this stage. You have to change the helping forces (strengthening them) and the hindering forces (reducing or eliminating them) in order to alter the current state of affairs.

- *Now decide on and implement the strategy.* This entails
  (a) selecting the alternatives that seem most likely to succeed
  (b) specifying the "know-how," methods, and other resources required to implement the chosen strategy.

- *Evaluate the outcome of applying the strategy.* This entails
  (a) defining what a successful outcome means—in terms of explicit criteria
  (b) specifying what the effects or consequences of the strategy were.

Group problem solving is generally more fruitful than individual effort, although there is no guarantee of this in particular instances.

In the problem-solving approach "small" is not so much "beautiful" as "manageable." Problems are not manageable when they are conceived in large global terms. (*"Everything* is going wrong"; "He will *never* change"; "There is *no hope*"; "I seem to have the world on my shoulders.")

You break through this rhetoric by trying to establish and obtain the relevant facts—attempting to "unpack" the complicated-looking dilemma. The more your clients can adopt a *mental set* that they *can* cope with a problem, the greater is the likelihood that with your help they will come up with a solution to it.

The feeling of being in control (and conversely, *not* helpless) is vital to the successful working through of difficult situations and is invaluable when you are involved in crisis interventions. You "relabel" the problem for the clients, defining what they once thought of as impenetrable as "manageable"—given thought and calm application of a series of interpersonal problem-solving strategies.

The Development of Problem-Solving Skills

Interpersonal problem-solving skills are learned from experiences beginning in the family and wherever the child interacts with others in situations that give rise to interpersonal difficulties. How well the developing child learns these skills is thought to reflect the extent to which the child's caregivers manifest these abilities themselves; also, the degree to which parents communicate in ways that encourage the exercise of such thinking in the child.

The emphasis is very much (but not exclusively) on *how* the person thinks; the goal in therapy or training is to generate a way of thinking, a way of using beliefs and values in making decisions at such times that problems arise.

George Spivack and his colleagues (Spivack, Platt, and Shure, 1976) have defined a number of differing interpersonal cognitive problem-solving skills. They suggest a series of skills rather than a single ability. The significance of each of these abilities in determining the degree of social adjustment is said to differ as a function of age.

The interpersonal cognitive problem-solving skills include:

• *Problem sensitivity*, which is the ability to be aware of problems that arise out of social interactions and a sensitivity to the kinds of social situations out of which interpersonal difficulties may arise. It also involves the ability to examine relationships with others in the here and now.

• *Alternative solution training*. A close parallel to this is "brainstorming." The key feature is the ability to generate a wide variety of potential solutions to the problem. Judgment about what is best is suspended, and the skill is to draw from a repertoire of ideas representing differing categories of solutions to a given problem.

• *Brainstorming* is the creative art of generating the greatest number of ideas in the shortest possible time. It is ideally suited to group participation as well as individual application.

There are some simple rules you apply to your chosen topic:

(a) Accept every idea that the topic or issue gives rise to *uncritically*.
(b) Aim for quantity of ideas rather than quality.
(c) At this stage do not initiate any discussion.
(d) List the ideas (e.g., write them on a blackboard or flip chart).
(e) Set a time limit.
(f) Code the ideas when the brainstorming session is over.

For example: (i) underline those that are not clear/understood; (ii) put a cross next to those that are impossible; (iii) put an asterisk against those that look useful and/or are worth exploring further.

Work out with the client the likely consequences of the better courses of action you have put forward. What is the utility of these consequences in resolving the problem as it has been formulated? For example, with regard to the proposed solutions put forward by Mrs. Hayes for managing Avril's tantrums;

(a) Punishment doesn't seem to work; in fact, it seems to make her more intractable.
(b) If I ignore her she'll probably follow me around, yelling more loudly. Like me she can be very stubborn.
(c) The idea of trying to reason with Avril sounds good, but I find it so hard to keep cool. And we may not be able to resolve things in the heart of the particular confrontation.
(d) My husband won't thank me for insisting that he back me up; he'll say "It's your problem."
(e) Putting Avril in time-out may work but it could also generate trouble, more sulking, and tantrums.
(f) Trying to find occasions to praise Avril should be a possibility; Avril can be reasonable when she's in a good mood—the trick is to catch her at the right time. She is vain and enjoys praise.

• *Means-ends thinking* reflects the ability to articulate the step-by-step means necessary to carry out the solution to a given interpersonal problem. The skill encompasses the ability to recognize obstacles, the social sequences deriving from these solutions, and a recognition that interpersonal problem solving takes time.

• *Consequential thinking* involves being aware of the consequences of social acts as they affect self and others and includes the ability to generate alternative consequences to potential problem solutions before acting.

• *Causal thinking* reflects the degree of appreciation of social and personal motivation and involves the realization that how one felt and acted may have been influenced by and, in turn, may have influenced how others felt and acted.

Any decision to change is likely to involve both benefits and "costs"; benefits for the client, for significant others, and for his or her network. There could also be costs to the client, to others and to his or her social setting. You might construct a list—with your client's help—of the likely benefits and costs of a particular planned change, in terms of these six categories.

Summary and Comment

Many, perhaps a majority of, clients who come for help to social workers and related disciplines, are deficient in life skills—most notably social and problem-solving skills. Fortunately there is a growing literature—theoretical and practical—for improving these skills. It is important not to think of them as a panacea for all social problems. It is also vital not to use them in cookbook fashion without a full and rigorous assessment.

PART IV

Empowerment of Families and Evaluation of Practice

The final two chapters bring us to our natural stopping point which is answering the questions each of us raises in our professional lives. First, Did our interventions in the lives of children and families help instead of harm; and did the help experienced have a lasting effect? Second, Are the practices and programs we deliver effective in attaining the problem solution hoped for; and were we efficient in their delivery?

Chapter 13 explains the importance of our intervention having lasting benefits for our clients in their daily lives as they continue to interact and cope in their families and communities. Long-term intervention and lengthy follow-up are giving way to demands for cost containment through briefer services as called for by managed care practices. The opportunity for ongoing support from community-based services is an extension of intervention beyond the agency. Healthy participation in social settings extends benefits of treatment into daily living. Focusing on client strengths is important to this extension. Having the capacity to be self-empowered and utilize their strengths, clients do take charge of their situations.

In addition to termination and whatever limited follow-up we provide, linking children and families with support networks is an important addition to our practice. Current mentoring practices are increasing as more and more evidence points to the benefit of mentoring in various life transitions. Examples of mentoring programs with youth are included in this chapter.

Chapter 14 calls for greater attention to ongoing evaluation of practices and programs as means to evaluating both processes and outcomes of our work. A comprehensive list of common purposes of evaluation is provided, not the least of which is the issue of responding to demands for greater professional accountability. Attention is brought to program evaluation and practice evaluation as important in identifying the costs and benefits of both our interventions and the many programs and agencies in the human services arena.

Finally, attention is given to ethical practices of evaluation. We are reminded that ethical, legal, and professional standards inform ethical practice and apply to service delivery, evaluation, and research methodology used in evaluating programs and practices.

Current literature is referenced to enable the reader to pursue the complex issues of research methodology and practice and program evaluation. The enormous challenge of mastering knowledge and techniques necessary for competent practice and its evaluation has implications for all of us.

CHAPTER 13

Beyond the Agency Door: Empowering and Mentoring Families

When children and families come to clinics or seek help from professionals such as social workers, psychologists, counselors, or medical professionals, such help comes in many forms. When help is in the form of counseling and therapeutic interventions, it will reflect theories of intervention and methods familiar to the therapist and believed to be helpful to the client. Other components contributing to the type of help offered reflect the agency's mission, usual service delivery practices to clients, range of professionals and ancillary service workers, and interprofessional linkages to the community. Regardless of the method of intervention, the overall goal of intervention generally is to help clients toward problem resolution and increased capacity for coping in their daily lives. Increased capacity for daily living and positive interpersonal relationships most often are desired outcomes of seeking and accepting help. As clients and their families take charge of their relationships and behaviors, increased self-confidence and self-esteem are likely to emerge as clients and families become empowered to multiply the benefits of the help received and to take control of their lives.

In the case of Avril Hayes, the family experienced great stress, loss of self-confidence, feelings of failure and guilt, and a sense of powerlessness to change the situation in the family. Her parents were seemingly powerless in the face of her demands. Avril's misbehavior, aggression, demands, and regressive behaviors escalated beyond her parents' control. Reinforced by the situation, Avril increased her aggressive and demanding behaviors. Through the helping process, Avril's parents were able to verbalize their need for her misbehaviors to stop and to identify new and appropriate behaviors. They were helped to learn to support desired behaviors and ignore or punish dysfunctional behaviors. Avril learned that her misbehaviors were no longer working for her as they were not being rewarded. Soon she learned to respond to her parents' rewards and punishments and to replace misbehaviors with new and positive behaviors for which she received attention.

This treatment example demonstrates the process and outcomes of treatment where dysfunctional behaviors in the family were directly related to interactions and communications. Avril's parents identified their own sense of personal failure and loss of self-esteem which they had experienced in their struggle to establish appropriate parent-child responses and behaviors. These negative feelings affected the family members in many areas of their lives and reduced their ability to feel rewarded in other interactions with friends, work and community activities, and social events. They had avoided taking Avril to social events because of their inability to manage her distracting and embarrassing demands. In situations like that of the Hayes family, family members often experience stress and frustration in various interpersonal relationships that cannot be contained within family boundaries but spill over into most areas of their lives. Behaviors, communication patterns, and feelings of failure and low self-worth extend to other realms of daily life, including systems such as schools, communities, work settings, and social organizations.

Not all families present with interpersonal and communication problems involved in a child's misbehavior. The range of problems and stresses that cause families to seek help from professionals is much broader. Domestic violence, marital dysfunctions, childhood disorders, adolescent adjustment, school failure, teen pregnancy, and medical crises are but a few of the problems that families present with. Many seek help with failure in their lives and with problems that are beyond the context of dysfunctional interpersonal relationships. These problems may be failure to have adequate resources for food, housing, clothing, education, and other necessities for living in today's society. Other problems relate to serious illnesses, medical crises, job failures, and unemployment. In Chapter 8, the mobilization of resources is discussed as an important intervention and can bring a supportive network together to help with various life crises. Many kinds of support are necessary as social workers, counselors, and other helping professionals join clients in their voyage to find solutions to problems and to gain satisfaction in their daily lives.

Helping Beyond the Agency Door

Intervening in the lives of clients is hard work! Individual helping, family therapy, and group problem solving all require specialized knowledge and skill to assess, treat, evaluate, and productively join clients in their voyage to problem solution.

How often is it that the social worker, counselor, psychologist, or health care professional asks the soul-searching questions, Did I help enough? Is my client going to be able to maintain progress? How realistic is long-term follow-up?

Fewer follow-up services are carried out by primary providers, particularly as managed care changes practices in services to children and families. Service provision now reflects briefer treatment, cost containment, and increased use of combined, "wrap-around," and triage services involving multidisciplinary teams and a variety of community-based services (Corcoran and Vandiver, 1996; Strom-Gottfried, 1997). Interventions that will have lasting impact for children and families are essential components of successful practice.

Briefer treatment and utilization of community-based support services are quickly becoming the model of practice for services to clients regardless of whether it is outpatient treatment such as that for the Hayes family or inpatient treatment for psychiatric disorders. Currently, managed care and cost containment are realities for the arena of health and human services across the range of emotional, psychological, and physical needs of children and families of all ages (Corcoran and Vandiver, 1996; Greene, 1992). Present practices and cost-containment efforts of managed care in health and human services arenas reduce the length of care and number of sessions for most types of service, including outpatient and inpatient treatment. Strom-Gottfried (1997) points out that consequences of briefer services and stronger outcome measures require that professionals build on client strengths and utilize social support and natural helping systems to support clients in their communities and homes.

Yes, many professionals would like to think that intervention toward problem resolution has strong and lasting effects that enhance resiliency of clients on their trajectory toward healthier and happier lives in a successful and self-directed manner. However, "practice wisdom," along with outcome studies and follow-up measures of long-term benefits from service, tells us that those who receive supportive or follow-up services after a period of intense care are more likely to sustain their progress or to prevent more serious or additional dysfunction (Mallon, 1998; Bloom, Fischer, and Orme, 1995; Jankowski, Videka-Sherman, and Laquidara-Dickinson, 1996). Community services and briefer services are increasingly important in service delivery involving placement of children in foster and adoptive homes or work with families to prevent delinquency or economic dependency.

Evidence of the importance of supportive networks and services in the lives of children and families can be found in nearly every model of care. For example, youth in out-of-home care have a high likelihood of leaving care for independent living, having missed the opportunity to learn life skills in a family environment. A study of 46 youths discharged from out-of-home care to independent living from Green Chimneys Children's Services in New York City reports the significance of follow-up life skills and support services for the youth (Mallon, 1998). Important supports identified by the youth included family, relatives, friends, teachers, employers, agencies, and churches. Sixty-seven percent reported maintaining contact with staff members of the agency after discharge. Mallon (1998) reports that linking youth with each other and with adult mentors are important measures in providing support for successful independence of these youth.

Another example that illustrates the importance of social support networks was demonstrated by clients who were participants in post–legal adoption counseling. These client families were adoptive families who were served by the Post Legal Adoption Services Project of Lucas County Children Services in Ohio, a project funded by the Department of Health and

Human Services (Harper and Loadman, 1992a). These adoptive children and parents, mostly families with children in early adolescence, were threatened with failed adoptions and were experiencing major stress and conflict in their families. Not unlike about 10% of families who adopt children in the United States and eventually experience failed adoptions (Barth and Berry, 1988), these families were on the edge of returning their children to the custody of the public agency. Throughout an eight-week period, parents and children from 40 adoptive families participated in post–legal adoptive family treatment groups of eight to ten members each. There they learned about and explored avenues for coping with problems which adoptive families sometimes experience. Parents and children gained skills in communication, explored expectations, gained self-esteem, and met other adoptive families through the group experience. Much empowered by their treatment experience and connected to a new network of adoptive families, these families set about developing community-based support groups for themselves and other adoptive families. Through this continuing social support network they hoped to gain confidence and help other families prevent adoption dissolution. For some, these support groups would complement the individual counseling they planned for themselves and their adoptive child. It is noteworthy that only one of the families served by the program terminated their adoption at the end of one year after the post–legal adoption treatment group intervention (Harper and Loadman, 1992b).

Examples of support systems and programs beyond the agency abound as people take charge of their lives and develop strength to become happier and more productive. In the case of Avril Hayes, she and her family would benefit greatly from support networks in their neighborhood and community. Such network linkage would provide them the opportunity to build upon their personal and family strengths and on the progress they made in therapy by ongoing relationships with other families with similar challenges. Such a group could help the family maintain its own progress and build upon strengths gained from improved family interactions, including not only sustaining the new management techniques for Avril's behavioral problems but anticipating changing behaviors and demands to be expected as she progresses to new ages and stages in her development.

As social workers, counselors, psychologists, and health care professionals we are confronted by ever increasing pressures for brief services, short-term stays, and community-based treatments. We see our clients return to their homes and communities, even after only one visit for assistance of some sort or after treatment such as that received by the Hayes family. People in search of assistance or treatment represent a plethora of strengths, needs, relationships, families, groups, and communities. It becomes our job to encourage, support empowerment, and assess to what extent our support is necessary to the situation at hand. It is at this juncture of assessment and decision making that referrals and linkages we make to support networks can extend our intervention further into the homes and communities of those we serve.

In many ways, the opportunity for ongoing support from community-based services is an extension of intervention beyond the agency. More affordable and consistent with the expectation of client independence, participation in natural and social support networks empowers members and allows children and families to utilize clinic-based treatment much less. It is the independence and participation in social settings that extend the benefits of treatment well beyond the agency door and into the daily lives of families.

Empowerment: The Glue That Can Hold!

Client empowerment is a concept and practice with roots in the charity and settlement house movements of the late 1800s, when poor, immigrant, and illiterate populations were provided aid and taught necessary language skills, placed in jobs, and included in the social and political ethos of the era. As the 1900s moved forward, social workers supported many dissolute and poor families and children through two world wars, the Great Depression, and the New Deal where public responsibility for private troubles, including retirement or disability, became legislated in the Social Security Act (Simon, 1998). During this period the psychological component of individuals increasingly gained attention. Freudian doctrine addressed pychological development and defense mechanisms of individuals. As concern for emotional and psychological well-being grew, existential thought evolved during postwar chaos. Not unlike Freudian doctrine, existentialists placed the locus for well-being in the individual but with a view toward having strength to overcome personal devastation caused by war and brutality and to search for and find meaning in life (Simon, 1998). In the last half of the 1900s, social work has been a primary force advocating for political action for social changes such as those represented by the civil rights and the women's movements. During this period, social work moved into change processes calling for client participation and social and political action, including client interests and rights in the spirit of equality and social justice (Simon, 1998; Kopp, 1989).

The history and evolution of empowerment reflect the social and political challenges of social work as a growing profession. From a theoretical perspective, empowerment entailed supporting capacities of oppressed and disenfranchised populations and clients based on identifiable strengths, whether political or personal. Based on Hodges, Burwell, and Ortega's (1998) summation of the literature, empowerment is a process that enhances self-image and self-efficacy, involves clients in the change process, facilitates access to needed resources and problem solutions, and enables assertive and proactive behaviors (Conger and Kanungo, 1988; Deming, 1984; Dunst, Trivette, and Deal, 1988). Empowering clients is a long-standing social work practice and comes from a strengths perspective wherein individual, social, and political power, or potentials for such power, within the client are built upon by the social worker. Working to increase clients' ability to identify and utilize their own personal, social, or political strength in their pursuit for happiness, self-esteem, and physical and emotional health continues the tradition of empowerment in current social work practice.

Building on personal and political strengths of clients and client groups is useful in gaining access and bringing about change. Four dimensions of practice for empowerment are identified by Parsons, Gutierrez, and Cox (1998). These dimensions call for client-professional partnering in the intervention process:

Dimension One targets the individual in need of help, the need for both a resource and interpersonal help. At this level, the worker and client identify and assess perceptions that contribute to feelings of powerlessness.

Dimension Two calls for educating and building skills to form networks and solve problems related to coping and inadequate life skills. Together the worker and client identify meaningful information useful in the particular life circumstance in the problem configuration.

Dimension Three identifies gaps and strains in the environment that impact personal problems. For example, together the worker and client identify deficits and gaps such as lack of jobs or absence of support systems, or the lack of information and actions needed to access opportunities or resources. Assistance with job preparation, interviewing, placement, and skills in negotiating the work setting may occur.

Dimension Four opens avenues for involvement in social and political issues and in group activity for change. Participation in action groups targeting issues of interest to others, including group action for change, can become an avenue for client involvement.

Worker-client partnership or teaming in these dimensions of intervention shape the process for empowerment. Targeting mostly resource acquisition and socially and politically oppressive issues and concerns, the process serves as a bridge across the chasm of powerlessness. It is important to note that this same process serves to inform the worker-client partnership for building bridges beyond feelings of helplessness or powerlessness such as those caused by a personal sense of failure or low self-esteem as a result of poor interpersonal relationships, family or marital problems, or other emotional or psychological problems. Empowerment is not only a process for bringing political and social change or developing resources; it is equally powerful for individuals, groups, and families in their daily lives and interpersonal exchanges.

Identifying and Using Client Strengths

It is indeed a rare occasion in the work of a social worker or counselor when a client stops by an office or agency to report what a great day it is! Instead, clients seek help with problems, report progress with problems, and hope that the helping process will keep problems away or find solutions that work. As a result, the function of helping relationships can become that of solving problems to the exclusion of defining client strengths. Focusing on client strengths is a shift from the traditional approaches of deficits and disease that have characterized much of social work practice (Cowger, 1997). Identifying strengths and supporting client capacities for growth and change are essential to the empowerment process. Empowerment in clinical practice is an internal process which is fueled by identification of strengths, encouraged through support from others, and fostered by growing self-esteem through experiencing success in coping with daily living.

Recognizing the strong capacities of people to access and utilize personal and community support systems and to grow in personal and social ways validates their resilience and strength. Some of these people could be (have been) our clients! Perhaps those who were would have been clients "differently" if our assessment had been focused to find their strengths, identify their capacities for growth and change, and record their behaviors as those of social creatures capable of contributing to their communities and discriminating their "fit" into our model of respect for humanity and creativity that people possess. Guided by Saleeby's (1997) "strengths perspective," we would approach our clients as "cups half full" and not as "cups half empty"! We would avoid diagnosing and assessing their deficits and failures as such, even as they define them. Having the capacity to become empowered, clients do take charge of their situations and become self-directed; it is the very life to be lived at home, at work, and in the community that is the desired outcome of intervention. In no way is it intended to discount the pain and suffering experienced by families such as Avril's, nor to underestimate the need for care of those experiencing life crises or mental and emotional mental illness seemingly powerful enough to immobilize and incapacitate. Nevertheless, the reality is that clients and their families seek help so that they may live their lives independently and be self-directed in all realms of being.

Strengths Perspective. Viewed as an approach or perspective rather than a theory, the strengths perspective is a way of viewing problem solutions which recognize the capacities of people to grow and change. According to Saleeby (1997), "Practicing from a strengths orientation means this—*everything* you do as a social worker will be predicated, in some way, on helping to discover and embellish, explore and exploit clients' strengths and resources in the service of assisting them to achieve their goals, realize their dreams, and shed the irons of their own inhibitions and misgivings" (p. 3). In the client-worker partnership for growth and change, the client becomes the expert about her/his life, hopes, and alternatives. For example, who knows better than a welfare mother of three children how to feed, clothe, shelter, and educate children while managing transportation and health care with a grossly inadequate income? She is also best able to identify how she manages (strengths) and what alternatives to inefficiencies in service systems are for her (change). She can explain her hopes for her children and some means for achieving them.

Consistent with the strengths perspective, families and children are vibrant and resourceful, capable of action and direction in the helping process. Upper limits of client capabilities and potential achievement are unknown to workers who can join clients in exploring and energizing their own motivation and potential for growth (Saleeby, 1997). Living in community-based family and social system networks, the client family becomes a consumer of services, integral in the helping process, and instrumental in effective community and network collaboration.

Children and families grow and change in both social and personal domains of their lives in response to a renewed sense of power that comes from exercising self-direction. Separating or trying to separately treat social and personal domains of clients' lives is not consistent with the strengths perspective, as these domains are interdependent and interactive. Growth and energy in one domain positively impacts the other (Cowger, 1997). Development in both personal and social domains of the Hayes family, discussed in Chapter 8, reports the progress experienced by Mrs. Hayes as her depression lifted and she gained confidence in her parenting role. Both she and Avril enjoyed social contacts with other families and reported looking forward to continued involvement with others outside the family. The case of the Hayes family is one example of increased life-skills development which builds upon their strengths and capacities, enabling them to gain new understanding of improved communications, discipline, rewards, and feelings of love and care for each other. Long-term follow-up in this case found that the Hayes family had been able to sustain progress in personal and social domains of their lives a year after treatment ended.

For helping professionals, meeting demands for cost containment requires brief treatment and reliance on community-based networks and teams found in various helping systems. We must make creative and innovative efforts to develop services for clients who desire or need ongoing support such as that available from paraprofessionals, role models, and mentors in their homes and communities.

Mentors: Extending Helping and Building on Strengths

Relatively new to helping professions like social work, counseling, and psychology, mentors are becoming a useful extension of helping professionals. Extension of support within familiar home and community contexts is an important follow-up for many clients, including those who benefit from more intensive interventions such as that described in the case of the Hayes family. Other types of client situations in need of some level of follow-up include those involving potential dangers of family violence, child abuse, school failure, teen pregnancy, and increasing frailty of elderly or disabled clients. Many children and families are now benefiting from mentors, either natural mentors in their social networks and communities or mentors made available through various community-based service programs.

Mentoring is not a phenomenon of the the recent past. Needing to learn wisdom and sensitivity, Telemachus was assigned a teacher named Mentor in *The Odyssey*. Mentor was old, experienced, ethical, wise, trusted, and compassionate. Mentor was more than a teacher of facts as he guided Telemachus in preparation to rule the kingdom. Mentor carried out his mission in preparing his protégé for roles involving power and leadership. Anderson and Shannon (1995) conclude from their analyses of Mentor and Telemachus that mentoring is an intentional and insightful effort to nurture, protect, support, and serve as a role model.

Mentoring, relatively new as an extension of professions like social work and counseling, has been a long-standing practice in fields such as business and education. The practice of setting examples, providing senior role models for junior managers and junior partners, has long been a practice in business, law, banking, organizational management, and corporate settings. Those in such partnerships are often protected, promoted, and in turn will mentor their partners and successors. It is noted that early models of corporate power and control have given way to practices of partnering, supporting, and enabling so that newcomers to professions and organizations can learn organizational practices (Bell, 1996). Serving as a path to power in corporate America, mentoring has a history of being a traditional male practice in which one who is older, more experienced, and powerful can create a path for successful growth and promotion of another. Mentoring involves a relationship and requires eventual separatism in which the mentee is free to go on, to exercise individual power and direction, and to surpass the mentor (Jeruchim and Shapiro, 1992).

Much the same as business and management, the field of education has long had mentors. Teacher education literature is rich with accounts of mentoring, particularly in areas of internships for student teachers. A major role for supervising teachers is to mentor student teachers in classroom teaching and to serve as experts to guide the student teacher in classroom teaching and student/teacher relationships (Campbell and Horbury, 1994; Aspinwall, Garrett, and Owen-Jackson, 1994). Learning opportunities occur for both student and mentor in a relationship that will not likely extend beyond the teaching internship.

Feminist literature calls for mentoring and credits mentoring as an important ingredient in many women's successes and achievements. Moving beyond severe oppression and eventual discrimination in the workplace, women and racial minorities have openly and actively developed networks and mentors for purposes such as employment, promotion, achievement, success, and gaining equal access. Different mentors may be helpful at different ages and stages according to Jeruchim and Shapiro (1992). Women enter careers at various times in their lives, often having reared children and sometimes entering the workforce as single parents. In her case, a middle-aged woman with such experiences would have mentoring needs very different from a twenty-year-old entering her first job. Perhaps better than men, women relate to and benefit from mentors of either gender. Women and minorities continue to need mentoring to enter the internal working relationships of organizations which are often male dominated and relatively closed. Many professional women and their mentors continue to chip away at the glass ceiling, the barricade between women and promotion within many organizations. At a different level, women who are clients experience similar exclusion from access to better jobs, resources, acceptance, and respect. Although different in content and context, mentoring is a process that is useful and appropriate for any woman.

Movements to find role models and mentors reflect the importance of mentoring as a step toward becoming whatever it is that an individual seeks to be (Jeruchim and Shapiro, 1992). Beginning a search for senior guidance is a form of self-empowerment that is often threatening and can cause much self-doubt. For client families, the search for self-empowerment without direction from the social worker or counselor may be prohibitively overwhelming, even if the need is felt.

Mentoring practices are on the rise in professions like social work, counseling, psychology, and allied health sciences professions. Numerous accounts of successful mentoring programs can be found in the literature. The benefit of mentoring as a means for curricular development and promoting understanding of cross-cultural knowledge, beliefs, and practices is reported by Mowry (1994), a social work educator who served as a mentor to relocated Hmong students.

Mentoring is a common practice in service delivery to youth. One study of twenty teen mothers with mentors assigned to them remained in school, held part-time jobs, and credited their mentors with influencing them to continue their education, evaluate options, and build self-esteem. Nearly half of the group maintained contact with their mentors after completing high school (Zippay, 1995). In another population of youth, mentoring is an important service for adolescents who move from foster care to independent living. According to Mech, Pryde, and Rycraft (1995), among programs designed to mentor youth, five model programs are as follows:

- Transitional Life Skills: Matching adults with adolescents to develop life skills and independent living.
- Cultural Empowerment: Same race/ethnicity mentors and gay/lesbian mentors
- Corporate/Business Mentors: Mentoring targets job preparedness and placement
- Mentors for Young Parents: Mentors assist young mothers and serve a preventive function
- Mentor Homes: Adult mentor guides four to six youths and serves as a group-home parent or manager

These mentoring models serve an important transitional function in the lives of adolescents, some of whom likely experienced multiple foster care arrangements. Although believed to be important preventive programs, little evaluation is available (Mech, Pryde, and Rycraft, 1995).

Client families affected by welfare reform and related welfare-to-work requirements are a population often served by multiple providers and sometimes for multiproblem situations. For some, strengths assessments and empowerment toward self-sufficiency likely are replaced by problem assessment and continuing poverty and despair. The Family Mentoring Program, operated by community action agencies in West Virginia, provides a training curriculum targeting paraprofessionals to serve as mentors to families affected by welfare-to-work requirements. Curricular areas include self-awareness, basic needs awareness, basic interviewing, and problem solving premised on respect, change, and action for independent living (Randall and Newfield, 1997). Once trained, family mentors work with families and children in their homes and communities and support them in their efforts to assess employable skills, search for employment, and reduce barriers such as child care and transportation problems to allow for successful return to the job market.

Summary and Comment

Given the scope of problems children and families seek help with, the importance of extending helping processes beyond the clinic door has never been more important than it is in today's world. The process of identifying strengths and increasing daily living skills builds personal and social capacities necessary for successful participation in increasingly complex demands experienced at all levels of living, particularly in view of the sophisticated information and technology systems spanning global communities and economies that impact personal and social domains of all our lives. Extending support and services into clients' homes and communities can be accomplished through the process models of empowerment and strengths perspective and through utilization of various community-based paraprofessionals and natural helpers in various mentoring arrangements.

CHAPTER 14

Evaluation: An Integral Component of Practice Processes and Outcomes

This book, written from the perspective of intervention with children and families in direct practice settings, brings us to the natural juncture of considering the value or quality of our practice. The nature of professional commitment causes practitioners to value treatment outcomes that are consistent with treatment plan goals and expectations. Questions like "Did intervention make a difference?" are asked by social workers and other helping professionals and by the clients themselves. Clients, not unlike practitioners, want their effort at problem solution to produce positive results toward solving the problem.

Intuitively, our own internal processes inform us a bit about benefits our clients gain in their healing processes through services we provide, whether these services are counseling, behavioral intervention such as that provided to the Hayes family, or resource provision through referrals to access food, housing, health care, or other supports. However positive our intuitive summation of our work and services, it does not provide internally consistent, reliable, or valid measurement of practice outcomes. Our intuitive assessment of our practice cannot be systematically communicated to others or used as justification for continued service or program support for future funding and development.

Over the past three decades, increasing demands have been placed on the helping professions for greater accountability and evaluation of efficient and effective service delivery. Historically, social workers, counselors, psychologists, and other helping professionals have not systematically conducted or communicated evaluation of their treatment outcomes. Creating a broad information deficit of the value of services delivered, this gap in outcome information resulted in human services professions being charged with accountability failures. This accountability gap is closing as practice and program evaluations are being done more consistently in response to changing service delivery systems. Careful and consistent attention to measuring and evaluating service delivery practices and programs is occurring in response to managed care and cost containment practices in health and human services in the current era (Corcoran and Vandiver, 1996).

Each era brings different political and economic philosophies as well as national and international catastrophes which affect human well-being. Changing philosophies and related programs reflect the social trends of the period in which they occur. Rossi and Freeman (1993) point out that shifts in political, social, and economic trends have influenced and continue to influence support for social service programs and their evaluation. For example, in the 1970s poverty movements and community mental health movements produced new demands for evaluation. In many instances, evaluative reports of costs and benefits of services and programs were unavailable. In response to demands for new services and greater service availability at the end of the 1970s, justification of funding for new and existing programs called for cost-benefit analyses of services delivered by human and social service agencies. Greater public expenditures were followed by a demand for greater accountability on the part of those using the funds.

In response to continuing pressure for performance evaluation and for program planning and service delivery, evaluation of human services and professional practices increased both locally and nationally. Social and political changes of the 1970s and 1980s produced new standards for consumer awareness and participation and for equal access to services for broader populations, including those represented in the civil rights, gay rights, women's, and other movements. As a result of broader awareness of human need, new services emerged in response to changing societal concerns.

Continuing the trends of the previous decade, the 1990s is an era of increased funding and growth of programs but with renewed emphasis on self-sufficiency and privatization of services. Many new service areas have developed, some of which are associated with problems such as homelessness, deinstitutionalization, AIDS, and increased violence in families and schools. Regardless of the type of service or the client system receiving the service, evaluation of our work is essential to determine its effectiveness and efficiency. Increasing requirements of accountability for effective and efficient service delivery can only be met through ongoing evaluation of practice and program outcomes that can be reported and disseminated.

Why Evaluate?

Overall, it is important to gain an estimate of the effectiveness and efficiency of our interventions in direct practice as well as an evaluation of programs which we have helped to shape and implement. The scope of this book does not include comprehensive presentation of strategies for evaluation or research methodology. However, a review of selected literature suggests much common ground in the practice of evaluation of services and service delivery systems (Rossi and Freeman, 1993; Royse, 1995; Tripodi, 1987; Reamer, 1998; Posavac and Carey, 1985; Sheafor, Horejsi, and Horejsi, 1994; Locke, Garrison, and Winship, 1998; Gershenson, 1995; Corcoran and Gingerich, 1994; Rossi, 1997). Many of these common purposes of evaluation are included in Figure 11.

Constraints in Evaluating Programs and Practices

Despite the many common and useful purposes associated with evaluating direct services which we deliver and the many programs that support the delivery of services, there are constraints that hamper conducting rigorous and ongoing evaluation of our work. One particular constraint is the availability of adequate funding to support the time and effort of expert personnel in designing and implementing ongoing evaluation. Related to organizational support, funding must not only be available, but the commitment of the organization is necessary in order to allocate resources and value the effort and results. Once outcome measurements are established and data are collected and analyzed, the findings provide a view of benefits and costs associated with the level and quality of services

Figure 11.   Common purposes of evaluation.

- Nature and scope of agency services, programs, and practices are defined.
- Nature and purpose of intervention(s) are defined.
- Populations intended to receive service and those receiving service are identified.
- Efficiency of effort and funding invested in programs and services is determined.
- Effectiveness of practices and programs is determined by service outcome measurements.
- Ethical practices including confidentiality and involvement of human subjects are reported.
- Planning for future service development and delivery is enhanced.
- Measurement of efforts and outcomes satisfies various accreditation standards.
- Measurement of efforts and outcomes informs administration and staffing patterns.
- Value of help received is determined.
- Rates of success and effort can be compared with previous and future periods.
- Measurement barometer for agency and practice performance over time is established.
- Program and practice continuation or change are informed.
- Outcome data useful for new and continued funding justification is provided.
- Valid and reliable performance measurement is produced.
- Professional accountability is established.
- Knowledge base of human services professionals is enhanced.
- Progression of ongoing measures of intervention and program delivery is identified.

---

delivered. These findings may support service and program continuation or may suggest change or termination of certain aspects of practices and services. It is the translation from evaluation to policy that can determine future directions for practices, programs, and even entire organizations.

In the event that available funding does not support systematic and ongoing evaluation, evaluation may be piecemeal and inconclusive. In some instances, evaluation may not occur. Failure to conduct ongoing evaluation produces major gaps in information and prevents comparison of data over time. Further, the lack of performance information may impede future funding efforts and result in continued funding shortfalls or program termination.

Available expertise among agency personnel is a second area of considerable concern. Information, knowledge, and technical skills are essential in conducting practice and program evaluation. Training existing personnel, employing evaluators, and utilizing external consultants are useful corrective actions often undertaken by organizations to increase skills in research and capacities for evaluation.

Third, changing practices, policies, and social concerns require constant attention to identified goals and outcomes to be measured. These demands not only place great expectations on program development and change, but require administrators, practitioners, and evaluators to continually upgrade knowledge and skills.

A fourth area of constraint is the area involving political issues and vested interests of all involved—practitioners, administrators, public, clients, and evaluators. Rossi and Freeman (1993) identify the challenge of clarifying the perspective from which evaluation is undertaken, particularly by those who have particular interests in outcome information. Evaluation has far-reaching professional and political implications, some of which may be powerful enough to affect the direction of social policies and human services delivered.

Program and Practice Evaluation

Program Evaluation

"Evaluation research is the systematic application of social research procedures for assessing the conceptualization, design, implementation, and utility of social intervention programs" (Rossi and Freeman, 1993, p. 5). According to Sheafor, Horejsi, and Horejsi (1994), the purpose of program evaluation is to assess the effectiveness and efficiency of a total program intended for serving a large number of people or perhaps even a whole community. Program evaluation involves applied research rather than research for the purpose of theory development or hypothesis testing. In this context applied research involves research design especially tailored to the program being evaluated. Reamer (1998) identifies four major issues which impact program evaluation design.

First, it is important that the "who" and "why" of evaluating a particular program are taken into consideration. Programs may be funded contingent on satisfactory program evaluation plans, with funders being interested as much or more in appropriate use of funds than in the quality of services so long as the program was implemented as agreed upon. Other situations of program evaluation may be more quality oriented and may call for projections about the program's potential long-range impact on populations served, including national trend comparisons. In other situations, program evaluation may be for organizational purposes ranging from simple accounting of instances of services rendered to various quantitative and qualitative studies which are designed to measure quality of services delivered. Given the breadth of human services delivered, there are nearly as many program evaluation designs as there are programs.

For example, the increasing use of mentoring programs is resulting in new and sometimes quite extensive evaluation designs. One such evaluative design measures the impact of mentoring youth who lack close adult attention in a Big Brothers/Big Sisters program (Grossman and Tierney, 1998). This evaluative model, based on a control group and a study group, reports a number of positive behavioral changes for youth who were paired with an adult mentor. This eigtheen-month comprehensive study included extensive data collection from 1,107 youth (97.3%) using baseline data, follow-up questionnaires, and interviews with 84.3% or 959 youths who were served. This effort evaluated quality of services, long-term outcomes, and costs and benefits of the program and had implications for program change and continuation.

A second important issue in program evaluation is that of clearly defining the scope and purpose of the evaluation itself so that program evaluation goals can be achieved. Just as programs have goals, so does program evaluation. Questions to be answered in identifying these goals include clarifying what the evaluation will be used for, for instance, justifying costs and benefits of program continuation or informing internal activities. Reamer (1998) emphasizes the importance of identifying goals for program evaluation and notes the potential impact of evaluation on staffing and workload patterns within agencies as well as on various segments of community and agency constituencies. Clarity about the goals of program evaluation are important in navigating the political and funding currents surrounding programs and human services agencies. Finally, clear program evaluation goals inform evaluators of their role and authority. Regardless of whether evaluators are internal or external to the agency, their project of evaluation takes on a structure and direction of its own once it gets underway. Evaluation demands time, energy, knowledge, and attention not only to goal achievement but to good practices in research and evaluation.

Third, Reamer (1998) identifies the issue of the intended use of information from program evaluation as being very important in developing the plan for evaluation. Whether the purpose of evaluation is for the agency's internal use or more for external purposes will determine what information is needed. Sometimes the information needed for internal assessment of service quality and agency expertise available or needed may not be the kind of information best shared broadly. Practicality, ethical practice, and objective measurement of performance outcomes enter into practices for evaluating direct practices and programs. Considering the use of evaluation information and potential audiences who will receive the information is important in developing goals for evaluation from the outset of both program planning and evaluative design.

The fourth issue identified by Reamer (1998) relates to the competence and capacity of evaluators to apply research methodology and analyses called for in implementing and completing program evaluation as designed. Evaluators may be internal or external to the organization. Those internal to the organization must have clarity about the purpose, implications, and expected use of their effort. Internal evaluators can be cost effective and can accomplish sound and useful program evaluation. Evaluation that is internally valued and incorporated as part of practice and program development can be an important learning experience for agency personnel. It is noted that funding organizations often require external evaluators. External evaluators are sometimes thought to bring greater objectivity to evaluation and may bring expertise not available internally. A common practice is to bring together both internal and external evaluators and to maximize the strengths of both in a team effort. Again, whatever the approach an agency takes, careful planning must occur at the outset so that goals for evaluation are articulated and become a natural extension of program implementation and service delivery.

Practice Evaluation

Evaluating our practice is necessary to gaining an understanding of the effectiveness of direct intervention with individuals, families, groups, and communities. Many practitioners take great pride in their competence and appraisal of their work. Self-introspection and self-assessment are important in our streams of thought and self-images as practitioners. This self-assessment and reflection are both painful and joyful in the journey of our professional careers and accomplishments. Visualizing a practice collage of clients' faces, sorrows, joys, growth, and resistance to change holds images of great accomplishments along with images of great need, both met and unmet, and even some images of failed interventions. Regardless of the pain or reward associated with self-assessment of professional practice, it does not replace internally consistent and methodologically sound evaluation of professional practices and direct services delivery.

The process of intervening in the lives of clients and client systems begins with encountering clients in the midst of their need for help and problem solution. Initially assessing the problem to be addressed, engaging clients in the plan for intervention, and identifying desired results is a process of learning and transitioning toward successful problem resolution and termination of intervention. Evaluating processes and products of intervention are important components in measuring effective and efficient service delivery in direct practice (Locke, Garrison, and Winship, 1998).

Evaluation of direct practice educates and informs practitioners and clients of both processes and outcomes of interventions or practice encounters. Intervening in the lives of clients and client systems calls for entering into a process that has both fluidity and vision for desired outcomes as lives change daily and hoped-for realities become informed. Gaining understanding of the importance of processes as well as outcomes is central to building knowledge and capacities for practice. Locke, Garrison, and Winship (1998) identify reasons which call for evaluation of practices and processes along the route to problem solution.

First, identifying and evaluating changes as the process of intervention unfolds determines accomplishments and barriers in the process of reaching intended problem solutions. For example, in the process of learning about parenting and behavioral management, Mrs. Hayes became aware of her feelings of anger and failure as a parent and was able to change her self-doubts in her mothering role and to gain new confidence and satisfaction as a parent when Avril's behavior began to change. For the Hayes family, the months of the treatment process involved milestones marking progress such as learning to give greater rewards for Avril's positive behaviors. They learned to evaluate eventual and lasting reduction of seriously distracting and aggressive behaviors. Evaluating changes in clients' behaviors and lives calls for repeated measures to understand and identify markers of progress. Establishing baseline measures of the problem at the outset of intervention and collecting multiple measures throughout the intervention process informs both practitioner and client(s) of progress and changes that occur (Bloom, Fischer, and Orme, 1995).

A second reason for identifying and monitoring even small steps toward accomplishing desirable changes is to inform the practitioner and clients of the direction that is occurring. Identifying markers of change which are expected and anticipated to occur in the process toward problem solution are supportive and empowering extensions of the intervention. Identifying instances of unexpected or troubling changes is equally important and helpful for all involved. Information and knowledge gained in the process of intervention may call for redirecting intervention and involving the client in renegotiating the intervention contract and redefining desired outcomes. New understanding of changes which occur has an educational function for building capacities for future problem solving.

A third reason for evaluating practice is that practitioners gain new understanding of the impact of their intervention and gain competencies for future intervention. Ongoing practice evaluation provides information about "how well we are doing" as practitioners.

Another reason for evaluating practice identified by Parsons (1998) is that practice evaluation provides a means of measuring progress in the context of clients' lives and not just from stark outcomes called for by theoretical perspectives. Linking practice evaluation to identifying client progress and capacities for growth brings a strengths perspective to the interface of practice and evaluation. Involving clients in the design, process, and evaluation of their experience in the practice encounter is empowering. To the extent possible, increasing client participation throughout the process of intervention and its outcome gives voice to clients in their voyage toward problem solution.

Professional Responsibility for the Practice of Evaluation

It is not within the scope of this chapter to provide a comprehensive overview of the extensive methodologies and techniques available for evaluating human services programs and practices. As mentioned previously, practice evaluation is as varied and unique as is the scope of human services programs and practices. A variety of techniques commonly used in evaluating practice are cited and briefly critiqued by Locke, Garrison, and Winship (1998) and include Goal Attainment Scale, Single-subject design, measurement scales for client system outcomes, case study analysis, reflective questioning, journaling, and client system satisfaction surveys. Numerous instruments and scales are available for measuring particular behaviors and functioning. Royse (1995) discusses ways to find, evaluate, and select scales and measures from existing resources. He provides comprehensive reviews of selected scales particularly designed to measure community living skills, empowerment, prosocial tendencies of children, attitudes toward long-term care, maternal characteristics, helping behaviors, role strains, and job satisfaction.

Numerous reports of practice evaluation are found throughout professional journals. One example of practice evaluation of treatment of depressed women reports a single-subject design incorporating standardized instruments in process and outcome measurement of intervention with nine clients. The Beck Depression Inventory was administered weekly and results indicating severity of depression were recorded and charted. Pre- and post-test measures of the women's adjustment were gathered by administering the Social Adjustment Scale. Both instruments were administered at the end of a six-month period after treatment ended. This evaluation model measures the impact of cognitive behavioral and interpersonal psychotherapies utilized and provides multiple measures of depression throughout the process of intervention. Post-test measures provide data for outcomes achieved and sustained for each of the women and provides overall indicators of the success of the intervention. Professional accountability for practice and evaluation of practice is met in this interesting report of intervention (Jensen, 1994).

There are few shortcuts to conducting valid and reliable evaluation of professional practice. Summaries of research and evaluation methods such as those cited educate and inform practitioners who are faced with evaluating their practice performances. Clearly, it is the responsibility of the practitioner to become familiar with research methodology literature on quantitative and qualitative approaches to evaluative design and with ethical practices in evaluating both programs and direct practices.

Ethical Practice

Competent evaluation of programs and direct practice with clients is a practice in its own right and calls for integrating practice and research knowledge and skills into everyday work. Just as professional ethics apply to program delivery and direct practice with clients, so do they apply to program and practice evaluation. At a minimum, ethically sound evaluation of pro-

grams and practices calls for informed consent, willing participation, and explanation of rights. Clients are not to be harmed
in the process of evaluation or in other situations including
control and experimental treatment groups. Determining practice effectiveness and efficiency, building knowledge, and planning programs and services delivery based on evaluation of
practice are not to be accomplished at any personal, social, or
other cost to clients involved. The concern of withholding or
delaying services for some in order to determine the impact
of services on others raises questions of potential harm in
instances where treatment or service is delayed or not provided. Debates about the benefits and harms encountered in
such practice are numerous and include concerns of whether
receiving delayed services will be harmful and even whether
the service or treatment in question is known to be helpful
(Williams, Unrau, and Grinnell, 1998).

"Being ethical is a matter of choosing morally 'right' actions,
being a professional who works within professional standards
is being a competent practitioner who (on current definitions)
uses scientifically verified generalizations to guide practice"
(Chambers, Wedel, and Rodwell, 1992). Ethical, legal, and professional standards inform ethical practice and apply to service
delivery, evaluation, and research methodology used in evaluation of programs and practices.

Ethical practice is essential in delivering services and
intervening in the lives of others. Ethical issues and concerns
arise despite our good intentions and sometimes require us
as professionals to seek guidance from supervisors and legal
experts. Sound and informed practices require that we extend
our knowledge base and follow best practices and professional
standards to the best of our ability. In addition to our knowledge and practice skills and our attention to informing clients,
protecting confidentiality, and avoiding potential harm, there
are many other concerns important to conducting practice and
evaluation of practice ethically and professionally. Bloom,
Fischer, and Orme (1995) call for client participation in identifying problem situations, treatment goals, data gathering, and
outcomes. Similarly, evaluation of intervention requires client
knowledge and participation and should not proceed or be

conducted if there is any risk of harm to clients or to the detriment of their progress or recovery. Evaluation of practice processes and outcomes must be independent of practice theory and objective in measuring behaviors, changes, and intended and actual results identified to be evaluated in order to be valid and useful.

Summary and Comment

Evaluating processes and outcomes of programs and practices designed to meet personal and social needs both individually and collectively for families and children is an area of practice with far-reaching implications. The common purposes of evaluation, although sometimes difficult to achieve, are professionally sound and respond to the ever-present demand for knowledge and greater understanding of the effectiveness and efficiency of our many programs and practices. Constraints of funding gaps, available expertise and knowledge, vested interests, and changing practices are hurdles to be overcome and not barriers to continuing our pursuit of evaluating our work with and on behalf of those we serve. Professional standards and conduct call for ethical practices, including their ethical evaluation. The challenge for professionals in both practice and practice evaluation is monumental in the face of changing practices and increased demands for services emerging in response not only to basic needs of people but also to their need to live their lives in today's increasingly complex and technological world. It is incumbent that professionals grow and develop in both practice and practice evaluation knowledge and skills as we, too, are part of the fluidity of the changing human condition.

Epilogue

This small volume contains so much about children and families and some of their stresses and struggles, as well as their capacities for change and growth. Indeed, there are numerous volumes in our libraries and on our shelves addressing theoretical perspectives that apply to children and families and interventions to help them in their processes of growing and developing. Nevertheless, this volume provides another lens through which to view concerns and celebrations which families experience in their own ways. We hope you will find the information we provide useful to you in your professional practice. Recognizing that our brief chapters are not comprehensive, it now becomes your task to explore practices and theories as they relate to your professional practice.

The experience of expanding this second edition has been rewarding in reminding us that, despite our limitations, we know so much about working with children and families. Yet, the potential to expand our knowledge and practices is more promising than ever. As you extend your work in evaluating processes and outcomes of practices and programs, there are increasing opportunities to disseminate your research and to contribute to existing knowledge bases. It is this opportunity that we encourage you to take very seriously, as well as the opportunity to share your expertise with those who are just entering helping professions. It will be through our involvement and contributions to knowledge and best practices that we will be able to help shape future services and construct a desired program and practice reality that will serve people in the changing world around us.

Parent Training

You may find it useful to train parents in behavioral methods and child management in a group setting. Here are some questions and answers on the choice of content of training programs:

- *Should parents rehearse or practice the skills they learn?*
  In principle the practice of child management skills would seem highly desirable. On balance the safe answer is *yes,* but there is no evidence to suggest that actual practice is a *necessary* or *sufficient* condition for helping parents develop such skills.
- *Should parent training focus on specific target problems or develop their knowledge of general behavioral principles?*
  It does seem that the latter is more cost-effective as it facilitates the implementation and generalization of newly acquired child management skills in situations.
- *Should parent training programs begin with easy or difficult problems?*
  There is no simple answer; problems are easy:
  (a) if they occur under conditions that permit ready observation by parents,
  (b) if they occur with relatively high frequency,
  (c) if they are maintained by stimuli from parents rather than others, and
  (d) if they occur naturally at a specified time (i.e., mealtime, bedtime, and so on).
- *Does early reinforcement arising from success with easy problems increase cooperation?*
  Beginning treatment with more or less difficult behavior problems does not seem to affect parental cooperation, but there is still some doubt about this issue. It may, however, increase parents' sense of self-conflicting or competence (self-efficacy).

- It seems probable that parents will maintain their enthusiasm and interest for the program as long as they perceive some progress in managing their offspring's actions, regardless of how difficult these behaviors are to deal with, in the therapist's opinion.

Telephone contact and carefully timed home visits also increase parent's cooperation.

- Teach only those behaviors that will continue to be reinforced after training.
- The parents' aim in using behavior modification procedures is to introduce the child to behaviors that are either intrinsically reinforcing or that make reinforcements available which he or she was not previously experiencing.
- In a sense there are top therapeutic objectives in training parents, and through them, their offspring:
  (a) to enhance a child's responses to the controlling factors in his or her environment without deliberately altering the latter. Assuming a family environment to be essentially satisfactory, one might attempt to adjust a child to it, or
  (b) to change the controlling factors in an unsatisfactory learning environment as a means of modifying problem behavior. Where the latter strategy is predominant the therapeutic objective is to program the environment so that it sustains the child's and parents' "improvement" after the formal program is terminated

At the Center for Behavioral Work for Families, Sue Milner and the second author have used the following program for training parents in groups—families referred by social services with multiple problems.

Content of the Sessions

Introductory home visit
- Introduce ourselves.
- Explain the nature of the program.
- Give time and place of the group, sort out arrangements for getting to the venue.
- Make a contract.
- Complete baseline measures.

- Observation of child interacting with family members.
- Leave a handout about the Center's approach.

Each session lasts two hours and includes a 20-minute coffee break.

Session 1
- Introduce ourselves and the other parents.
- Explain the nature of the program; discuss how other parents have similar problems with their children.
- Video of "Claire"—one of our training tapes; a family mismanaging a disobedient toddler.
- Discussion of tape and what constitutes a problem.
- Discussion of the specific behavior manifested by their children that cause them concern.
- Explain red, green, and yellow code.
- Small subgroups to specify what each parent's *priorities* are (discipline/child-rearing).
- Fill in parent rating scale individually.
- Parents individually choose two problem behaviors to work on; parents also describe two prosocial behaviors to record.

Homework: Parents are given a recording sheet and are asked to record the frequency of prosocial behaviors and the chosen problem behavior. Parents are asked to bring the records with them next week.

Session 2
- Greetings.
- Discussion of successes and difficulties of the previous week.
- Video of a mother discussing her child's problems.
- Introduce the ABC of behavior as a basis for discussion of *learning*.
- Repeat the video of Claire. Illustrate the ABC analysis by group discussion.

Homework: Record ABCs of target problem behaviors; parents given record sheets and an example.

Session 3
- Greetings.
- Discussion of successes and difficulties of previous week; discuss records.

- Collect records.
- Discussion of *differential attention*—planned ignoring, attention to good behavior (handouts on these subjects).
- Practice being precise about *reinforcing specific behavior*.
- Role play and rehearsal of making eye-contact, being close by when giving instructions; showing firmness and warmth.
- Discussion of the behaviors that cannot be ignored.

Homework: Try out these methods, continue ABC recording.

Session 4
- Greetings.
- Discussion of successes and difficulties of previous week.
- Small groups looking at the records.
- Collect the records.
- Discuss incentives, star charts, and time-out.
- Video on time-out; role play and rehearsal of time-out.
- The importance of consistency.

Homework: Try out these methods, continue ABC recording.

Session 5
- Greetings.
- Discussion of successes and difficulties of previous week.
- Small groups looking at the records.
- Discussion of coping strategies—self-talk, relaxation, and self-reinforcement.
- Problem solving (discussion and exercises) (see chapter 12).

The remaining three sessions include revision of learning principles and management techniques. There is a thorough discussion of individual problems (e.g., disobedience, tantrums, etc.); also a discussion of expectations regarding developmental norms for children. Methods rehearsed include response cost and overcorrection:

- *Phasing out* the program is planned on an individual basis during the final (eighth) session.
- A further session is arranged for a *debriefing* and *evaluation* of the program. Home visits are made for observations of parent-child interactions and repeat testing on the questionnaires used in the introductory home visit.

Treatment Options in Cases of Child Abuse and Neglect

Likely target problems (of the excess/deficit/inappropriate categories) that occur in relation to:

- Characteristics of the parents (e.g., alcohol abuse; deficits in bonding and child-rearing skills, faulty expectations of the child).
- Characteristics of the child (e.g., noncompliant aggressive problems, incontinence, inappropriately inflexible response to different situations).
- Unique interaction of the child and his/her parents (e.g., coercive/aversive communications; mutual avoidance; inappropriate, inconsistent (perhaps noncontingent) reinforcement/punishment).
- Significant others in the family (interference, subversion of maternal authority by grandparents; sexual/physical abuse by relative/lodger, etc.).
- Environmental factors (poverty, overcrowding, social isolation).

Social workers are likely to be faced with any of the following *specific problems* when child abuse cases are referred to them.

Specific Areas of Intervention

1. *Deficits*

   - Skill deficits (poor problem-solving skills; ineffective communication skills; ineffective reinforcement skills).
   - Social isolation.

	• Withholding attention (ignoring) until there's a crisis (i.e., very annoying activities).
Poor care-giving/ socializing skills	• Failure to *track* minor incidents before they blow up in major confrontations (e.g., fighting).
	• Failure to acknowledge/notice/ reward prosocial behavior.
	• Few family recreational activities together.
	• Low self-esteem/low perception of self-efficacy.
	• Less positive emotional expression.

2. *Excessive/surplus problems*

- Use of *aversive* (negative, coercive, punitive) means of influencing/changing others (criticism/physical assaults).
- Parental yelling, shouting, nagging, threats, complaints.
- Punishment of prosocial behavior.
- High parental stress/distress (marital discord/inadequate income, poor housing, lack of emotional/social support).
- Alcohol/drug use.
- Acting out, antisocial, conduct problems.

3. *Inappropriate beliefs/attitudes/knowledge/behavior*

- Faulty attributions (cause-and-effect inferences)
- Reinforcement of inappropriate/deviant actions
- Unpredictable/inconsistent
- Mutual avoidance
- Faulty expectations due to absence of basic knowledge about child development
- Inflexible in response to child-disciplinary situations

Potential Treatment Strategies

1. Systemic Level (*Family*)	• Written contracts.
	• Negotiation training.
	• Conflict resolving (settling differences).

- Contingency contracting (exchange theory).
- Communication enhancement.
- Clarification of roles and rules.
- Enhancement of social contacts.
- Improvement of physical environment, resources (e.g., child-minding/day care).

2. Dyadic Level
(*Interactions/ relationship*)

- Enhancing positive interactions.
- Operant programs (increasing positive reinforcement—"catching the child out in good behavior").
- Decreasing threats, criticism, negative injunctions.
- Play.
- Increasing consistency.
- Negotiating fair/few/clear rules.
- Marital work.

3. Individual Level
Parents:

- Training in more effective child-rearing practices
- Developmental counseling to improve knowledge/decrease family expectations/attributions
- Cognitive restructuring
- Decreasing inappropriate anxiety/anger reactions
  (i) relaxation
  (ii) self-talk
  (iii) self-control training
- Improving skills
  (i) social skills
  (ii) problem-solving skills
- Addiction/substance abuse
- Self-esteem, self-efficacy enhancement (performance accomplishments)
- Depression/learned helplessness

Children:

- Training/therapy as in chapter 11

A Case Vignette

Behavioral Casework With a Family Referred for Child Abuse: Failure to Thrive in a Two-Year-Old

The names are fictitious, the identities disguised. The case is paraphrased (with permission) from the one reported by Dr. Dorta Iwaniec (the key worker) and the author (co-therapist) in *The Australian Journal of Child and Family Welfare.*

Jimmy and Wayne Grant are twins. To see them on one of our home visits is to understand something of what the terms "child abuse" and "failure to thrive" mean. Jimmy is a chubby, rose-cheeked boisterous two-year-old. He appears to be a happy, mischievous boy, running, playing, talking, and laughing. He comes to his mother for help and comfort and cuddles up to her spontaneously. He responds readily to her attention and affection. She smiles at him, picks him up, sits him on her lap, plays with him, answers his questions, watches his movements, warns him when he is in danger.

On the edge of the room, like a stranger, stands Wayne— posture rigid, staring fixedly at us. He is a sad, lethargic-looking child, very small, and extremely thin. His pale face throws into relief the dark shadows under his eyes. He remains in one spot, as if at attention; by now he is gazing unswervingly at his mother. She takes no notice of him. When asked to call Wayne over to her she looks in his direction; as she does so her face hardens and her eyes are angry. She addresses him with a dry command; when he hesitates she shouts at him.

Our observation of his interactions with his mother (several visits over four weeks, which gave us baseline data) indicated that she *never* smiled at him, *never* picked him up, *never* sat him on her knee, *never* played with him, or read to him. The only physical contact came about when she fed, bathed, or dressed him, and at such times, her handling was rough and silent. When she approached him he appeared to be frightened and occasionally burst into tears. He would never come to her for comfort or help and she never approached him except to carry out the bare essentials of care and control. The children were both meticulously clean and well-dressed.

Home-based observations allowed us to see that when his father returned from work, Wayne brightened a little; he became somewhat more alert and lively, especially when his mother was out of sight. When she entered the room he stiffened up. Jimmy and Wayne didn't play together. Jimmy frequently pushed his brother and smacked him; Wayne's cries were largely ignored by his mother.

Looking at Wayne and Jimmy it is hard to believe that they were of the same weight at birth. Wayne's small stature was now reflected in a height and weight that were below the third percentile curves of normal growth. Wayne had been hospitalized several times because of his failure to gain weight. During the latest hospitalization, Wayne's mother refused to visit him and requested his reception into care; she appeared to be very depressed and said that she could no longer cope with trying to feed him (he would refuse food, or spit it out screaming loudly). She added that she could no longer tolerate his behavior ("defiance," whining, and crying) and her hostile feelings toward him. At the state of our entry into the case, Wayne had to be fed by a combination of the health visitor, father, or neighbor.

Failure to Thrive

Failure to thrive has become a popular term to describe infants and children whose growth and development are significantly below expected standards. It is thought of as a pattern (syndrome) of severe retardation of growth that is frequently associated with a specific disturbance of parental (often maternal) behavior and family disorganization. Certainly, in Wayne's case, it was clear (after the essential, exhaustive, medical tests) that his retarded growth at this stage of his life was not due to physical (organic) disease. Research findings suggest that organic abnormalities cause such failures to thrive in only a minority of children.

Studies of such children and their families have shown that the most commonly identified forerunners to these problems are emotional disturbance and environmental deprivation—with the wide range of psychological and social disorganization that these concepts imply. The deprivation often involves rejection, isolation from social contacts, and neglect. Occasionally, physical abuse enters the picture. On several occasions Wayne showed severe bruising. The health visitor had placed him on the "at risk" register.

The association of poor growth with adverse environmental factors has often been pointed out in the context of the maternal deprivation and child abuse literature. The mechanisms of the growth failure, in fact, are not clear. It is suggested that maternally deprived infants can be underweight because of under-eating (which is secondary to being offered inadequate food), *or* because of the refusal of the adequate nourishment offered, rather than as a result of some psychologically induced defect in absorption or metabolism.

Assessment: Behavioral Psychotherapy Approach

To return to the Grant family—now in acute crisis—they were referred to the authors for a form of assessment and a broadly based form of behavior therapy which we call "behavioral psychotherapy." This family-oriented approach, which combines behavioral methods of assessment and modification with family-casework methods is being used (and evaluated) at the "Center for Behavioral Work With Families" at the University of Leicester Clinical Psychology Department.

Wayne was hospitalized five times during his two years and three months of life. Altogether he had spend 68 days in the hospital. The first admission was at the age of four weeks. He

273

had been a difficult baby to feed from the word "go." He vomited frequently and seemed to cry or scream incessantly for the first few weeks of life. He was suffering from pyloric stenosis. After the operation he improved a little. His sucking became more vigorous although he took a long time to feed. The situation deteriorated when solids were introduced at the age of five months. He persistently refused to take them and gradually stopped taking liquids as well. From that time onward, feeding time became a battle.

Wayne was 14 months old (weight 6 kg, height 69 cms) when his mother finally found it impossible to cope with his reluctance to eat. She screamed at him, smacked him, shook him, getting angrier and more frustrated each day. When she forced him to eat, he screamed, vomited immediately, and then had diarrhea. Soon Wayne began to scream at the sight of his mother. She could not touch him or come near him. In anger and helpless despair she would take him up upstairs and leave him there for hours. Wayne took some food from his father and next door neighbor, and was fed only when they were available. Because he was losing weight rapidly, he was admitted to the hospital for investigation.

In the hospital, Wayne cried a lot, was at first unresponsive to nurses and movement around him. When not crying he looked blank and lethargic. Gradually he began to take food and became more alert and lively, doing well enough in the end to be discharged. This pattern of "failure to thrive," improving in the hospital, and deteriorating soon after going home, was to be repeated several times. All of this increased his mother's feelings of hostility and rejection toward the child, not to mention her feelings of inadequacy as a mother. He seemed better when he was in different places with different people. In the end she refused to have Wayne back home from the hospital.

Our work, after some initial sessions in the hospital, was carried out in the home with both parents and children. In order to be able to institute a full program of assessment and treatment, we had to teach Mrs. Grant to relax and to structure small, manageable daily tasks to counter her tensions and her inertia and apathy. We diagnosed her depression as learned helplessness. So as not to exacerbate her feelings of helplessness and demoralization, we underlined the point that we were not there as "experts" to take over the burden of the child's problem from the parents, but that we would be partners in a cooperative venture with a major part of the responsibility rightfully in their hands. A period of counseling and support-giving and relaxation-training was embarked upon and covered seven weeks. We arranged for full-time attendance by the twins at a day-nursery.

Looking at the history we took at this time, it seems likely that the child learned to avoid food by associating feeding with painful experiences, such as, forcing, hurrying, shaking, smacking, scolding, and throwing. Finally, mother's person became a stimulus to evoke fear which (in proximity) brought physical symptoms like vomiting and diarrhea, if she was angry. He expressed fear at the sight of his mother approaching him. Being reared in social isolation and lacking stimulation it is not surprising that Wayne manifested serious delay in the development of his speech. His brother was more generally advanced but also showed speech retardation.

Treatment Program

A variety of measures is used in the provision of services. This provision of methods and resources falls into two categories.

(1) *Immediate.* A variety of methods play their part. During the early stages of the Center's involvement, attention in this sort of case is paid to immediate needs (crisis intervention) of the child and family. This has involved, in general:

(a) Ensuring that the child was safe, fed, and stimulated;
(b) Arranging attendance at a day nursery (in part a safety measure). This allowed us to monitor the child for a substantial part of the day. It provided mother with a "break" and the space to work on her problem with the social worker. It also gave the child some much needed social stimulation.
(c) Arranging for health visitors, home-start volunteers, and neighbors to assist mothers with feeding and child-care and to provide moral support;

(d) Assisting parents with problems of housing, financing, welfare rights, and so on, where and when appropriate;

(e) Providing supervision by regular visits and phone calls (also emotional support);

(f) Placing children on the "at risk" register because of extreme rejection and/or abuse (failure to thrive);

(g) Beginning and supporting self-help parents groups (composed of earlier clients) which parents could attend;

(h) Desensitizing (where necessary) the mother's tension, anger, and resentment when in the child's company. It was almost always necessary for the mother of these children to learn to control and resolve feelings of anger and resentment and to deal with high levels of anxiety. This was sometimes achieved (before any formal feeding program could be initiated) by training in relaxation, stress management, and self-control.

(2) *Longer term.* After the attention to the immediate safety and needs of child and family, the intervention focuses on critical issues such as the mother's relationship with her infant, her ability to feed her child, and his to receive (and benefit from) sustenance; the depression and or anxiety she so often suffers from; the parents' relationship, and so on.

During this phase the treatment of failure to thrive cases consists of a "package" of psychosocial methods ranging from "talking" (personal and developmental counseling) to behavior modification. This family-oriented approach combines behavioral methods of assessment and modification with family casework methods (including discussion, clarification of problems, task-setting, and support giving). It is carried out in the home with both parents (generally speaking) and the child, but mother–child transactions become the main focus of therapy because of the acute crisis we meet in most cases. This *was* the case for Mrs. Grant and Wayne.

Before we could initiate a program dealing with the interactions between Mrs. Grant and her child, we had to cope with the crisis issue of the mother's feeding her child. After all, Wayne was wasting away.

Phase I: This was tackled in a highly structured (and thus, directive) manner. At first we had to make the mealtimes more relaxed. She agreed (albeit reluctantly and sceptically) to desist from screaming, shouting, and threatening the child over his meals. The period of eating was made quiet and calm. Mrs. Grant was asked to talk soothingly and pleasantly to him.

This was extremely difficult for her. The social worker joined the family for a few meals, helping to reassure Wayne, prompting the mother to help him eat in a gentle manner when he was in difficulties. Mrs. Grant was encouraged to look at him, smile, and occasionally touch him. If Wayne refused his food she was to leave him. We encouraged her to coax him by play or soft words. The food was arranged to look attractive.

This aspect of the program (lasting several weeks) was purely "symptomatic" in the sense of encouraging the child to eat by creating less stressful circumstances. As long as the mother kept to this schedule, Wayne would eat (not much, but sufficient to sustain life). If she broke the rules because she was moody or unstable, Wayne would not sit in his high chair. We added another rule (on the basis of this observation), that she never feed the twins when feeling acutely angry or tense. There should be a period of quiet relaxation (using the relaxation tape and the training we had given her) if this was difficult to achieve.

Phase II: This phase (as with earlier stages of treatment) was discussed in detail with both parents. A contract was drawn up specifying the mutual obligations and rules for the family and ourselves.

Objectives

1. To deliberately, and in planned fashion, increase positive interactions and decrease negative interactions between mother and child.
2. To desensitize Wayne's anxieties with regard to mother's caregiving (and other) activities.
3. To desensitize mother's tension, anger, and resentment when in Wayne's company.

4. To increase and make more general the interactions with other members of the family (e.g., as a group, between Wayne and his brother, etc.).

Methods

Mrs. Grant agreed to play exclusively with Wayne every evening after her husband returned from work, for 10 minutes during the first week; 15 minutes during the second week, 20 minutes during the third week, and 25 minutes during the fourth and subsequent weeks. The father took Jimmy for a walk, or to another room, while Wayne had this period of play. Afterward they would join in for a family play session. The mother was asked to play with Wayne on the floor—this was demonstrated and rehearsed—and she was encouraged to talk to him in a soft reassuring manner, encouraging him to participate in the play.

She was also instructed to smile at Wayne, look at him, touch him briefly, or praise him for each positive response she detected from him. (His tentative approaches toward her were "shaped" by just such a series of successive approximations.) After a period of weeks she was guided to seek proximity to him by hugging him briefly and then holding him close, but gently, while reading him a story.

There is no doubt that Mrs. Grant found these times difficult, and, at times, distasteful; but they became gradually less so as time passed and especially as Wayne began to seek her out shyly and to smile and talk to her. We had to provide a good deal of support and encouragement to both parents during frequent visits or by phone calls. (Reinforcing the reinforcer is critical in this work.) Three months were occupied in this stage of the intervention.

Phase III: The final phase took two weeks and deliberately involved an intensification of Mrs. Grant's interactions (now much improved) with Wayne.
1. She was to take him (as far as possible) everywhere she went. She was instructed to talk as much as possible to him in a soft measured way, smiling, and cuddling him at appropriate times. These had to be discussed as Mrs. Grant frequently put Wayne in a double-bind by giving contradictory verbal and nonverbal cues.

2. She was asked to read to him and Jimmy, encourage them to play together, and read to them both at bedtime. *Their* positive interactions were to be reinforced socially.

The formal program was phased out gradually (over a period of several weeks) after discussing with both parents the importance of a stimulating environment and a rich reinforcement schedule for the maintenance of the improvements they both detected in the family interactions and mother's feelings and attitudes (she monitored these for us). Our assessment of Wayne's improved health, weight, and height (and indeed his general psychological well-being) were confirmed by the assessments of the pediatrician, the dietary consultant, and a health visitor. Mrs. Grant's sense of attachment (bonding) to Wayne had returned; what is of interest is that although we discussed her feelings and attitudes with her they were not the primary focus of treatment. She found it difficult and, in the end, refused to discuss them. We hoped that old feelings of affection and nurturance would return if we countered the avoidance situations (and sense of helplessness) that stood in the way of her learning to love him again. Feelings (and insights) *followed* actions.

Relative Importance of Screening Characteristics for Child Abuse

Relative importance as determined by step-wise discriminant function analysis.

	Abusing families (n = 62) %	Non-abusing families (n = 124) %
1. Parent indifferent, intolerant, or overanxious toward child	83.9	21.8
2. History of family violence	51.6	5.6
3. Socioeconomic problems such as unemployment	85.5	34.7
4. Infant premature, low birth weight	24.2	3.2
5. Parent abused or neglected as a child	43.5	6.5
6. Stepparent or cohabitee present	35.5	4.8
7. Single or separated parent	38.7	8.1
8. Mother less than 21 years old at the time of birth	40.3	23.4
9. History of mental illness, on drug or alcohol addiction	61.3	21.8
10. Infant separated from mother for greater than 24 hours post-delivery	17.7	5.6
11. Infant mentally or physically handicapped	1.6	0.8
12. Less than 18 months between birth of children	22.6	15.3
13. Infant never breast fed	46.8	40.3

(*From Browne, 1988, with permission.*)

Bibliography

Amato, P. R. & Keith, B. (1991). Parental divorce and the well-being of children: A meta-analysis. *Psychological Bulletin*, 110, 26–46.

Anastasi, A. (1997). *Psychological testing* (7th ed.). Upper Saddle River, NJ: Prentice Hall.

Anderson, E. M. & Shannon, A. L. (1995). Toward a conceptualization of mentoring. In T. Kerry and A. S. Mayes (Eds.). *Issues in mentoring*. NY: The Open University.

Anderson, R. E. & Carter, I. (1990). *Human behavior in the social environment: A social systems approach* (4th ed.). NY: Aldine de Gruyter.

Aponte, H. (1978). The anatomy of a therapist. In P. Papp (Ed.). *Full length case studies*. London: Gardner Press.

Argyle, M. & Henderson, M. (1985). *The anatomy of relationships*. Harmondsworth: Penguin Books.

Aries, P. (1973). *Centuries of childhood*. Harmondsworth: Penguin Books.

Arlow, J. A. (1995). Psychoanalysis. In R. J. Corsini and D. Wedding (Eds.). *Current psychotherapies* (5th ed.). Itasca, IL: F. E. Peacock Publishers, Inc.

Aspinwall, K., Garrett, V., & Owen-Jackson, G. (1994). 'In at the beginning': A pilot partnership. In I. Reid, H. Constable, and R. Griffiths (Eds.). *Teacher education reform*. London: Paul Chapman Publishing Ltd.

Axline, V. M. (1947). *Play therapy: The inner dynamics of childhood*. Boston, MA: Houghton Mifflin.

Bandura, A. (1976). *Social learning theory*. Englewood Cliffs, NJ: Prentice-Hall.

Bannister, D. & Fransella, F. (1980). *Inquiring man*. Harmondsworth: Penguin Books.

Barlow, D. (1981). *Sexually transmitted diseases—the facts*. Oxford: Oxford University Press.

Barth, R. P. & Berry, M. (1988). *Adoption and disruption: Rates, risks, and responses*. NY: Aldine de Gruyter.

Becker, W. C. (1964). Consequences of different kinds of parental discipline. In M. L. Hoffman and L. H. Hoffman (Eds.). *Review of child development research*. NY: Russell Sage Foundation.

Becvar, D. S. & Becvar, R. J. (1996). *Family therapy: A systemic integration*. Boston, MA: Allyn and Bacon.

Beech, R. (1985). *Staying together.* Chichester: John Wiley.
Bell, C. R. (1996). *Managers as mentors: Building partnerships for learning.* San Francisco: Berrett-Koehler Publishers.
Benjamin, A. (1974). *The helping interview* (2nd ed.). NY: Houghton Mifflin.
Berg, I. K. (1994). *Family based services: A solution-focused approach.* NY: W.W. Norton and Company, Inc.
Bigner, J. J. (1979). *Parent-child relations: An introduction to parenting.* NY: Macmillan.
Biller, H. B. (1971). *Father, child and sex role.* Lexington, MA: Heath.
Bloom, M., Fischer, J., & Orme, J. G. (1995). *Evaluating practice: Guidelines for the accountable professional* (2nd ed.). Needham, MA: Allyn and Bacon.
Bogolub, E. B. (1995). *Helping families through divorce: An eclectic approach.* NY: Springer Publishing Company, Inc.
Bonnie, R. J. & Lynch, B. S. (1997). Teenagers underestimate the risk of addiction. In P. A. Winters (Ed.). *Teen addiction.* San Diego, CA: Greenhaven Press, Inc.
Bowen, M. (1978). *Family therapy in clinical practice.* NY: Jason Aronson.
Bowlby, J. (1982). *Attachment and loss* (2nd ed.). NY: Basic Books.
Brown, G. W. & Harris, T. (1978). *Social origins of depression.* London: Tavistock.
Browne, K., Davies, C., & Stratton P. (1988). *Early prediction and prevention of child abuse.* Chichester: John Wiley.
Browne, K. D. (1988). The naturalistic context of family violence and child abuse. In J. Archer and K. D. Browne (Eds.). *Human aggression: Naturalistic approaches.* Beckenham, Kent: Croom Helm.
Budney, A. J. & Higgins, S. T. (1998). A community reinforcement plus vouchers approach: Treating cocaine addiction. (NIH Publication No. 98-4309). Rockville, MD: NIH.
Cahill, M. M. (1984) *The aids epidemic.* London: Hutchinson.
Campbell, B. & Horbury, A. (1994). Mentoring articled science teachers. In I. Reid, H. Constable, and R. Griffiths (Eds.). *Teacher education reform.* London: Paul Chapman Publishing Ltd.
Carter, E. A. & McGoldrick, M. (1989). *The family life cycle* (2nd ed.). Boston, MA: Allyn and Bacon.
Chambers, D. E., Wedel, K. R., & Rodwell, M. K. (1992). *Evaluating social programs.* Boston: Allyn and Bacon.
Clarke, A. & Clarke, A. D. B. (1976). *Early experience: Myth and reality.* London: Open Books.
Conger, J. V. & Kanungo, R. N. (1988). The empowerment process: Integrating theory and practice. *Academy of Management Review, 13,* 471–482.
Corcoran, K. & Vandiver, V. (1996). *Maneuvering the maze of managed care.* NY: Free Press.

Corcoran, K. L. & Gingerich, W. J. (1994). Practice evaluation in the context of managed care: Case-recording methods for quality assurance reviews. *Research on Social Work Practice, 4,* 326–337.

Cowger, C. (1997). Assessing client strengths: Assessment for client empowerment. In D. Saleeby (Ed.). *The strengths perspective in social work practice.* NY: Longman.

Crain, W. C. (1985). *Theories of development: Concepts and applications.* Englewood Cliffs, NJ: Prentice-Hall.

Cunningham, C. & Davis, H. (1985). *Working with parents: Frameworks for collaboration.* Milton Keynes. London: Open University Press.

Deming, B. (1984). Empowerment: A vehicle to peace. In M. S. White and D. Van Soest (Eds.). *Empowerment of people for peace* (p. 8). Minneapolis, MN: Women Against Military Madness.

Diagnostic and statistical manual of mental disorders, (1994) (4th ed). Washington, DC: American Psychiatric Association.

Dominian, J. (1968). *Marital breakdown.* Harmondsworth: Penguin Books.

Duncan, D. E. & Petosa, R. (1955). Social and community factors associated with drug use and abuse among adolescents. In T. P. Gullotta, G. R. Adams, & R. Montemayor, (Eds.). *Substance misuse in adolescence.* Thousand Oaks, CA: Sage Publications.

Dunst, C., Trivette, C., & Deal, A. (1988). *Enabling and empowering families.* Cambridge, MA: Brookline.

Egan, G. (1986). *The skilled helper.* Monterey, CA: Brooks/Cole.

Eliot, G. (1929). *Silas Marner.* NY: The Macmillan Company.

Epstein, J. F. & Gfroerer, J. C. (1998). Estimating substance abuse treatment need from a national household study. *Analyses of substance abuse and treatment need issues.* (DHHS Publication No. [SMA] 98-3227). Rockville, MD: SAMHSA, Office of Applied Studies.

Erikson, E. (1965). *Childhood and society* (Rev. ed.). NY: W. W. Norton.

Erikson, E. (1985). *Childhood and society* (35th anniversary ed.). NY: W. W. Norton.

Faller, K. C. (1988). *Child sexual abuse: An interdisciplinary manual for diagnosis, case management, and treatment.* NY: Columbia University Press.

Faller, K. C., Bowden, M. L., Jones, C. O., & Hildenbrandt, H. M. (1981). Types of child abuse and neglect. In K. C. Faller (Ed.). *Social work with abused and neglected children.* NY: Free Press.

Finkelhor, D. (1979). *Sexually victimized children.* NY: Free Press.

Fiske, M. (1979). *Middle age: The prime of life.* London: Harper & Row.

Forward, S. & Buck, C. (1981). *Betrayal of innocence: Incest and devastation.* Harmondsworth: Penguin Books.

Frank, Jerome D. (1973). *Persuasion and healing: A comparative study of psychotherapy* (Rev. ed.). Baltimore, MD: Johns Hopkins University Press.

Fraser, M. W. (1997). The ecology of childhood: A multisystems perspective. In M. W. Fraser (Ed.). *Risk and resilience in childhood*. Washington, DC: NASW Press.

Freud, S. (1974). *Introductory lectures on psychoanalysis*. Harmondsworth: Penguin Books.

Frude, N. (Ed.) (1980). *Psychological approaches to child abuse*. London: Batsford.

Furstenberg, F. & Cherlin, A. (1991). *Divided families: What happens to children when parents part*. Cambridge, MA: Harvard University Press.

Gale, A. & Chapman, A. J. (Eds.) (1984). *Psychology and social problems*. Chichester: John Wiley.

Garbarino, J. & Binn, J. L. (1992). The ecology of childbearing and child rearing. In J. Garbarino (Ed.). *Children and families in the social environment* (2nd ed.). NY: Aldine de Gruyter.

Garvin, C. D. (1997). *Contemporary group work* (3rd ed.). Needham Heights, MA: Allyn and Bacon.

Gelles, R. J. & Cornell, C. P. (1997). *Intimate violence in families*. (3rd ed.). Thousand Oaks, CA: Sage Publications.

Germain, C. B. (1991). *Human behavior in the social environment: An ecological view*. NY: Columbia University Press.

Germain, C. B. & Gitterman, A. (1987). Ecological perspective. In A. Minahan et al. (Eds.). *Encyclopedia of social work* (18th ed.) (pp. 488–499). Silver Spring, MD: NASW Press.

Gershenson, C. (1995). Social policy and evaluation: An evolving symbiosis. In P. J. Pecora, M. W. Fraser, K. E. Nelson, J. McCroskey, and W. Meezan (Eds.). *Evaluating family-based services*. NY: Aldine De Gruyter.

Gil, E. (1991). *The healing power of play*. NY: The Guilford Press.

Ginott, H. (1969). *Between parent and child: New solutions to old problems*. NY: Avon Books.

Gittelman, R. (Ed.) (1986). *Anxiety disorders of childhood*. Chichester: John Wiley.

Goldenberg I. & Goldenberg H. (1991). *Family therapy: An overview*. Monterey, CA: Brooks-Cole Publishing.

Gorell Barnes, G. (1984). *Working with families*. London: Macmillan.

Gottlieb, B. H. (1981). *Social networks and social support*. Beverley Hills, CA.: Sage Publications.

Greene, R. R. (1992). Case management: An agenda for social work practice. In B. S. Vourlekis and R. R. Greene (Eds.). *Social work case management*. NY: Aldine De Gruyter.

Greenspan, S. I. & Greenspan, N. T. (1991). *The clinical interview of the child*. Washington, DC: American Psychiatric Press, Inc.

Grossman, J. B. & Tierney, J. P. (1998). Does mentoring work? An impact study of the Big Brothers Big Sisters Program. *Evaluation Research, 22*, 403–426.

Guerney, B. C. (Ed.) (1977). *Relationship enhancement*. San Francisco, CA: Jossey-Bass.

Haley, J. (1987). *Problem solving therapy* (2nd ed.). San Francisco: Jossey-Bass.

Harper, K. V. & Loadman, W. E. (1992a). *Prevention of adoption disruption/dissolution: Special needs of special children*. Report of funded project, Post Legalization Adoption Services. Toledo, OH: Lucas County Childrens Services.

Harper, K. V. & Loadman, W. E. (1992b). Adoption disruption/dissolution: A predictive model. In *Discovering the new world of research and statistics: A federal-state partnership*. Proceedings of the 32nd National Workshop of the National Association for Welfare Research and Statistics. Columbus, Ohio, August 1–5, 1992, Vol. II, 107–131.

Harper, K. V. & Shillito, L. S. (1991). Group work with bulimic adolescent females in suburbia. In A. Malekoff (Ed.). *Group work with suburbia's children: Difference, acceptance and belonging*. NY: The Haworth Press.

Helton, L. R. & Jackson, M. (1997). *Social work practice with families*. Boston, MA: Allyn and Bacon.

Herbert, M. (1974). *Emotional problems of development in children*. London: Academic Press.

Herbert, M. (1986). *Psychology for social workers* (Rev. ed.). London: British Psychological Society/Macmillan.

Herbert, M. (1986). Social skills training with children. In C. R. Hollin, & P. Tower, (Eds.). *Handbook of social skills training: Applications across the life span*. Vol. I. Oxford: Pergamon Press.

Herbert, M. (1987). *Living with teenagers*. Oxford: Basil Blackwell

Hinde, R. (1979). *Towards understanding relationships*. NY: Academic Press.

Hodges, V. G., Burwell, Y., & Ortega, D. (1998). Empowering families. In L. M. Gutierrez, R. J. Parsons, and E. O. Cox (Eds.). *Empowerment in social work practice: A sourcebook*. Pacific Grove, CA: Brooks/Cole.

Holmes, T. H. & Rahe, R. H. (1967). The social adjustment rating scale. *Journal of Psychosomatic Research*, 11, 213–218.

Hopson, B. & Scully, M. (1980). *Lifeskills teaching: Education for self-empowerment*. NY: McGraw-Hill.

Horne, A. M. (1991). Social learning family therapy. In A. Horne & J. Passmore (Eds.). *Family counseling and therapy*. Itasca, IL: F. E. Peacock Publishers.

Horne, A. M. & Sayger, T. V. (1990). *Treatment of conduct and oppositional defiant disorders of children*. NY: Pergamon Press.

Hudson, A. (1987). *Personal communication*. Second Author.

Institute for Sex Research (1953). *Sexual behavior in the human female by the staff of the Institute for Sex Research, Indiana University; Alfred C. Kinsey, et al*. Philadelphia: Saunders.

Iwaniec, D. (1983). *An investigation of non-organic failure-to-thrive.* Unpublished dissertation. University of Leicester: Psychology Department.

Jankowski, S., Videka-Sherman, L., & Laquidara-Dickinson, K. (1996). Social support networks of confidants to people with AIDS. *Social Work*, 41, 206–213.

Janzen, C. & Harris, O. (1997). *Family treatment in social work.* Itasca, IL: F. E. Peacock Publishers, Inc.

Jensen, C. (1994). Psychosocial treatment of depression in women: Nine single-subject evaluations. *Research on Social Work Practice*, 4, 267–282.

Jeruchim, J. & Shapiro, P. (1992). *Women, mentors, and success.* NY: Fawcett Columbine.

Johnson, D. & Johnson, F. P. (1987). *Joining together: Group therapy and group skills* (3rd ed.). Englewood Cliffs, NJ: Prentice-Hall.

Kagan, J. (1984). *The nature of the child.* NY: Basic Books, Inc.

Kazdin, A. E. (1978). *History of behaviour modification.* Baltimore, MD: University Park Press.

Kelly, G. A. (1955). *The psychology of personal constructs.* NY: Norton.

Kempe, R. S. & Kempe, C.H. (1978). *Child abuse.* Cambridge, MA: Harvard University Press.

Kennedy, E. (1981). *Crisis counselling.* Dublin: Gill and Macmillan.

Kids Count Data Book (1997). *Kids count data book: State profiles of child well-being.* Baltimore, MD: The Annie E. Casey Foundation.

Kirkpatrick, A. C. & Holland, T. P. (1995). *Working with families.* Boston, MA: Allyn and Bacon.

Kopp, J. (1989). Self-observation: An empowerment strategy in assessment. *Social Casework*, 70, 276–284.

Kubler-Ross, E. (1969). *On death and dying.* NY: Macmillan.

Lask, B. (1980). Evaluation: Why and how. *Journal of Family Therapy*, 2, (2), 119–210.

Lee, S. G. & Herbert, M. (Eds.) (1970). *Freud and psychology.* Harmondsworth: Penguin Books.

Lewin, R. (Ed.) (1975). *Child alive.* London: Temple Smith.

Lidz, T. (1976). The person, his and her development throughout the life cycle (Rev. ed.). London: Basic Books.

Locke, B., Garrison, R., & Winship, J. (1998). *Generalist social work practice: Context, story and partnerships.* Pacific Grove, CA: Brooks/Cole Publishing Company.

Long, D., Wood, R. G., and Kopp, H. (October, 1994). *The educational effects of LEAP and enhanced services in Cleveland.* Cleveland, OH: Manpower Demonstration Research Corporation.

Longres, J. F. (1995). *Human behavior in the social environment* (2nd ed.). Itasca, IL: F. E. Peacock Publishers, Inc.

Lorenz, K. (1973). *Motivation of human and animal behavior: An ethological view.* NY: Van Nostrand Reinhold Co.

Madanes, C. (1981). *Strategic family therapy.* San Francisco: Jossey-Bass.
Madanes, C. (1984). *Behind the one-way mirror: Advances in the practice of strategic therapy.* San Francisco: Jossey-Bass.
Madanes, C. (1990). *Sex, love and violence: Strategies for transformation.* NY: W. W. Norton.
Maddox, B. (1975). *Step-parenting.* London: Urwin Paperbacks.
Mallon, G. (1998). After care, then where? Outcomes of an independent living program. *Child Welfare, 76,* 61–78.
Mason, M. A., Skolnick, A., & Sugarman, S. D. (1998). *All our families.* NY: Oxford University Press.
McDonald, T. P., Allen, R. I., Westerfelt, A., & Piliavin, I. (1996). *Assessing the long-term effects of foster care.* Washington, DC: CWLA Press.
Mech, E. V., Pryde, J. A., & Rycraft, J. R. (1995). Mentors for adolescents in foster care. *Child and Adolescent Social Work Journal, 12,* 317–328.
Meichenbaum, D. H. (1974). *Cognitive behaviour modification.* NY: Plenum.
Minuchin, S. (1974). *Families and family therapy.* Cambridge, MA: Harvard University Press.
Minuchin, S. & Fishman, C. (1981). *Family therapy techniques.* Cambridge MA: Harvard University Press.
Moon, B. L. (1990). *Existential art therapy.* Springfield, IL: Charles C. Thomas Publisher.
Morgan, R. (1984). *Behavioural treatments with children.* London: Heinemann Medical Books Ltd.
Mothner, I. & Weitz, A. (1986). *How to get off drugs.* Harmondsworth: Penguin Books.
Mowry, D. D. (1994). Mentoring the Hmong: A practice outlet for teaching faculty and a possible community development tool. *Journal of Community Practice, 1,* 107–112.
Nichols, M. P. & Schwartz, R. C. (1991). *Family therapy: Concepts and methods.* Boston, MA: Allyn and Bacon.
Novaco, R. H. (1975). *Anger control: The development and evaluation of an experimental treatment.* Lexington, MA: Heath.
O'Connor, R. D. (1969). Modification of social withdrawal through symbolic modeling. *Journal of Applied Behavior Analysis, 2,* 15–22.
O'Connor, R. D. (1972). Relative efficacy of modeling, shaping and the combined procedures for modification of social withdrawal. *Journal of Abnormal Psychology, 79,* 327–334.
O'Hanlon, W. H. (1993). Possibility therapy: From iatrongenic injury to iatrogenic healing. In S. Gilligan and R. Price (Eds.). *Therapeutic conversations.* NY: W. W. Norton.
O'Hanlon, W. H. & Weiner-Davis, M. (1989). *In search of solutions: A new direction in psychotherapy.* NY: W. W. Norton.
Ollendick, T. H. & Cerny, J. A. (1981). *Clinical behaviour therapy with children.* NY: Plenum.

Open University Course Organizers (1982). *Parents and teenagers*. London: Harper and Row.

Parke, R. D. (1981). *Fathering*. London: Fontana/Open Books.

Parkes, C. M. (1972). *Bereavement: Studies of grief in adult life*. NY: International Universities Press.

Parsons, R. J. (1998). Evaluation of empowerment practice. In L. M. Gutierrez, R. J. Parsons and E. O. Cox (Eds.). *Empowerment in social work practice*. Pacific Grove, CA: Brooks/Cole Publishing Company.

Parsons, R. J., Gutierrez, L. M., & Cox, E. O. (1998). A model for empowerment practice. In L. M. Gutierrez, R. J. Parsons and E. O. Cox (Eds.). *Empowerment in social work practice: A sourcebook*. Pacific Grove, CA: Brooks/Cole Publishing Company.

Patterson, G. (1982). *Coercive family process*. Eugene, OR: Castalia.

Payne, M. (1991). *Modern social work theory: A critical introduction*. Chicago, IL: Lyceum Books, Inc.

Posavac, E. J. & Carey, R. G. (1985). *Program evaluation: Methods and case studies*. Englewood Cliffs, NJ: Prentice-Hall.

Price, R. H. (1978). *Abnormal behaviour: Perspectives in conflict* (2nd ed.). NY: Hall, Rinehart & Winston.

Randall, E. & Newfield, N. (1997). *West Virginia visions: Mentoring manual*. Morgantown, WV: School of Social Work, West Virginia University.

Rapoport, R. N., Fogarty, M. P. & Rapoport, R. (Eds.) (1982). *Families in Britain*. London: Routledge & Kegan Paul.

Reamer, F. C. (1998). *Social work research and evaluation skills*. NY: Columbia University Press.

Richards, M. and Dyson, M. (1982). *Separation, divorce and thc development of children: A review*. Cambridge: Child Care and Development Group.

Rogers, C. R. (1951). *Client-centered therapy*. Boston, MA: Houghton-Mifflin.

Rossi, P. H. (1997). Program outcomes: Conceptual and measurement issues. In E. J. Mullen, & J. L. Magnabosco, (Eds.). *Outcomes measurement in the human services*. Washington, DC: NASW Press.

Rossi, P. H. & Freeman, H. E. (1993). *Evaluation: A systematic approach*. Newbury Park, CA: Sage Publications.

Royse, D. (1995). *Research methods in social work*. Chicago: Nelson-Hall Publishers.

Rutter, M. (1972). *Maternal deprivation reassessed*. Harrnondsworth: Penguin Books.

Rutter, M. (1975). *Helping troubled children*. Harrnondsworth: Penguin Books.

Rutter, M. (1981). Stress, coping and development. *Journal of Child Psychology and Psychiatry*, 22 (4), 323–357.

Rutter, M. & Madge, N. (1976). *Cycles of disadvantage*. London: Heinemann.

Saleeby, D. (1997). Introduction: Power in the people. In D. Saleeby (Ed.). *The strengths perspective in social work practice.* NY: Longman.

Satir, V. (1982). The therapist and family therapy: Process model. In A. M. Horne and M. M. Ohlsen (Eds.). *Family counseling and therapy.* Itasca, IL: F. E. Peacock Publishers.

Satir, V. (1983). *Conjoint family therapy* (3rd ed.). Palo Alto, CA: Science and Behavior Books.

Schaefer, E. S. (1959). A circumplex model for maternal behavior. *Journal of Abnormal and Social Behaviour,* 59, 226–235.

Schaffer, H. R. (1971). *The growth of sociability.* Harmondsworth: Penguin Books.

Schaffer, H. R. (1977). *Mothering.* London: Fontana/Open Books.

Seligman, M. & Darling, R. B. (1997). *Ordinary families, special children.* NY: The Guilford Press.

Seligman, M. E. P. (1975). *Helplessness: On depression, development, and death.* San Francisco, CA: Freeman.

Sgroi, S. (1982). *Handbook of clinical intervention in child sexual abuse.* Lexington, MA: Lexington Books.

Sheafor, B. W., Horejsi, C. R., & Horejsi, G. A. (1994). *Techniques and guidelines for social work practice* (3rd ed.). Boston: Allyn and Bacon.

Shulman, L. (1999). The skills of helping individuals, families, groups, and communities (4th ed.). Itasca, IL: F. E. Peacock Publishers, Inc.

Simon, B. L. (1998). *The empowerment tradition.* NY: Columbia University Press.

Skolnick, A. (1998). Solomon's children: The new biologism, psychological parenthood, attachment theory, and the best interests standard. In M. A. Mason, A. Skolnick, and S. D. Sugarman (Eds.). *All our families.* NY: Oxford University Press.

Sluckin, W. & Herbert, M. (Eds.) (1986). *Parental behaviour.* Chichester: John Wiley.

Sluckin, W., Herbert, M., & Sluckin, A. (1983). *Maternal bonding.* Oxford: Basil Blackwell.

Spivack, G., Platt, J. J., & Shure, M. B. (1976). *The problem-solving approach to adjustment.* San Francisco, CA: Jossey-Bass.

Stern, D. (1977). *The first relationship: Infant and mother.* London: Fontana/Open Books.

Strom-Gottfried, K. (1997). The implications of managed care for social work education. *Journal of Social Work Education,* 33, 7–18.

Substance Abuse and Mental Health Services Administration, Office of Applied Studies (1996). *National household survey on drug abuse: Main findings 1994.* (DHHS Publication No. [SMA] 96-3085). Rockville, MD: SAMHSA, Office of Applied Studies.

Sutton, C., Smith, B., & Rosenberg, B. (1970). *The sibling.* London: Holt, Rinehart & Winston.

The State of America's Children Yearbook (1996). Washington, DC: Children's Defense Fund.

Thurman, S. (1997). LSD on the playground? Teen drug trends: Users get younger, substances harder. *Christian Science Monitor*, 89, 3.

Tower, C. C. (1996). *Understanding child abuse and neglect*. Boston, MA: Allyn and Bacon.

Treacher, A. & Carpenter, J. (Eds.) (1984). *Using family therapy*. Oxford: Basil Blackwell.

Tripodi, T. (1987). Program evaluation. In S. M. Rosen, D. Fanshel, and M. E. Lutz (Eds.). *Encyclopedia of social work* (19th ed.). Silver Spring, MD: National Association of Social Workers.

U.S. Bureau of the Census (1993). *Current population reports. Population profile of the United States*. Washington, DC.

Vetere, V. & Gale, A. (1987). *Ecological studies of family life*. Chicester: John Wiley.

Visher, E. B. & Visher, J. S. (1979). *Step families*. NY: Brunner Mazel.

Walczak, Y. (1984). Divorce, the kid's stories. *Social Work Today*. June, 12–13.

Wallerstein, J. & Blakeslee, S. (1989). *Second chances*. NY: Ticknor and Fields.

Wallerstein, J. S. & Kelly, J. B. (1980). *Surviving the breakup*. NY: Basic Books.

Walvin, J. (1982). *A child's world*. Harmondsworth: Penguin Books.

Watzlawick, P., Weakland, P., & Fisch, R. (1974). *Change: Principles of problem formation and problem resolution*. NY: Norton.

Webb, N. B. (1991). Play therapy crisis intervention with children. In M. Herbert, (Ed.). *Play therapy with children in crisis*. NY: The Guilford Press.

Williams, M., Unrau, Y. A., & Grinnell, Jr., R. M. (1998). *Introduction to social work research*. Itasca, IL: F. E. Peacock Publishers, Inc.

Winnicott, D. (1958). *Collected papers*. London: Tavistock.

Winters, K. (1998). Treatment recognizes link between delinquency and substance abuse. *Corrections Today*, 60, 118–123.

Yelloly, M. A. (1980). *Social work theory and psychoanalysis*. London: Van Nostrand Reinhold.

Zastrow, C. & Kirst-Ashman, K. K. (1997). *Understanding human behavior and the social environment*. Chicago, IL: Nelson-Hall Publishers.

Zippay, A. (1995). Expanding employment skills and social networks among teen mothers: Case study of a mentor program. *Child and Adolescent Social Work Journal*, 12, 51–69.

Index

and problem solving, 227–32
and role playing, 204–5
and self control training, 206–7
and settling differences, 202–4
and stress management, 207–8
individuality (of clients), 30–31, 240
and adolescence, 100
and communication, 181, 183–184,
187–88
and excessive closeness, 51
and family therapy, 81–83, 172
and play therapy, 186–87
and psychotherapy, 184–86
and rules, 47
and society, 44
and solution-focused family
therapy, 45
and systems theory, 20–21
infants, 64
developmental tasks for, 94–96
emotional needs of, 119
life tasks for, 12–13
socializing of, 16
instrumental conditioning, 63
integration, 2
intelligence quotient (IQ), 68–69
interactional references, 30
inter alia, 69
interdependence. *See* systems theory
internalization, 138
interpretive-insight approach, 69
intervention, 2–3, 44–48, 55, 85,
98–99, 147–48
briefer service of, 237–240
and counseling, 188–92
and cultural factors, 149–50
example of, 279–283
illustrated case. *See* Hayes, Avril
and individual helping, 198–209
methods for
child abuse, 271–73
coercive families, 174–76
cognitive approach, 226–27
evaluating impact, 250–62
family therapy, 45, 81–83
groupwork, 194–198
operant learning, 214
planned ignoring, 216–18
sexual abuse, 114
time-out procedure, 218–20

other support sources for, 237–38
and Phase I-III procedures,
154–58
selecting goals of, 160–162
interviews
and "ABC" terms, 31–37, 63–64
of baby-sitter, 146
and baseline data collection, 55
importance of, 6
techniques and skills for, 22–24
isolation, 76
Iwaniec, Dorta, 275–76

Joining Phase (family therapy), 170

Kelly, George, 69–73
Kemp, C. Henry, 114
Kinsey, Alfred, 112

letting go, 137
life-event information, 40–43
life skills, 12–13, 38–39, 93–96
and child abuse, 271–72
and empowerment, 242
for children, 118, 224–26
evaluation scales for, 259–60
for parents, 9–10, 17, 52–53,
230–32
and problem solving, 227–32
and strengths perspective, 244–45
for teenagers, 53–55
training for, 223–37
See also social skills training
listening, 6–13, 55
Lorenz, Konrad, 125–26
Love-Hostility, 9–10

marital-work contract, 167–68
marriage
and first child birth, 39
and life-event information, 40
and middle age, 41–42
work needed for, 166–68
maternal bonding theory, 119–25
maternal deprivation, 120–26
and child abuse, 277
means-end thinking, 231
medical model, 8
medical neglect, 50
mentors, 245–49
evaluation of, 255